THE PROBLEMATIC PUBLIC

RHETORIC AND DEMOCRATIC DELIBERATION
VOLUME 30

EDITED BY CHERYL GLENN AND STEPHEN BROWNE
THE PENNSYLVANIA STATE UNIVERSITY

Co-founding Editor: J. Michael Hogan

EDITORIAL BOARD:

Robert Asen (University of Wisconsin–Madison)
Debra Hawhee (The Pennsylvania State University)
J. Michael Hogan (The Pennsylvania State University)
Peter Levine (Tufts University)
Steven J. Mailloux (Loyola Marymount University)
Krista Ratcliffe (Marquette University)
Karen Tracy (University of Colorado, Boulder)
Kirt Wilson (The Pennsylvania State University)
David Zarefsky (Northwestern University)

Rhetoric and Democratic Deliberation focuses on the interplay of public discourse, politics, and democratic action. Engaging with diverse theoretical, cultural, and critical perspectives, books published in this series offer fresh perspectives on rhetoric as it relates to education, social movements, and governments throughout the world.

A complete list of books in this series is located at the back of this volume.

THE PROBLEMATIC PUBLIC

LIPPMANN, DEWEY, AND DEMOCRACY
IN THE TWENTY-FIRST CENTURY

EDITED BY KRISTIAN BJØRKDAHL

The Pennsylvania State University Press | University Park, Pennsylvania

This volume is published with the generous support of the Center for Democratic Deliberation at The Pennsylvania State University.

Library of Congress Cataloging-in-Publication Data

Names: Bjørkdahl, Kristian, editor.
Title: The problematic public : Lippmann, Dewey, and democracy in the twenty-first century / edited by Kristian Bjørkdahl.
Other titles: Rhetoric and democratic deliberation ; v. 30.
Description: University Park, Pennsylvania : The Pennsylvania State University Press, [2024] | Series: Rhetoric and democratic deliberation ; volume 30 | Includes bibliographical references and index.
Summary: "Explores the reception history of Walter Lippmann's and John Dewey's ideas about publics, communication, and political decision-making and assesses the relevance of these ideas for addressing contemporary crises"—Provided by publisher.
Identifiers: LCCN 2023041469 | ISBN 9780271096773 (hardback)
Subjects: LCSH: Lippmann, Walter, 1889–1974. | Dewey, John, 1859–1952. | Democracy. | Political science.
Classification: LCC JC423 .P869 2024 | DDC 320—dc23/eng/20230918
LC record available at https://lccn.loc.gov/2023041469

Copyright © 2024 The Pennsylvania State University
All rights reserved
Printed in the United States of America
Published by The Pennsylvania State University Press, University Park, PA 16802–1003

Chapter 3 is an abridged English translation of "Le fantôme de l'esprit public: Des illusions de la démocratie aux réalités de ses apparitions," which appeared as the preface in Walter Lippmann, *Le Public Fantôme*, edited by Bruno Latour (Paris: Éditions Demopolis, 2008). This chapter was translated from the original by Catherine Porter.

The Pennsylvania State University Press is a member of the Association of University Presses.

It is the policy of The Pennsylvania State University Press to use acid-free paper. Publications on uncoated stock satisfy the minimum requirements of American National Standard for Information Sciences—Permanence of Paper for Printed Library Material, ANSI Z39.48–1992.

CONTENTS

Acknowledgments | *vii*

Introduction: Lippmann, Dewey, and Democracy in a Hailstorm | 1
KRISTIAN BJØRKDAHL

1 A "Constituency of Intangibles": Walter Lippmann's Plea for a Better Democracy | 17
MICHAEL SCHUDSON

2 The Lippmann/Lippmann Debate: What Role Do Social Movements Play in Democratic Politics? | 29
NATHAN CRICK

3 From the Illusions of Democracy to the Realities of Its Appearances | 45
BRUNO LATOUR

4 Debates Conjured, Debates Forgotten | 68
ANNA SHECHTMAN AND JOHN DURHAM PETERS

5 Societal Embedding of the Lippmann/Dewey Debate: From Opinion Expression to Opinion Polling and Mining | 88
SLAVKO SPLICHAL

6 The Lippmann/Dewey Debate in the History of Twentieth-Century Progressivism | 111
STEVE FULLER

7 Propaedeutic Rhetorical Citizenship: Deweyan Impulses in Danish Community-Building | 138
LISA S. VILLADSEN

8 A Public and Its Solutions: Lippmann and Dewey Through the Prism of Norwegian Social Democracy | 160
KRISTIAN BJØRKDAHL

9 Democracy Now: Recovering the Political Pragmatism of Walter Lippmann and John Dewey | 182
SCOTT WELSH

10 Democratic Deliberation, Identity, and Information | 200
PATRICIA ROBERTS-MILLER

11 Rhetorical Sociology and the Management of Public Discourse | 217
ROBERT DANISCH AND WILLIAM KEITH

List of Contributors | 239

Index | 241

ACKNOWLEDGMENTS

No matter how hard they might try, books are nothing like sushi. For one thing, they cannot be procured and served fresh, but must accumulate over time, in an often prolonged and painstaking process—as their content is sketched and developed, rewritten and revised. Furthermore, books—at least the good ones—cannot necessarily be consumed and digested with ease: serious books need time, effort, and sometimes frustrated engagement to be read properly. The work that books in the end can do belongs not to days or weeks, but to months and years, or, if one should be so lucky, to decades and centuries. So if the present book has been rather too long in the making, I nevertheless hope it will offer ample stimulation to its readers, and also, that it—like its objects of study, Walter Lippmann and John Dewey—will *last*. More simply put, I hope this book has been worth the wait, for the patient people at Penn State University Press, for its well-willing and forbearing authors, as well as for potential readers who were placed in a state of anticipation along the way. I would like to acknowledge and thank especially Cheryl Glenn, Catherine Porter, John Durham Peters, Bill Keith, and Slavko Splichal, as well as the two reviewers, who in various ways offered support when this project needed it the most.

INTRODUCTION: LIPPMANN, DEWEY, AND DEMOCRACY IN A HAILSTORM

Kristian Bjørkdahl

"Optimism about democracy is to-day under a cloud," wrote John Dewey, in 1927, in *The Public and Its Problems*.[1] As we began our effort to assemble the present volume, almost one hundred years later, optimism about democracy had taken a turn for the worse: it now found itself in the midst of a violent and seemingly never-ending hailstorm of obnoxious and divisive tweets emanating from the White House, Air Force One, Mar-a-Lago, or whatever posh golf course was currently hosting the forty-fifth president of the United States of America—each shower washing out even further the hopes anyone might still have had in the rule of the people. The *people*, a score of academics and commentators now suggested, was precisely the problem, for it was what had enabled Trump's ascent to the presidency in the first place.

One much-cited contribution to the debate about the state of democracy in the second decade of the twenty-first century made this implication explicit: in *The People vs. Democracy*, Yascha Mounk warned that "the preferences of the people are increasingly illiberal" and added that the current moment amounted to an "existential crisis of liberal democracy."[2] Mounk argued that we were witnessing a parting of the ways of liberalism and democracy, and he explained how this development had opened up avenues for "elites [who] are taking hold of the political system and making it increasingly unresponsive," concluding that "the powerful are less and less willing to cede to the views of the people."[3] Others ventured much further into democratic skepticism and suggested that the long-standing democratic romance with the people needed to be left behind. The solution to our ills could be found in *10% Less Democracy*, one book proclaimed in its title, and offered reasons "why you should trust elites a little more and the masses a little less."[4] From every corner of the academic world, not to mention from the newspaper columns, came fresh analyses of the troubles of democracy, the threats of populism, or the mechanics of demagoguery.

As adept as Donald Trump was at making himself the center of attention within this turbulent moment, it soon dawned on most that he was only a player, and that a more disconcerting circumstance was how the game of politics itself appeared to have changed. We had allegedly entered a "post-truth" era, where regard for science, knowledge, and the very notion of truth had vanished or been dethroned.[5] With a long line of ominous book titles, scholars and authors suggested that we were witnessing the "end of democracy," the "death of democracy," or the "twilight of democracy."[6] All these bearers of bad omens did appear to have a point: in 2016, the *Economist* for the first time categorized the United States as a "flawed democracy" on its Democracy Index—an event that, just as one would expect, sparked a flood of news stories in various outlets across the world. More recently, Freedom House has noted that the United States between 2010 and 2020 experienced a significant decline on the Freedom in the World index, placing it behind countries such as Panama, Romania, Argentina, and Mongolia, though still ahead of Ghana and Trinidad and Tobago.[7] As embarrassing as these indexes are for the United States, this type of "democratic backsliding" is not unique to America,[8] but can be observed across countries and continents—for instance in Turkey, Hungary, Poland, and Brazil—in what many have come to think of as a new populist moment.[9]

More recently, Russia's war in Ukraine has seen the emergence of a form of territorial authoritarianism that appears old and new at the same time. It is old in the sense that its aims are roughly those of similar movements of the past (i.e., power), but new in the sense that its methods have been adapted to the circumstances of our time: authoritarianism today is not fixed within any grand ideology but fueled by a more straightforward belief in the strongman. Interestingly, though disconcertingly, this means that "democracy," too, can be used as a sort of placeholder for authoritarianism. This is what Victor Orbán famously did when he expressed "the [need] to state that a democracy is not necessarily liberal," and adding, in a sort of slogan for "illiberal democracy," that "just because something is not liberal, it still can be a democracy."[10]

While these tendencies have terrified many, and led some to double down on their defense of science or expertise or otherwise urge a "return to normalcy," others have discouraged such a response and explained why "we can't have our facts back."[11] Some even find in the contemporary predicament a scene of opportunity and potential positive change. Chantal Mouffe, for instance, has suggested that the current moment carries great promise, since it has been articulated not just within the authoritarian, far-right version represented by the likes of Erdoğan, Trump, Orbán, and Bolsonaro, but also within leftist movements like Occupy in the United States (and elsewhere), Aganaktismenoi and later Syriza in Greece, and Indignados and later Podemos in Spain. In *For a Left Populism*, she argues that the current era is seeing a reanimation of politics after decades of bland, "third way" consensualism, and that the chains of equivalence between various democratic demands—which she, with Ernesto Laclau, has called for since the mid-1980s—have now finally begun to form.[12] A different, but equally optimistic, assessment comes from Steve Fuller, who argues that the current moment is characterized not so much by the alleged novelty of "post-truth" as by the ascendancy of foxes over lions—that is, of those who want to topple the current order above those who want to preserve it—and that we can understand what is now surfacing as a further democratization of society.[13] These authors help us see that perhaps the most important characteristic of the present political moment is the way it has exploded calcified attitudes and practices of politics, opening up a new space for political creativity.

This more hopeful rendering of our situation is perhaps more inclined to highlight the flaws of the regime that remained hegemonic up to 2015 or so, and to consider that the liberal democracy of the recent few decades has been overdue for exposure to the "masses." This reading is more likely to acknowledge and even promote the sentiment at the core of the current movement, namely that the old elites had *already* left ordinary citizens behind. From this perspective, the problem is not, as Mounk argues, that powerful demagogues suddenly have become "less and less willing to cede to the views of the people"; it is that these allegedly benign elites have not ceded to the views of the people for a long while. The fact that this insight appears to have struck many politicians, pundits, advisers, and scholars only late in the game[14] is perhaps a sign of just how important the insight is. Before Brexit and Trump's win, the elites of established liberal democracy had grown so disinclined to consider the concerns and complaints of ordinary citizens that they solipsistically thought that "Brexit will not happen" and "Trump cannot win." While such pronouncements might have had the air of expert opinion at the time, it soon became clear that these were not manifestations of political insight, but only the latest instance of elites parading their arrogant ignorance. Hilary Clinton's infamous "basket of deplorables" trope served only to underline what many had known for a long time, namely that "Washington" did not have the people's best interests at heart.

Not all members of the elite were as oblivious to the growing estrangement between the elites and "the rest": almost immediately after Trump's win, the internet meme machine dived into its archives and resurfaced with an excerpt from philosopher Richard Rorty's then eighteen-year-old book, *Achieving Our Country*, where he appeared to prophesy the future coming of a strongman in the United States. If such a situation did come to pass, Rorty had argued, it would be as a consequence of the elites' infatuation with symbolic "identity politics" at the expense of more tangible, redistributive, class politics, a shift of priorities that over time would leave large parts of the population estranged from and dismayed by the urban elites.[15]

One of the most striking attempts to portray the elites' failure to listen to the concerns of common folk came in the form of the based-on-true-events film *Brexit: An Uncivil War*. The film opens with the Leave campaign manager, Dominic Cummings, giving a to-camera speech about the *sound* of popular discontent: "Britain makes a noise. An actual noise, did you know that? It *groans*. It's been groaning for some time. A hum, that only very few people can hear. Never stopping. A million important questions to be asked of our nation, our species, our planet, and no one's asking the right ones." To ask the right questions and listen when ordinary people respond is exactly what Cummings does, and this inclination is what the film puts forth to explain the Leave campaign's success. In a key scene, Cummings and his colleagues visit a poor, elderly couple whose everyday existence falls firmly outside the radar of the political parties. The couple are somewhat perplexed—no political party has knocked on their door "since about the eighties"—but soon enough they express the apathy they feel in the face of their neighborhood's deterioration. All of a sudden, Cummings hears a noise and leaves the room; he goes out onto the street, where he lays down on the asphalt, with his ear to the ground, *listening*. A voice-over says, "The noise, it's getting louder. Much louder. What does it mean? What's it trying to tell us?" As Cummings comes to realize, the noise is telling us that people want to "take back control" of their lives. He puts the phrase to use as the Leave campaign's populist slogan—and wins.[16]

Brexit: An Uncivil War renders the zeitgeist in another way: Importantly, Leave's success did not come only, or even predominantly, from knocking on people's doors and listening to what they had to say, but also, notably, from the magic offered by the tech companies—more specifically, the collection of great masses of personal data used for unprecedented online microtargeting. The current moment, then, is very much about how certain groups of people feel they have been left behind, and about how this sentiment—or even ressentiment—can be transformed into politics. It is, at the same time, about the technological means of doing just that, by way of big data, social media, echo chambers, filter bubbles, fake news, and all the other—still unfolding—aspects of what some call "surveillance capitalism."[17]

Even if one acknowledges the value of the current moment, and appreciates how calcified structures have been taken apart, one must confront the issue of how one might exploit this moment *well*, maybe even responsibly. In this, the Leave campaign is surely no model, since it was involved in shady methods of collecting personal data and circulating demonstrably fake news. This is arguably just to say that if this is a moment of political opportunity and potential, it is also, at the same time, and for many of the same reasons, a moment of *risk*.

Lippmann/Dewey: The Indispensable Distinction?

From this brief attempt to encapsulate some of the tendencies of our political present, it should be clear that what has recently been put into play—in a way that was never the case in the decades leading up to ours—is democracy itself. Gone are the days when liberal democracy was taken for granted: the question of what kind of democracy we should have, if we should even have one at all, has recently come alive with renewed force and urgency—to the point where some scholars have called for a *reinvention of popular rule*. The book from which that phrase is borrowed, Hélène Landemore's *Open Democracy*, is symptomatic of the times: even those who are committed to liberal democracy are now beginning to question some of its workings, and, like Landemore, draw on democratic experiments like Citizens' Councils and Citizens' Conventions for inspiration "to imagine and design more participatory, responsive, and effective institutions."[18]

Such proposals often sound as echoes of the past—whether this is openly acknowledged or not. The starting point for this book is that among the most important ideas to echo in the present, and which should in fact *continue* to do so, is the work of Walter Lippmann and John Dewey. As recent, "revisionist" scholarship has shown, a somewhat peculiar picture of Lippmann's and Dewey's respective contributions to political thought began to form in the 1980s, and perhaps even before that, which construed the relation between the two as a "debate," and which in turn painted this debate as one between thesis and antithesis. Their respective approaches to democratic deliberation and decision-making have often been taken to represent opposing poles, to the point where the differences between them were ingrained as a sort of typology of democracies: on the one hand, the expert-oriented, elitist, centralized type favored by Lippmann; on the other, the grassroots, bottom-up, participatory type favored by Dewey.

The critics of this picture have argued that its originator was the noted communication scholar James Carey, who, as Anna Shechtman and John Durham Peters put it in this volume, painted a "tendentiously rosy portrait of Dewey for field-reforming purposes." More specifically, critics have suggested that Carey rendered the opposition between Lippmann and Dewey in far starker terms than the evidence could support, in order to establish a distinction between an "administrative" or "realist" approach to political communication and his (or was it Dewey's?) "critical" or "participatory" ideal. What went by the wayside in this account was, quite simply, Walter Lippmann—of whom Carey made a "straw man" caricature and an "anti-democrat."[19] But contrary to what Carey suggested, these critics argued, Lippmann was no anti-democrat, and he did not denigrate the common citizen. All he did was think realistically through what we could sensibly expect from the common citizen and what we could not. This scholarly pushback against Carey's representation of Lippmann and Dewey, has in turn been met with countercriticism, not least the work of Lana Rakow, who not only has targeted the empirical base of these critics' revisionism but has also mounted a defense and a restatement of Carey's Deweyan emphasis.

In the context of this volume, the debate about the Lippmann/Dewey "debate" is an important backdrop, not least because it, in many ways, has rekindled the interest in these two undeniably important political thinkers. The purpose of the present book, though, is not primarily to set the record straight on this issue, but to ask, first, how we can tell a richer story of the contributions of Lippmann and Dewey, and second, what each of them—or both, in concert—has to offer our attempt to think through our own predicament. In part, the book looks back in time, to consider the historical context of these two thinkers, and in part, it looks toward the present and future, to inquire into their enduring relevance. What might these two thinkers help us understand, but also take advantage of, in the current political moment? More specifically, the book asks what can be gained from revisiting their writings on democracy and democratic publics—notably, though not exclusively, Lippmann's *Public Opinion* (1922) and *The Phantom Public* (1925), and Dewey's *The Public and Its Problems* (1927)[20]—in order to further the cause of democracy, in a situation where democracy appears to face greater challenges than it has since World War II.

We realize that this question might strike some as strange, for if the current moment is really such an anomaly, why would one want to rummage about in the archives and inspect what happened one hundred years ago? There are two main reasons.

The first is that the era that produced these writings has some clear parallels with our own. They are both marked by great social and political shifts, which constantly border on, and sometimes erupt in, conflict—and which are seen and even used as opportunities to enact change. They also share the aspect of risk, the feeling—or even the real possibility—that space opens up to those with less than democratic agendas. This situation stands in contrast to the post–World War II decades, which were characterized rather by stability and steady growth within the frame of the Cold War. Even after the fall of the Berlin Wall and the dismantling of the Soviet Union, a great deal of postwar stability lingered. Only with great difficulty was anyone able to imagine that the global triumph of liberal democracy was less than permanent. But however strong the convergence around liberal democracy grew—and by the mid-1990s it had grown very strong—it could always be broken, and that is in fact what has begun to happen in our day, as new political space has opened up and as questions of the relation between rich and poor, elites and commoners, experts and layfolk, again have been put at the center of politics. In this context we are, at least in some ways, back where Lippmann and Dewey were in the 1920s, when they felt that things were changing rapidly and dramatically, that one could not know which way things would go, but where it, precisely for this reason, was imperative to take hold of one's moment in time. As they tried to diagnose their present, Lippmann and Dewey asked themselves what, given these new and rapidly changing circumstances, would be apposite means to our democratic ends. To the extent our situation is like theirs—and while it is not perfectly so, there are some clear parallels—it should be more obvious why we should take an interest in Lippmann and Dewey.

This leads to the second reason, which is that the Lippmann/Dewey axis—understood not just as a series of analyses of democratic publics, but as a pair, as an expression of opposite democratic emphases—has proven to be remarkably productive. In short, the Lippmann/Dewey distinction has to a large extent become constitutive of the scope of democratic alternatives. As hinted at above, this situation is not just for the good; as several of the contributors to this volume point out, there were and are still other ways of construing democratic deliberation and decision-making than those highlighted by the Lippmann/Dewey axis, and this distinction has been the root of a certain calcification by which no one is well served. There was, historically, a much larger universe of discourse around Lippmann and Dewey than what the model-oriented representation lets us believe, and many political diagnoses and cures circulate today that have nothing much to do with either of them. That said, it should be just as clear that many of the issues at stake in their writings from the 1920s have not at all gone away. And even if recent efforts to tone down the opposition between them have been worthwhile and sensible, we cannot deny that their respective visions for democracy were, in significant ways, very different, and that they represent live options for us today. To put it simply, we are either justified in placing our hopes in broad popular participation in democracy—or we are not.

Today, the stakes are perhaps even higher than they were one hundred years ago. In circumstances where the sustainability of the democratic way of life appears to be challenged from many sides at once—climate change and biodiversity loss, racism and xenophobia, wars and territorial ambition, economic inequality and political polarization—we are faced not just with the doomsayers' concern with *whether democracy will survive*, but just as important, with the question of *what democracy can and will become*. On the latter issue, Walter Lippmann and John Dewey are still indispensable guides to the options available to us.

Excavations, Appreciations, Rediscoveries, Elaborations

In writing for this book, the authors have faced no "partisan" premise to which they had to align their contributions. Instead, they were free to explore the history of Lippmann/Dewey opposition or its continued relevance, to focus on Lippmann or on Dewey or on both, and to take any "side"—if any at all. The only requirement was to keep the conversation about these two authors going. Naturally, they have chosen to approach this task in many different ways.

First, a few of the contributors issue what we might call appreciations of the protagonists, in part to respond to recent scholarship, in part to establish a framework to think through our own time.

Michael Schudson, in his chapter, refines his position on the debate about Lippmann/Dewey. He underlines here the importance of distinguishing between singling out *citizens'* lack of capacity for oversight, knowledge acquisition, and rational decision-making (which Lippmann did *not* do) and making a general point about *human beings'* lack of such capacity (which

Lippmann *did* do). For Lippmann, the incompetency in question is certainly real and represents a problem for democracy, but he never suggested it had something to do with the people qua people. Rather, when Lippmann says that citizens are not sufficiently equipped for self-governance, this reflects a "situational condition and not an individual trait." Ordinary citizens are incapable of self-government simply because government, in a modern mass society, involves all sorts of things that "they are not personally and professionally acquainted with." This point had no particular reference to "the people." Rather, as Lippmann wrote, "every one of us is an outsider to all but a few aspects of modern life."

Nathan Crick starts from the idea that there is not one Walter Lippmann, but (at least) two. Specifically, the Lippmann of *A Preface to Politics* (1913) is in many ways an entirely different thinker than the Lippmann of *The Phantom Public* (1925). While the former, according to Crick, renders social movements as "instruments of progress," the latter is dotted with statements to the effect that no great hope should be placed on "public opinion and the action of masses." Excavating the earlier Lippmann, Crick finds that central terms of the Lippmann/Dewey debate can already be found in the "debate" that the late Lippmann had with his earlier self. Crick argues that the two positions are distinguished not so much by matters of epistemology but by trust—"namely the trust in ordinary people to contribute something positive to the creative life of politics in the form of social movements."

In his chapter, Bruno Latour reads Lippmann as a latter-day Machiavelli—one who wanted to free politics from all its ingrained illusions. The value of Lippmann's work, as Latour sees it, is the conviction and clear-sightedness with which he pursues his goal; Lippmann is an open and flexible thinker who bravely takes on broad thoughts that others relate to as taboos. No grounds to believe in the idea of "the Public"? Let's get rid of it! More specifically, Latour argues that "Lippmann has identified with maximum precision what is paralyzing the apprenticeship of liberty: the very idea of society." Only by going along with Lippmann, and exposing the appearances of democracy, can we give ourselves "the means to obtain the necessary adjustments," he writes. As for Dewey's role, Latour aligns himself with Dewey's insistence that the adjustments to be had from Lippmann's realism will never be sufficient to "compose a viable world," and that Lippmann leaves us without any impulse toward the creation of a common good.

Another set of authors use this book as an opportunity to build a wider context around the alleged debate, to counter the somewhat flat distinction that has come down to us. Not only was the "Lippmann/Dewey debate" not really a debate, it also was not a concern for this pair alone. In fact, there is much more to be said about both where Lippmann and Dewey were coming from, and about the intellectual environment of which their books and articles were but a part.

Anna Shechtman and John Durham Peters note that while James Carey's construal of the difference between Lippmann and Dewey was overdrawn and schematic, Carey was nevertheless right "to locate in these figures and this moment important precedents for the problems we continue to face around media and democracy." Importantly, though, the issues that Lippmann and Dewey raised were not theirs alone. In fact, a whole host of scholars and commentators responded to that moment in time, and Shechtman and Peters resurrect some of the many intellectual figures and exchanges that, in the shadow of the Lippmann/Dewey debate, have been largely forgotten, among them Randolph Bourne, Floyd Allport, Max Horkheimer, Lewis Mumford, and Reinhold Niebuhr. Unlike Lippmann, many of these thinkers were explicit critics of Dewey. According to Shechtman and Peters, these critics have tested and adjusted Dewey's legacy, but they have not thereby put it to rest—since democracy, for Dewey, was a "project of liberating humanity" that involved "a socializing of the means of communication"—and hence, an ongoing project.

Slavko Splichal emphasizes that Lippmann's and Dewey's ideas about public opinion are still relevant today, but that they are now surrounded by a new context, where issues of "transnationalization" and "datafication" of public opinion are among the central concerns. To take hold of the current moment, however, we need to recognize that the study of public opinion did not spring "fully panoplied" from Lippmann's and Dewey's publications in the 1920s; serious inquiry into the issue had already gone on for some time before this pair, and can even be traced back so far as to Machiavelli. Significant work was also ongoing alongside Lippmann and Dewey, including by such prominent thinkers as Gabriel Tarde and Ferdinand Tönnies. Later, substantially new approaches were added, including polling and, more recently, data mining. Reflecting on this history, Splichal concludes that, while the current technological moment offers democratic potential, it will not materialize by itself. Neither authoritarian powers nor commercial corporations will make it happen, and instead we should reignite the call, which unites Lippmann and Dewey with Tarde, to expand citizens' level of education.

In his chapter, Steve Fuller reads the differences between Lippmann and Dewey as a "struggle for the soul of Progressivism" and retraces some of the stakes of that struggle, focusing mostly on Lippmann's trajectory. Fuller suggests that the two in this pair were indeed distinct in their respective construals of the State: While Dewey was an "emergentist" on this issue, Lippmann was a "dualist." Importantly, however, Fuller introduces a much wider set of characters to his story, so as to downplay the binary framing that the Lippmann/Dewey contrast has often served. Both of them were actors in wider historical processes and projects, and they had various—not to mention changing—roles within them. Fuller doubts the usefulness of the pair as intellectual resources today since, as he writes, "If Dewey was clearly on the losing side of history, it doesn't follow that Lippmann was clearly on the winning side." They were both important historical actors, however, and their lives and works are central sites from which to write history—say, of Progressivism and its fate.

A final set of authors transpose Lippmann and/or Dewey to other places and settings—like Europe, the present, or practical politics—than the ones we normally associate with them—like the United States, the past, or intellectual culture.

Lisa Villadsen starts from what many have felt is a romantic weakness in Dewey's account, namely his idea that democracy, in order to flourish, requires face-to-face interaction among citizens. Although this type of interaction is not always directly involved in high-level decision-making, that does not mean it is irrelevant or marginal. In fact, for Dewey, as for Villadsen, this type of interaction is crucial, and arguably even more important than the "results" of democratic decision-making, since "the communicative processes undergirding public and political life" are what enable people to come together and form a public at all. Seen in this way, the central importance of *The Public and Its Problems* is that it shifts our priorities from Lippmann's results orientation toward an ideal of democracy as a process—or as he himself put it, as a way of life. Villadsen's argument is that practical sites and processes of engagement and interaction have a propaedeutic function, that they enable and build rhetorical citizenship. She provides an illustration of this point by way of an in-depth account of Denmark's Borgerlyst initiative (whose name means Civic Desire)—a semiorganized series of events designed to foster democratic discussion and agency.

Kristian Bjørkdahl, in his chapter, suggests that the Lippmann/Dewey complex has unduly constrained our political imaginations, to the point where we fail to see that there exist practical ways of overcoming the choice between them. Specifically, he argues that the tradition of tripartism in Scandinavian social democracy strikes a compromise between the pair. As a political mechanism, tripartism is both top-down and bottom-up; it creates bridges between experts and citizens; and it encourages various sorts of traffic back and forth between insiders and outsiders. That does not mean it aligns with either Lippmann or Dewey, but that is exactly the point: real politics does not conform to models or ideals; rather, it is messy, full of compromise and second-best solutions. Norwegians have usefully made a cultural virtue of the will to compromise, which they see encapsulated in the tripartite arrangement, but the flip side of this "culturalization" of tripartism is that it tends to underestimate the contingent and largely coincidental history of this mechanism, instead presenting tripartism as a sort of gift given to the Chosen People of the North. In this way, it gets in the way of a discussion of whether the Norwegian experience could hold lessons for other countries.

In a meditation that traffics back and forth between Lippmann and Dewey, as well as between their age and ours, Scott Welsh aims to find out how we can find inspiration in this pair today. Without discounting the differences, Welsh points out that even Dewey underlined the difference between *political* democracy and the *idea* of democracy, and that his hopes, just like Lippmann's, were rather constrained on behalf of the first. Still, there is no way around political democracy and all its restrictions. A problem with both writers, Welsh argues, is that they "demeaned the practice of democratic politics in the moment" by setting up a future democracy that allegedly would be more satisfactory or sufficient, thus making actually existing democracy look "somehow compromised, tawdry, or democratically second-rate." To counter this problem, Welsh sets out to reclaim the pragmatism that is also inherent in both writers, by focusing on what each actually does appreciate in existing democracy—an exercise that is important to our current democratic hopes, since those cannot be sustained without an appreciation of the day-to-day work of politics.

Patricia Roberts-Miller, in her chapter, points out that what Lippmann and Dewey share is an inclination to think that the problem of the public is somehow connected to (mass) mediation and that "direct knowledge is preferable." Thus, they both assumed that the problems they were grappling with were consequences of the huge demographic and societal changes of the late nineteenth and early twentieth century. But this, Roberts-Miller contends, is a "very problematic assumption." She puts Lippmann's and Dewey's assumption to the test of more recent research, which leads us to think that to privilege direct knowledge is deceptive and false. Indeed, Roberts-Miller claims that this tendency is "at the base of how and why people reason badly." More specifically, this tendency makes us overlook or discount such phenomena as confirmation bias and in-group favoritism, which science has shown to be far more ubiquitous than either Lippmann or Dewey—or indeed most of us—would like to admit. The implication of this, Roberts-Miller says, is that we "keep trying to solve the wrong problem," that is, to identify the entity (the people? the experts?) whose judgments best qualify it to govern. We are thus fooled by the opposition between Lippmann and Dewey not to reflect on the basic—but wrong—assumption, that the best judgments come from those with direct knowledge. Against the pair, we should not see good decision-making as the outcome of an *identity*, but of a *process*.

Robert Danisch and William Keith start from the point that Lippmann and Dewey addressed a common set of problems, but that those problems had little to with the viability of deliberative democracy as such. Rather, the core of the problem, they suggest, is that US society by the 1920s had grown so big and complex that the systems that had seemed to work up to the past century now seemed insufficient and mismatched to the current predicament. What both Lippmann and Dewey did, in that situation, was to formulate a new rhetorical sociology, which is to say that they offered new accounts of how "social structures, institutions, and forms of individual agency are both guided by and constituted by communicative practices." As Danisch and Keith see it, there is good reason, still today, to be inspired by their respective formulations, but there is no point in assuming that our rhetorical sociology cannot combine elements from both thinkers. What we need to take from Dewey, they suggest, is the need for "institutional mechanisms capable of forming, building, and maintaining social relationships between diverse sets of strangers," while from Lippmann we should take "institutional mechanisms for ensuring that the information circulating in public discourse is reliable and accurate."

Notes

1. Dewey, *Public and Its Problems*, 304.
2. Mounk, *People vs. Democracy*, 12, 16.
3. Mounk, 12.
4. Jones, *10% Less Democracy*.
5. For an insightful, though in many ways atypical, account of post-truth, see Fuller, *Post-Truth*.
6. Runciman, *How Democracy Ends*; Levitsky and Ziblatt, *How Democracies Die*; Applebaum, *Twilight of Democracy*.
7. Economist Intelligence Unit, *Democracy Index 2016*; Repucci, *From Crisis to Reform*, 2. The downward trend continues in the latest EIU report (*Democracy Index 2021*).
8. Silva-Leander, *Global State of Democracy*.
9. Müller, *What Is Populism?*

10. Tóth, "Full Text of Viktor Orbán's Speech."
11. Marres, "Why We Can't Have Our Facts Back."
12. Mouffe, *For a Left Populism*. See also Laclau and Mouffe, *Hegemony and Socialist Strategy*; as well as much of the pair's subsequent publications.
13. See Fuller, *Post-Truth*.
14. Mudde, "Why Is American Political Science Blind on the Right Eye?"
15. See Helmore, "Something Will Crack"; and Senior, "Richard Rorty's 1998 Book." An argument much in the same vein was offered in real time, as it were, by Mark Lilla in *The Once and Future Liberal*.
16. If this film is an instantiation in popular culture of a growing awareness of the importance of *listening*, this tendency has also been notable in scholarship; see, for example, Dobson, *Listening for Democracy*; Scudder, *Beyond Empathy and Inclusion*; Ercan, Hendriks, and Dryzek, "Public Deliberation."
17. Zuboff, *Age of Surveillance Capitalism*.
18. Landemore, *Open Democracy*, xviii.
19. The main entries in the debate have been Jansen, "Phantom Conflict"; Jansen, "Walter Lippmann, Straw Man"; Schudson, "'Lippmann-Dewey Debate'"; Schudson, "Trouble with Experts"; Schudson, "Walter Lippmann's Ghost"; Rakow, "Family Feud"; and Rakow, *John Dewey*. Other central contributions include Crick, "Search for a Purveyor of News"; Tell, "Reinventing Walter Lippmann"; and Goodwin, "Walter Lippman, the Indispensable Opposition."
20. Lippmann, *Public Opinion*; Lippmann, *Phantom Public*; Dewey, *Public and Its Problems*.

Bibliography

Applebaum, Anne. *Twilight of Democracy: The Seductive Lure of Authoritarianism*. New York: Doubleday, 2020.

Crick, Nathan. "The Search for a Purveyor of News: The Dewey/Lippmann Debate in an Internet Age." *Critical Studies in Media Communication* 26, no. 5 (2009): 480–97.

Dewey, John. *The Public and Its Problems* (1927). In *John Dewey: The Later Works, 1925–1953*, edited by Jo Ann Boydston, 2:235–372. Carbondale: Southern Illinois University Press, 1984.

Dobson, Andrew. *Listening for Democracy: Recognition, Representation, Reconciliation*. Oxford: Oxford University Press, 2014.

Economist Intelligence Unit. *Democracy Index 2016: Revenge of the "Deplorables."* London: Economist Intelligence Unit, 2017.

Economist Intelligence Unit. *Democracy Index 2021: The China Challenge*. London: Economist Intelligence Unit, 2022.

Ercan, Selen, Carolyn M. Hendriks, and John S. Dryzek, "Public Deliberation in an Era of Communicative Plenty." *Policy and Politics* 47, no. 1 (2019): 19–36.

Fuller, Steve. *Post-Truth: Knowledge as a Power Game*. London: Anthem, 2018.

Goodwin, Jean. "Walter Lippman, the Indispensable Opposition." In *Trained Capacities: John Dewey, Rhetoric, and Democratic Practice*, edited by Gregory Clark and Brian Jackson, 142–58. Columbia: University of South Carolina Press, 2014.

Helmore, Edward. "'Something Will Crack': Supposed Prophecy of Donald Trump Goes Viral." *The Guardian*, November 19, 2016.

Jansen, Sue Curry. "Phantom Conflict: Lippmann, Dewey, and the Fate of the Public in Modern Society." *Communication and Critical/Cultural Studies* 6, no. 3 (2009): 221–45.

———. "Walter Lippmann, Straw Man of Communication Research." In *The History of Media and Communication Research: Contested Memories*, edited by David W. Park and Jefferson Pooley, 71–111. New York: Peter Lang, 2008.

Jones, Garret. *10% Less Democracy: Why You Should Trust Elites a Little More and the Masses a Little Less*. Stanford, CA: Stanford University Press, 2020.

Laclau, Ernesto, and Chantal Mouffe. *Hegemony and Socialist Strategy*. London: Verso, 1985.

Landemore, Hélène. *Open Democracy: Reinventing Popular Rule for the Twenty-First Century*. Princeton, NJ: Princeton University Press, 2020.

Levitsky, Steven, and Daniel Ziblatt. *How Democracies Die*. New York: Broadway Books, 2018.

Lilla, Mark. *The Once and Future Liberal: After Identity Politics*. New York: HarperCollins, 2017.

Lippmann, Walter. *The Phantom Public* (1925). Abingdon: Routledge, 2017.

———. *Public Opinion* (1922). Abingdon: Routledge, 2017.

Marres, Noortje. "Why We Can't Have Our Facts Back." *Engaging Science, Technology, and Society* 4 (2018): 423–43.

Mouffe, Chantal. *For a Left Populism*. London: Verso, 2018.

Mounk, Yascha. *The People vs. Democracy: Why Our Freedom Is in Danger and How to Save It*. Cambridge, MA: Harvard University Press, 2018.

Mudde, Cas. "Why Is American Political Science Blind on the Right Eye?" *HuffPost*, August 29, 2016. https://www.huffpost.com/entry/why-is-american-political_b_11764330.

Müller, Jan-Werner. *What Is Populism?* Philadelphia: University of Pennsylvania Press, 2016.

Rakow, Lana F. "Family Feud: Who's Still Fighting About Dewey and Lippmann?" *Javnost—the Public* 25, no. 1 (2018): 75–82.

———. *John Dewey: A Critical Introduction to Media and Communication Theory*. New York: Peter Lang, 2019.

Repucci, Sarah. *From Crisis to Reform: A Call to Strengthen America's Battered Democracy*. Washington, DC: Freedom House, 2021.

Runciman, David. *How Democracy Ends*. London: Profile Books, 2018.

Schudson, Michael. "The 'Lippmann-Dewey Debate' and the Invention of Walter Lippmann as an Anti-Democrat, 1986–1996." *International Journal of Communication* 2 (2008): 1031–42.

———. "The Trouble with Experts—and Why Democracies Need Them." *Theory and Society* 35, no. 5 (2006): 491–506.

———. "Walter Lippmann's Ghost: An Interview with Michael Schudson." *Mass Communication and Society* 19, no. 3 (2016): 221–29.

Scudder, Mary F. *Beyond Empathy and Inclusion: The Challenge of Listening in Democratic Deliberation*. New York: Oxford University Press, 2020.

Senior, Jennifer. "Richard Rorty's 1998 Book Suggested Election 2016 Was Coming." *New York Times*, November 20, 2016.

Silva-Leander, Annika, ed. *The Global State of Democracy 2019*. Stockholm: International IDEA, 2019.

Tell, Dave. "Reinventing Walter Lippmann: Communication and Cultural Studies." *Review of Communication* 13, no. 2 (2013): 108–26.

Tóth, Csaba. "Full Text of Viktor Orbán's Speech at Băile Tuşnad (Tusnádfürdő) of 26 July 2014." *Budapest Beacon*, July 29, 2014. https://budapestbeacon.com/full-text-of-viktor-orbans-speech-at-baile-tusnad-tusnadfurdo-of-26-july-2014/.

Zuboff, Shoshana. *The Age of Surveillance Capitalism: The Fight for a Human Future at the New Frontier of Power*. New York: PublicAffairs, 2019.

I
A "CONSTITUENCY OF INTANGIBLES":
WALTER LIPPMANN'S PLEA FOR A BETTER DEMOCRACY

Michael Schudson

If there is a single sentence in Walter Lippmann's *Public Opinion* that refutes, by itself, the mess that has been made of his ideas in media and communication studies, it would be this one: "It is no accident that the best diplomatic service in the world is the one in which the divorce between the assembling of knowledge and the control of policy is most perfect."[1] That diplomatic service, Lippmann says, is the British Foreign Office. Lippmann reported that during World War I in many British embassies and in the Foreign Office in London there were nearly always personnel who "quite successfully discounted the prevailing war mind. They discarded the rigmarole of being pro and con, of having favorite nationalities, and pet aversions, and undelivered perorations in their bosoms. They left that to the political chiefs" (240).

They were, in short, experts, people able to collect and report the cold facts relevant to policy makers, but not people in a position to make policy decisions themselves. And individual experts, Lippmann argued in his next paragraph, gain their authority only if they are distinctly *not* the decision-makers and only if each of them takes on the attitude of "not caring, in his expert self, what decision is made" (241). Experts are not employed to see what they wish to see but "to represent the unseen"—not voters but something more abstract—"mute people, unborn people," and even "relations between things and people." The expert is not responsible to the voters but has nonetheless "a constituency of intangibles" (241). (I do not know what Lippmann had in mind with "relations between things and people," but the National Park Service had just been established a few years before, in 1916. Its charter legislation declared that its aim should be "to conserve the scenery and the natural and historic objects and wildlife therein . . . by such means as will leave them unimpaired for the enjoyment of future generations." The aim of conservation of natural resources to endow a future, regardless of whether voters of the present might care deeply about it, is much in people's minds today. Perhaps something like this was on Lippmann's mind a century ago.)

There are two crucial ideas in this passage. First, the ideal function of experts in government should be simply "the assembling of knowledge" and passing it on to decision-makers. The job of experts is to present to the decision-makers a picture of the "unseen" world fuller and more accurate than they would otherwise have had before them. There is no ground here for the sort of accusation that would be later tossed at Lippmann as someone seeking to place experts at the helm of democratic leadership. That was never his position. Whether Lippmann is realistic in assuming that experts can "assemble knowledge" without any intrusion of their values or policy preferences is a different matter (that I will return to).

Second, Lippmann looks to the experts to bring to decision-makers not only a broader sense of relevant materials across geographic space, that is, information of what is known across a state or region or nation or globe that would not be available to legislators and bureaucrats from their own personal experience or acquaintance, but also to bring to them relevant materials across time—urging that they keep in mind future generations, a part of their constituency of intangibles.

Experts today don't have a good reputation even among experts. We know how easy it is for them to protect one another and to fall into a habit of talking only to one another and reinforcing one another's assumptions. Incorporating expertise into democracy is hazardous—although not as risky, it seems to me, as operating without it.

Just what are the hazards of experts for democracy? We often get this wrong. We often forget what David Halberstam's book about the Vietnam War, *The Best and the Brightest*, refers to in its famous title. The phrase has been understood again and again to be pointing at the power and arrogance of experts. In fact, it is unrelentingly a defense of experts. It decries Secretary of Defense Robert McNamara's ignorance of Vietnam and judges him "the last man to understand and measure the problems of a people looking for their political freedom." No one, Halberstam writes, was more forceful in the Kennedy administration than McNamara in blocking information from the government's own experts so that it did not influence decisions on Vietnam. Halberstam criticizes Secretary of State Dean Rusk for putting down the State Department's own top authority on Vietnam. He complains that the Joint Chiefs of Staff ignored the judgments of the government's Vietnam experts.[2]

For Halberstam, the ironic phrase "the best and the brightest" refers to the high-flying political appointees and military leaders who could not be bothered to listen to people whose whole careers were devoted to the study of Southeast Asia. There may be a problem with a democracy that gives too much decision-making authority to experts, but the larger problem is that democracies are often inclined to give experts too little attention and too minimal a role in governing. Halberstam was criticizing not experts but the smugness of the quasi-aristocratic corps of tough-minded men around John F. Kennedy whose arrogance derived neither from professional training nor from expertise but from class rearing, and this led them as agency heads or White House advisers to ignore or silence subordinates. The tragedy of Vietnam policy, for Halberstam, is that this rule of arrogance overrode the well-informed cautions of State Department officers. Not incidentally, he criticized the military commanders who castigated his own reports from Vietnam for the *New York Times*—reports later confirmed as true.

Lippmann has been broadly understood as an unrepentant elitist since the lively discussion among communication scholars in the 1980s about a so-called Dewey/Lippmann debate. He was supposed to be deeply suspicious of democracy, strongly identified with placing American politics in the hands of elites, specifically, subject-matter experts. But that interpretation is, at best, caricature and often sheer distortion. Lippmann's ideas are richer, more nuanced, more powerful, and with more relevance to our own day than this allows. I will get to this through a rereading of *Public Opinion* with particular respect to how Lippmann assessed the capacities of the general public for democratic participation and how he viewed the capacities of government to govern.

Rereading *Public Opinion* I: The General Public and Its Limitations

In *Public Opinion*, Lippmann makes no distinction between experts, elites, and the general public in their capacity for learning, their general intelligence, or their fitness for participating in a democratic society. All of us—he is scrupulous and insistent about this—*all of us* are subject to accepting fiction as reality. All of us have partial vision. All of us are more able to absorb information about things we are interested in than about things we are not interested in, things that relate closely to our occupation, our family, and our friends than those that do not. Journalists who regularly write about foreign policy or State Department officials who deal with foreign policy every day are more likely to be informed about foreign policy than you or me regardless of our native intelligence or years of schooling.

Lippmann's critics have repeatedly and stubbornly misread him on this point. James Carey, not alone in this but the most influential culprit, held that Lippmann believed that "voters are inherently incompetent to direct public affairs."[3] Using an argument he made at a 1986 conference at the Center for the Study of Democratic Institutions in Santa Barbara, California, and publishing in that organization's journal, *The Center*, in 1987, Carey wrote that Lippmann confirmed "the psychological incompetence of people to participate" in democracy.[4]

"Psychological incompetence" like "inherently incompetent" strongly suggests an individual characteristic, a failure of untrained or unschooled people. But, for Lippmann, the insufficiency of people for democratic self-governance is a situational condition and not an individual trait. It is not a sociological difference between rich and poor or educated and uneducated or a psychological difference between intelligent and unintelligent or dutifully attentive and lazily inattentive. It is a positional or situational difference that Lippmann consistently, from a 1915 article in the *New Republic* to *Public Opinion* in 1922 to *The Phantom Public* in 1925, discussed as the difference between "insiders" and "outsiders."

It's illuminating to look at the chapter of *Public Opinion* where Lippmann judges the ordinary person or voter or citizen to be not incompetent but approaching "omnicompetence." This chapter helps to clarify what Lippmann intended in the book as a whole. Lippmann argued, throughout *Public Opinion*, that what he called "democratic theory" depended on an understanding of citizens as "omnicompetent" and thereby able to evaluate candidates and parties and policies from the foundation of being well-informed. One weakness in the book, I think, is that "democratic theory" is waved before the reader without citing any individual thinker or group of thinkers or set of principles that constitutes it. "Democratic theory," in Lippmann's hands, is a vague straw man he attacks with his psychological realism about how human beings process information—although it is not exactly a straw man because something like it does seem to pervade, at least in the United States, a broad understanding of how democracy is supposed to work. But for Lippmann, people actually *are* "omnicompetent" when they live in a "self-contained community" where they have firsthand acquaintance with most of what goes on in their community: "The doctrine of the omnicompetent citizen is for most practical purposes true in the rural township. Everybody in a village sooner or later tries his hand at everything the village does. There is rotation in office by men who are jacks of all trades. There was no serious trouble with the doctrine of the omnicompetent citizen until the democratic stereotype was universally applied, so that men looked at a complicated civilization and saw an enclosed village" (173). These are Lippmann's words. In small towns and rural communities, everyone is nearly omnicompetent in public affairs. But in the complex, cosmopolitan world we all share today, incompetence is the fate of all of us. This is through no fault of ours as individuals; it is simply that comprehending the complex world we inhabit is impossible, that our world is "out of reach, out of sight, out of mind" (18). He never held that the general public is "incompetent" (as opposed to competent experts), and he never wrote or implied that the general public is "inherently incompetent." It is clear throughout *Public Opinion* that "incompetence" for intelligent participation in democratic life is not a matter of "class" and it is not a matter of "inherent" incapacity. The public's incapacity, for Lippmann, was entirely situational.

Rereading *Public Opinion* II: Government and Its Limitations

What was omitted by the 1980s and 1990s readers of Lippmann is that he spends a lot of time discussing the limitations of Congress and government bureaucrats alike for decision-making. "There is no systematic, adequate and authorized way for Congress to know what is going on in the world" (182), he complains. Even here, when he might have taken off after the dunderheads that ill-informed people elect to Congress, he takes quite a different tack. For Lippmann, the limitations of knowledge of members of Congress "is no fault of the individual Congressman's, except when he is complacent about it" (183). The difficulty is far deeper: "The cleverest and most industrious representative cannot hope to understand a fraction of the bills on which he votes. The best he can do is to specialize on a few bills, and take somebody's word about the rest" (183). Writing half a century before John Kingdon's study of how members of the US Congress make decisions on legislation before them, Lippmann anticipated Kingdon's findings—that members of Congress do precisely what he said and depend on other members of Congress to determine their voting on bills of which they have little or no knowledge. Other politicians can offer the best advice, notably those who are of the same party and who share general values and preferences. These people can give advice that recognizes the political needs of the member seeking advice and, not incidentally, are "readily available at the time of voting, a consideration of paramount importance" (183). This pattern is less pronounced in the Senate than in the House, as senators are better equipped with staff aides of their own they can turn to than are members of the House.

Lippmann offers a cognitive psychology and a social psychology in *Public Opinion*. He does not offer a sociology. He does not say what characterizes the mental outlook of the general population as opposed to experts, or the people of one class or region compared to others. He is consistently interested to report on the outlooks of people in general, and not, say, the masses as opposed to elites. So Carl Bybee is mistaken to hold that Lippmann has "grave doubts over the capacity of the average citizen to engage in rational self-government."[5] No, he did not criticize the "capacity of the average citizen." He insisted—over and over, in fact—that "we"—all of us—have a limited capacity to attend to matters beyond our immediate concerns. That is the guiding framework for the whole of Lippmann's *Public Opinion*.

The general public's poor grasp of public and political issues arises not because ordinary people are poorly educated or because their mental capacities are inferior to those of experts, but because they are human beings and share with experts a great ignorance of matters they are not personally and professionally acquainted with.

And what, for Lippmann, is the role of experts in all of this? It is secondarily to inform journalists and through them the public. But that will not take us very far toward better democratic government because all of us, when we are outsiders, have limited time, attention, and familiarity with the questions at issue: "The outsider, and every one of us is an outsider to all but a few aspects of modern life, has neither time, nor attention, nor interest, nor the equipment for specific judgment. It is on the men inside, working under conditions that are sound, that the daily administrations of society must rest" (251). He repeated this again and again in *Public Opinion*: all of us are outsiders to most public issues most of the time.

Lippmann looks forward to a world where experts have a more institutionalized place in governing, but he is no fool about their virtues and limitations. He writes, "Our knowledge of human institutions is still extraordinarily meager and impressionistic. The gathering of social knowledge is, on the whole, still haphazard; not, as it will have to become, the normal accompaniment of action" (256). For Lippmann, "As our minds become more deeply aware of their own subjectivism, we find a zest in objective method that is not otherwise there" (251).

Who is this "we"? Everyone, experts included. What experts have that nonexperts do not is enough information about a specific subject and enough acquaintance with a variety of authoritative voices (of varying opinion) on that subject to possess a check on their own subjectivism to pay other voices heed.

Public Opinion gives an important place to journalism in democracy, but reforming journalism is not the reformist heart of the book; reforming the informational resources for public administration is more central to the book's agenda. Public administration should have embraced Lippmann as much or more than journalism and communication studies.

In *The Phantom Public* (1925), Lippmann is more critical than ever of unrealistic hopes for popular democracy. But he separates himself from critics who judge public opinion to be "uninformed, irrelevant and meddlesome." These (unnamed) critics usually find "a congenital difference between the masterful few and the ignorant many." But this, Lippmann concludes, is wholly mistaken. What is "congenital" has nothing to do with it. What matters, as he insisted already in *Public Opinion*, is the difference between insiders and outsiders. "The outsider is necessarily ignorant, usually irrelevant and often meddlesome" but not as the "aristocratic theorists" suppose, congenitally so but only in relation to their location in the social, political, and institutional order. For Lippmann, "competence exists only in relation to function." Insiders are not better people or smarter people than outsiders, but they are located in positions where they can know more and competently decide more. The insider is "so placed that he can understand and can act."[6]

Lippmann did not by any means forsake democracy. In his chapter on the "Self-Contained Community," Lippmann concedes too much, I think. He argues that democracy—participatory democracy, if you will—operates well enough in the "self-contained community." What leads to the complications in modern society is that we do not live in self-contained communities any longer. Most of the relevant information about the world reaches us only through the news media—we have little or no firsthand experience of it. Where we experience the world firsthand, democracy operates well. But in this he joins John Dewey in picturing the small community through rose-colored glasses. If you read Michael Zuckerman on early New England town meetings or Jane Mansbridge on Vermont town meetings she studied in the 1970s, it is clear that most decisions in these settings did not operate "democratically," even in a putatively egalitarian town meeting.[7] The town selectmen carefully prepared the agenda for the meeting, and debate was strongly discouraged. The town meeting was less an occasion for reasoned discussion than for a public confirmation of what the selectmen had already concluded was the best policy.

Afterword

It is the recurrent theme of many social critics that we once knew how to be citizens but now are failing at the task. Even Lippmann himself suggests this view in picturing a world of "omnicompetent citizens" in the small, "self-contained community." The persistence of the theme cannot help but make one wonder about its empirical basis. Lippmann complained about civic participation in the 1920s. For that matter, so did his putative critic John Dewey: "In most circles it is hard work to sustain conversation on a political theme; and once initiated, it is quickly dismissed with a yawn."[8] Sociologist David Riesman in the 1950s complained about the rise of the suburbs and the new suburbanite who, "if he is political at all—rather than parochially civic-minded, tending to a 'garden' which includes the local schools and waterworks—he is apt to be an Eisenhower Republican, seldom informed, rarely angry, and only spasmodically partisan."[9] In 1961, Robert Dahl noted that politics for most people lies at "the outer periphery of attention," while at the center of people's interest are "primary activities involving food, sex, love, family, work, play, shelter, comfort, friendship, social esteem, and the like."[10] He might just as well have used Lippmann's term—most of us most of the time are "outsiders."

I drafted this chapter as the first televised, public hearings on the impeachment of President Donald Trump began. Responding to the hearings, David Brooks picked up a Lippmannesque theme. Brooks, the conservative op-ed writer for the *New York Times*, has looked more and more liberal in the past several years—or, to put it perhaps more accurately, more and more distressed that the Republican Party has abandoned any relationship to recognizably conservative moral and political values rather than a sheer opportunistic embrace of a president whose popularity with those who embrace a far-right and explicitly racist white nationalism makes it politically dangerous for Republicans running for office to speak against such values. At any rate, his column ran under the headline "In Praise of Washington Insiders." And reminiscent of Lippmann's high praise for the British Foreign Service, Brooks praised the likes of William Taylor, George Kent, Marie Yovanovitch, and Fiona Hill, career public servants who "tend to be self-effacing and deeply knowledgeable about some small realm of public policy. They're generally not all that interested in partisan politics but are deeply committed to the process and substance of good government." Brooks noted that "we don't celebrate these people." Trumpians see them as "unelected bureaucrats" (as indeed they are), "denizens of the swamp, the cesspool or a snake pit." And some on the left have long attacked them as "the establishment, the power elite, the privileged structures of the status quo." And yet these individuals, their outlook, their ethics, and their knowledge—shaped powerfully by the institutions they have pledged to serve and the Constitution they have vowed to defend—have an integrity that could not be matched in Trump's White House. That is to say, they have integrity while Trump, as president, had at most an expressive authenticity, which is not the same thing. To blurt rather than to speak is not a good model for us or for our children, but it is the only model the president offered. Institutions are designed to protect us from such random, unpredictable, superficial, and unstudied attention-grabbing. Trump's opinions are sometimes foolish, often impulsive, regularly in violation of everything his closest advisers counsel so that he looks for support more and more to the lunatic fringe or to people (like his daughter and son-in-law) he can fully dominate. Brooks spoke on behalf of institutions and the people whose sense of public service has been shaped by them. That is very much where Lippmann put his trust in 1922.

In the 1980s and 1990s when media scholars began to attend to Lippmann and Dewey, they were drawn in by the unrealistic but romantically appealing dreams of Dewey, and they were repulsed by the democratic realism of Lippmann that hoped elected leaders might be guided through an increasingly complex world by informed advice from experts. To be guided—but not controlled—by informed advice from experts looks today, however modest a proposal it is, well worth defending. Amid the global COVID-19 pandemic where governments ignored expert warnings about the prospects of a pandemic occurring, the vital importance of finding ways to assure that government leaders hear and respond to the views of experts has been tragically reinforced.

Lippmann did, indeed, think the general public had limitations—but he included himself and anyone who might be reading his book as members of the general public. We all suffer from the same cognitive shortcomings as every other man and woman in the street. That is what Lippmann argued in *Public Opinion*. There, over and over, when Lippmann discusses human limitations for operating a democracy, he speaks of "we" and not of "they."

And, yes, Lippmann did indeed think experts were a necessary component of democratic governance—but as advisers, not as decision-makers. He could not have been clearer about this. And he understood that expertise is always incomplete and knowledge structures always unfinished, and that experts worth their salt knew this better than anyone. For him, expertise was not simply a matter of knowing a lot of facts about a specific subject but a "multiplication of the number of aspects we are prepared to discover, plus the habit of discounting our expectations" (76). It is worth lingering on that last phrase—"the habit of discounting our expectations." Expertise is in part an accumulation and mastery of a specialized body of information, but it is also a moral attitude, a recognition that even experts stand in a certain place, see the world from a particular vantage, and arrive at conclusions that may be influenced by their own views and values, hopes and fears—and experts should thus be wary of and find protections against their own positions. That is the whole point of scientific "peer review," for all its shortcomings. Experts require themselves to be skeptical and require especially that they be skeptical of themselves, and that they demonstrate their knowledge of their own individual limitations by submitting their work to the review of their peers before publishing it. Expertise is not only a cognitive achievement but a social institution and a moral stance. Lippmann did not discuss the institutional underpinnings of expertise; he was writing *Public Opinion* before a robust sociology of science developed and well before what would be known as the "sociology of scientific knowledge" and, in other hands, "science studies" or "science and technology studies."

In the digital era, with its new enthusiasm for broadly distributed civic expertise, for the virtues of participatory or citizen journalism, there are additional complexities to how a reliable structure of knowledge can be produced and maintained. It's a wild new world, technologically speaking, and not one where Lippmann offers direct guidance. But we can at least clarify that Lippmann thought the kind of knowledge ordinary people possessed about public questions demonstrated their knowledgeability on matters close to their local communities or to their domestic or occupational experience, but not matters of public politics far from home. As for certified experts on public questions, Lippmann believed they contributed crucially to democratic governance without being elected to decision-making roles and without stepping into decision-making themselves.

Walter Lippmann thought government decision-making should be guided by information scrupulously and expertly assembled. Journalism should do likewise. He doubted that journalism would ever be able to confront fully the complexities of the twentieth century, but in *Liberty and the News* he recommended two reforms he believed would help. First, he recommended that journalists be better educated as professionals. That has happened, perhaps more than he could have imagined. Second, he observed that even professional journalists in the complicated modern world must rely on outside expertise to arrive at reliable, trustworthy, and perceptive stories. Institutional sources of expertise outside news organizations he called "political observatories," and he hoped that more of them would arise in independent nonprofits, in universities, and inside government itself.[11]

In both government and journalism, Lippmann called for experts to play a role. In this, he was a standard early twentieth-century progressive, if an unusually articulate one. But when scholars in the 1980s and 1990s took up Lippmann's work in media and communication studies, they did so to denounce it and to argue that to champion expertise as Lippmann did was to align oneself with an antidemocratic, elitist project. I have argued before, as have also Sue Curry Jansen and John Durham Peters in related work, that this was a profoundly mistaken effort.[12] I reprise these arguments now, in this moment of a global pandemic where remarkable scientific advances have saved millions of lives and blatant ignorance, embraced with enthusiasm, has operated to strangle a recovery. Today expertise is as much in need of a full-throated defense as democracy itself.

Notes

1. Lippmann, *Public Opinion*, 240. Further citations of this work in this chapter are given in the text.
2. Halberstam, *Best and the Brightest*, 214, 259, 267, 280, 307.
3. Carey, "Press and the Public Discourse," 7.
4. Carey, "Chicago School," 246.
5. Bybee, "Can Democracy Survive," 32.
6. Lippmann, *Phantom Public*, 139–40.
7. Zuckerman, *Peaceable Kingdoms*; Mansbridge, *Beyond Adversary Democracy*.
8. Dewey, *Public and Its Problems*, 139.
9. Riesman, "Suburban Sadness," 377.
10. Dahl, *Who Governs*, 279.
11. Lippmann, *Liberty and the News*, 56.
12. Schudson, "'Lippmann-Dewey Debate'"; Peters, "Public Journalism and Democratic Theory"; Jansen, "Phantom Conflict" and "Walter Lippmann, Straw Man."

Bibliography

Bender, Thomas. *New York Intellect*. New York: Alfred A. Knopf, 1987.
Brooks, David. "In Praise of Washington Insiders." *New York Times*, November 15, 2019.
Bybee, Carl. "Can Democracy Survive in the Post-factual Age? A Return to the Lippmann-Dewey Debate About the Politics of News." *Journalism and Communication Monographs* 1, no. 1 (1999): 28–66.

Carey, James W. "The Chicago School and the History of Mass Communication Research." In *James Carey: A Critical Reader*, edited by Eve Stryker Munson and Catherine A. Warren, 14–33. Minneapolis: University of Minnesota Press, 1997.

———. "The Press and the Public Discourse." *Center Magazine* 20 (March–April 1987): 6–15.

Dahl, Robert. *Who Governs?* New Haven, CT: Yale University Press, 1961.

Dewey, John. *The Public and Its Problems* (1927). Athens: Ohio University Press, 1954.

Halberstam, David. *The Best and the Brightest*. New York: Random House, 1972.

Jansen, Sue Curry. "Phantom Conflict: Lippmann, Dewey, and the Fate of the Public in Modern Society." *Communication and Critical/Cultural Studies* 6, no. 3 (2009): 221–45.

———. "Walter Lippmann, Straw Man of Communication Research." In *The History of Media and Communication Research: Contested Memories*, edited by David W. Park and Jefferson Pooley, 71–112. New York: Peter Lang, 2008.

Kingdon, John W. *Congressmen's Voting Decisions*. New York: Harper & Row, 1973.

Lippmann, Walter. *Liberty and the News* (1920). Princeton, NJ: Princeton University Press, 2008.

———. *The Phantom Public* (1925). New Brunswick, NJ: Transaction, 1993.

———. *Public Opinion* (1922). New York: Free Press Paperbacks, 1997.

Mansbridge, Jane. *Beyond Adversary Democracy*. New York: Basic Books, 1980.

Peters, John Durham, "Public Journalism and Democratic Theory: Four Challenges" in *The Idea of Public Journalism*, edited by Theodore L. Glasser, 99–117, New York: Guilford Press, 1999.¶

Pozen, David E., and Michael Schudson, eds. *Troubling Transparency: The History and Future of Freedom of Information*. New York: Columbia University Press, 2018.

Riesman, David. "The Suburban Sadness." In *The Suburban Community*, edited by William M. Dobriner, 375–408. New York: Putnam's, 1958.

Schudson, Michael. "The 'Lippmann-Dewey Debate' and the Invention of Walter Lippmann as an Anti-Democrat, 1985–1996." *International Journal of Communication* 2 (2008): 1031–42.

Zuckerman, Michael. *Peaceable Kingdoms: New England Towns in the Eighteenth Century*. New York: Alfred A. Knopf, 1972.

2

THE LIPPMANN/LIPPMANN DEBATE: WHAT ROLE DO SOCIAL MOVEMENTS PLAY IN DEMOCRATIC POLITICS?

Nathan Crick

Social movements are at once the symptoms and the instruments of progress. Ignore them and statesmanship is irrelevant; fail to use them and it is weak.

—Walter Lippmann, *A Preface to Politics*

The reputation of Walter Lippmann might make it hard to believe that he ever associated social movements with progress. In *The Phantom Public*, after all, Lippmann writes, "I set no great store on what can be done by public opinion and the action of masses." Lippmann writing in 1925 preferred relying on "the private labor of individuals" who were capable of genuinely understanding the situation and generating intelligent modes of action.[1] What Lippmann called "statesmanship" (and I shall refer to as political leadership) thus "consists in giving the people not what they want but what they will learn to want," and as such required a "capacity to act upon the hidden realities of the situation in spite of appearances."[2] But for these political leaders to be able to act on these realities required an important condition, namely that "the public must be put in its place . . . so that each of us may live free of the trampling and roar of a bewildered herd."[3] From this perspective, political leaders were better off seeing social movements as obstacles, not allies, to progress. These and many other like-minded passages from Lippmann's later work thus contributed to his reputation as an irredeemable elitist with hardly disguised contempt for popular democracy who has little to offer contemporary politics.[4] One would thus suspect that the man who saw social movements as instruments of progress were written by a different person.

In a way, it was. In 1913, when he wrote those words, Lippmann had embraced a popular vision of democratic leadership that saw it as necessarily partnering with social movements to achieve reform. Far from relegating the public to the back of the theater of history, Lippmann argued that it should be, in fact, on the forefront of social and political change. He writes, "In fact, unless a political invention is woven into a social movement it has no importance. Only when that is done is it imbued with life."[5] By "life," Lippmann meant energy, vitality, innovation, reality, and solidarity—if not always clarity, effectiveness, and direction. Any social movement is necessarily a mixed bag, for "each one carries along a quantity of inert and outworn ideas,—not infrequently there is an internally contradictory current" (52). To become useful, confused beliefs and obsolete habits would "need to be expurgated by an unceasing criticism" (53). But for the Lippmann of 1913, the contributions that flow from the life of the movement outweigh these constraints, such that "in bulk the forces I have mentioned, and many others less important, carry with them the creative powers of our times" (53). Genuine political leadership thus situates itself at the forefront of the life of social movements: "Statesmanship, if it is to be relevant, would obtain a new perspective on these dynamic currents, would find out the wants they express and the energies they contain, would shape and direct and guide them" (51). The public, far from a bewildered herd, is here represented by a dynamic current, surging forward. Indeed, his tone often seems close to defending the same vision of democratic social change often attributed to John Dewey in their famous debate in the 1920s.

The striking difference between Lippmann's early and later writings merits closer attention. In his classic treatment of Lippmann's intellectual development, for instance, Benjamin F. Wright argued that Lippmann actually articulated five distinct philosophies in his career, beginning with an optimistic reading of Theodore Roosevelt's forward-looking Progressivism and ending on a nostalgic "vision of an idealized past—and a hopeless present."[6] This chapter, however, focuses on the contrast between the early and middle phases of his work, spanning the years between *A Preface to Politics* and *The Phantom Public*. Consequently, this chapter focuses on what I call the "Lippmann-Lippmann debate" between his prewar and postwar selves. In this debate Lippmann had with himself, the central point of contention came down to a matter of trust, namely the trust in ordinary people to contribute something positive to the creative life of politics in the form of social movements. Lippmann had trust in 1913; he lost it in the war. Specifically, the war showed him how easily the masses were manipulated, how propaganda could justify the greatest vices through the most noble virtues, and how social movements were just one more manifestation of people reacting to manufactured pictures placed in their heads. Today one could point to any number of examples that would reinforce this position, from climate denialism to anti-vaccine movements to the fascist political resurgence. Yet there are also counterexamples to bolster the case that Lippmann may also have given up hope too quickly, and that his early vision may still have something to teach us.

The Early Lippmann: Iconoclast and Socialist

The voice of the youthful Lippmann has long been buried by the established terms of the Lippmann-Dewey debate as James Carey famously defined them. That is to say, it has been buried by philosophy. Carey argued that the debate should be understood as being situated along the "ragged ambulating ridge dividing the Enlightenment from the Counter-Enlightenment—Descartes from Vico."[7] From this perspective, Lippmann and Dewey were articulate representatives of counter philosophical traditions that in turn represented the conflict "between objectivist and expressivist views of the world" (73). To take sides in this debate was therefore to join one or another philosophical position and commit oneself to a whole system of epistemological, political, and ethical imperatives. For instance, Carey contends that the "philosophical side of Lippmann is arguing for a general theory of representation that divides culture into the areas that represent reality well (such as science), those that represent it less well (such as art), and those that do not represent it at all (such as journalism), despite their pretense of doing so" (77). By contrast, Carey saw Dewey as proposing that "conversation, not photography, is the ultimate context within which knowledge is to be understood" (80). As a result, Dewey is said to have argued that "the purpose of news is not to represent and inform but to signal, tell a story, and activate inquiry" (82). As Dave Tell recently summed up this legacy, Carey saw "in Lippmann a manifestation of what he most argued against: a scientific epistemology in which politics and knowledge, activity and truth are isolated from one another."[8] In Carey's framework, the debate thus forced its interpreters to make a judgment between two competing epistemologies and their consequences. To side with Dewey was to embrace pragmatic and community-centered way of knowing and of acting together.

Yet the Dewey/Lippmann debate takes on a different character situated within a biographical and historical context rather than in an artificially constructed philosophical one. For instance, the environment of Lippmann's upbringing created a young man who was far from the caricature of the scientific epistemologist that Carey sketches for us. Born to German-Jewish parents in 1889, Lippmann grew up in a comfortable home on Lexington Avenue in New York City where he absorbed the "cultural cosmopolitanism" of the urban elite.[9] His early education at the Sachs School for Boys was traditionally classical and "included eleven hours of Greek and five hours of Latin each week" (6). When he entered Harvard in 1906, "he had no doubt that he would become an art historian, pursuing, with Ruskin as his model, the pleasures of art poetic in inspiration and reformist in spirit" (11). Although growing up in a traditional environment, he wanted nothing more than to break out of tradition and be a part of the creative set of cutting-edge thinkers, artists, and writers prepared to launch America forward in world leadership. Lippmann in his early years was an ambitious representative of the cosmopolitan upper class of the American Northeast, eager to make his mark on the world as an iconoclastic freethinker.

More important, his experience at Harvard introduced him to an intellectual environment in which his aesthetic interests turned toward politics and a philosophically informed social criticism with a pragmatic character. Namely, William James and George Santayana heavily influenced him. The most intimate relationship he had was with James, with whom he shared tea and conversation every Thursday morning. James inspired the young Lippmann with his praise of experimentation, pluralism, and action; "downgrading intellectualism, he exulted will over reason, and urged his young disciples to give up logic" and substitute for it "reality, life, experience, concreteness, immediacy" (17). James provided him justification for "idol-smashing" (18) in the name of radical experimentalism unfettered by tradition. And Santayana, too, influenced Lippmann as "a Catholic freethinker who valued religion aesthetically rather than as a guide to morality" (19). The influence of Santayana would over time outlast that of James, for it was "Santayana who instilled in him a striving for excellence as the highest goal of a life guided by reason" (21). But these two voices both competed for the young Lippmann's allegiance, one inspiring radical iconoclasm, the other appealing to transcendent ideals toward which society could rationally strive.

The early culmination of these influences was Lippmann's embrace of Progressive Era socialism. What inspired this position was Lippmann's first direct encounter with poverty. This occurred when he volunteered with other Harvard students to help the victims of an Easter fire that ravaged the slums of nearby Chelsea in 1908: "On returning to the yard he began to relate what he had seen to the social criticism he had been reading," and "now he began to question the system that produced such inequality" (23). In fact, he wrote to a friend soon after attending a lecture on socialism at Faneuil Hall, "I have come around to socialism as a creed. I do believe in it passionately and fearlessly."[10] He would soon join the Harvard Socialist Club, which was "organized with the avowed object of examining all schemes of social reform designed to achieve a radical transformation of society."[11] But Lippmann retained something of Santayana's rationalism and elitism. Lippmann was drawn to the British Fabian Society, who were "convinced that nothing constructive could be done by the masses[;] they favored the creation of a small core of selfless leaders" (24). Lippmann's socialism thus allowed him to give voice to his iconoclasm, which would shatter the old conservative order, while simultaneously expressing his rational faith that a more just society could be produced by having leaders strive to actualize ideal aims in concrete practice.

The years leading up to his first book, *A Preface to Politics*, saw him writing for numerous magazines with a muckraking or socialist character as he sought to find ways to channel his attitudes and ambitions. He quickly left his first job at the moderate Progressivist *Boston Common* for an opportunity in 1910 to join *Everybody's Magazine*, the latest venture by the investigative journalist Lincoln Steffens. Lippmann was hired to work with Steffens on researching the system of financial power, "burrowing through financial reports and investigating scores of people from stockbrokers to messenger boys" (35). In the end, his efforts revealed how "the economic life of the country was organized by small groups of men," largely concentrated in the banking house of J. P. Morgan, and his reporting "helped trigger the Pujo Committee investigations, which in turn paved the way for the attempt to control the giant banks to the Federal Reserve Act of 1913" (36). On the side, he also wrote for the "socialist monthly the *International*, and the socialist-anarchist *Masses*," an outlet that drew him less for their ideological doctrine or even for a "fiery passion for justice and equality" as much as a chance to vent to his "impatience with how badly society was managed" (39–40). His experience, particularly with Steffens, cultivated certain attitudes that would become characteristic of Lippmann in his later years, namely "his skepticism about the inherent goodness of the average man, his belief that corruption was an inherent part of the system, his insistence on uncluttered declarative writing, his emphasis on intelligence, his admiration for strong leaders, and his faith in science" (38). All these attitudes were developed not through philosophical reading of Descartes but his personal relationships with professors, journalists, and politicians alongside a practical, on the ground, investigative reporting into events.

The result of all these experiences led to the writing of *A Preface to Politics* in 1913. It was a youthful, brash exercise in iconoclasm, what Barry Riccio calls "an indictment of mechanical and unimaginative thinking about public affairs."[12] But at the core of the book was a fairly simple idea he had developed in conversation with his Harvard friend Alfred Booth Kuttner, with whom he shared a cabin in Maine in 1912 while he was writing his book. Kuttner had recently become a disciple of Sigmund Freud, and "around the fire at night, as Kuttner explained what Freud meant by words like 'taboo' and 'sublimation,' Lippmann glimpsed a new analytical tool. . . . Freud's analysis of the unconscious showed why reason alone could not explain human behavior and at the same time suggested how emotions could be channeled by reason" (46). Articulating the Freudian position thus allowed him to break idols on all sides. On the one hand, he was able to criticize socialists for what was, in his perspective, an idealist belief that "social revolution would be brought about by developing individual initiative and self-reliance among the toiling masses."[13] On the other hand, he was able to criticize conservatives for their failure to recognize that genuine leadership is not repressive or authoritarian but rather "seeks to sense the thrust of mass human desires and to provide healthy opportunities for the expression of human impulses."[14] The result was an embrace of leader-centered structural reform to improve the quality of life for the general welfare.

A Preface to Politics: In Search of Political Leadership

The problem Lippmann confronted in *A Preface to Politics* was one of political indifference, not epistemological uncertainty. In the opening pages, he laments that when youthful, idealistic reformers finally confront the difficulty of constituting and channeling public opinion, they often take refuge in "their ancient comforter, self-deception: they complain about the stolid, inert masses and the apathy of the people."[15] This indifference on the part of political leaders was derived, he thought, from "un-criticized assumptions" that have culminated in "blunders in our political thinking which confuse fictitious activity with genuine achievement, and make it difficult for men to know where they should enlist" (4). Lippmann argued that too often our image of politics is influenced by false rationalist assumptions. Contemporary rationalists were those whose "minds construct a utopia—one in which all judgments are based on inference from syllogisms built on the law of mathematical probabilities" and who then made it "their will to impose that method upon other men" (163). But Lippmann argued that people were not just passive material to be formed into whatever ideologues desired. Political conceptions are not imposed from outside but are rather "the servants of men's purposes. Good or bad, that it seems to me is the way we work. We find reasons for what we want to do" (161). It was only after we accepted this premise that we could really begin to construct a realistic political philosophy.

The proposition about human nature that Lippmann defends in *A Preface to Politics* is this: "Man when he is most creative is not a rational, but a wilful animal" (161). Notably, this proposition does not deny the rational faculty of human beings; it says only that rationality is not the *source* of creativity or will. For Lippmann, "original genius sees the dynamic purpose first, finds reasons afterward" (161). The function of rationality is not to stimulate creative action but to justify desires and systematize impulses. Reason therefore is not the primary mover of political life; it simply puts in order what the impulsive will initiates in both individual and the mass. It is for this reason that "only the pathetic amateur deludes himself into thinking that, if he presents the major and minor premise, the voter will automatically draw the conclusion on election day. The successful politician—good or bad—deals with the dynamics—with the will, the hopes, the needs and the visions of men" (164). Therefore, just as misplaced faith in rationality leads rapidly from utopian dreaming to disillusionment, a genuine assessment of the creative capacity of the will can produce a genuine leadership that transforms politics from a soulless bureaucratic machine to a dramatic theater of action.

Before turning to Lippmann's positive recommendations, it is important to clarify the dual nature of the problem that stems from what he felt to be a false understanding of human nature. The first problem is rhetorical. Too often, even the most well-meaning politicians and social actors place too much confidence in the persuasive power of reason, particularly when it is embodied in what they believe to be a true and coherent ideology. For instance, one of Lippmann's criticisms of socialism was that it "assumes that men are determined by logic and that a false conclusion will stop a moving, creative force" (169). One effect of this rationalistic rhetoric is a fairly rapid disillusionment, culminating in indifference and cynicism. Thus even the most high-minded idealist "recognizes the willful character of politics: then he shakes his head, climbs into an ivory tower and deplores the moonshine, the religious manias and the passions of the mob. . . . With all his learning he is ineffective because, instead of trying to use the energies of men, he deplores them" (169). The modern academy is full of such individuals. What these well-meaning advocates fail to realize is that reason always follows on the heels of action; it doesn't initiate it: "Real life is beyond his control and influence because real life is largely agitated by impulses and habits, unconscious needs, faith, hope and desire" (169). Socialism will come into being not because it is ideologically true but because people desire the immediate changes it promises in their lives.

The second problem, however, is more pervasive, structural, and difficult to dislodge. This is the problem of overcoming the inertia of the political machine that has been built on top of this disillusionment. What Lippmann means by a "political machine" is embodied in the workings of Tammany Hall in New York City, a tight system of control that represented "an accretion of power around a center of influence, cemented by patronage, graft, favors, friendship, loyalties, habits,—a human grouping, a natural pyramid" (20). One could blame such political machines on the existence of "corruption," but that is to engage in sloppy moralism. The real reason such machines exist is because of what Lippmann calls "the paradoxes of the democratic movement—that it loves a crowd and fears the individuals who compose it—that the religion of humanity should have had no faith in human beings" (18). The central paradox, in other words, is that even though democratic publics fear tyrants and refuse to concentrate power in a single individual, democratic leaders fear the masses and seek to distance them from the levers of power. Thus, "jealous of all individuals, democracies have turned to machines" (18). The benefit of the machine is that it is an impersonal system that is neither a tyranny nor a mob. It is simply a system of inputs and outputs that removes actual governance from the influence of living human beings with all their reactive impulses, fickle desires, and fantastic hopes.

From the atmosphere of machine politics emerges a particular class of political actor that Lippmann calls the *routineer*. Routineers simply regard "government as a routine to be administered" (9), and thus see their job as designers or caretakers of machinery. These individuals appear in many different forms. The most familiar would be that of the traditional conservative.

This is an individual "who will follow precedent, but never create one," one to whom "government is something given as unconditionally, as absolutely as ocean or hill. He goes on winding the tape that he finds" (11). But routineers also include reformers. Indeed, for Lippmann, "the tinkering reformer is frequently one of the worst of the routineers" for the very reason that while defending the need for adaptation this individual nonetheless props up the existing machinery and rarely makes more than "a poor rickety attempt to adapt the machine to changing conditions" (11). Lastly, Lippmann even considers certain self-proclaimed "radicals" as types of routineers insofar as they "simply to substitute some other kind of machine for the one we have" (12). These radicals may represent an advance over the prior ones insofar as their "perceptions are more critical" and "they do see that humanity is badly squeezed in the existing mould," but they nonetheless retain "an infinite faith in moulds" (12). They accept the necessity for political machinery, desiring simply a new and improved machine.

Against the routineer, Lippmann opposes what he calls a "political creator or a political inventor" (13). The hallmark of a political creator is not any specific model of democratic governance; it is a set of experimental attitudes about government itself. For the political creator, "systems, institutions and mechanical contrivances have for him no virtue of their own: they are valuable only when they serve the purposes of men" (12). In other words, the political creator is thoroughly pragmatic; government exists as a tool for individuals to use to attain ends that arise within their specific historical context. When those contexts change, so too must the tool change to best solve the problem. The political creator thus "has no faith whatever in automatic governments," but rather uses state institutions "with a constant sense that men have made them, that new ones can be devised, that only an effort of the will can keep machinery in its place" (13). But perhaps most important of all, the political creator is not another breed of enlightened tyrant; democracy matters insofar as the best political machine grows out of the needs and desires of the people that a government serves. And here Lippmann draws the starkest contrast: "While the routineers see machinery and precedents revolving with mankind as puppets, [the political creator] puts the deliberate, conscious, willing individual at the center of his philosophy. . . . He serves the ideals of human feelings, not the tendencies of mechanical things" (13). The language Lippmann uses here sounds more radical than it actually is; nonetheless, it does capture his relative openness to creative human initiative both on the part of political leaders and ordinary people that animated his political thought before the war.

In sum, the political philosophy that Lippmann advances in *A Preface to Politics* encompasses three basic practices. The first concerns the public at large. Lippmann calls for a healthy iconoclasm willing to criticize and ultimately abandon outworn beliefs, structures, and political machinery that obstruct intelligent reform: "I have tried again and again to point out the iconoclasm that is constantly necessary to avoid the distraction that comes of idolizing our own methods of thought. Without an unrelaxing effort to center the mind upon human uses, human purposes, and human results, it drops into idolatry and becomes hostile to creation" (229). This is perhaps the most long-term project that Lippmann envisions, something that pervades culture and engages "the work of publicists and educators, scientists, preachers and artists" whose task is to make a citizenry "interested in invention and freed from the authority of ideas" (229). Before we can invent the new, we must deconstruct the old.

The second practice is to be "sympathetic to agitations" (76) on the part of the public for changes that would directly impact their lives. At the core of *A Preface to Politics* is the belief that "the yearnings of to-day are the symptoms of needs, they point the course of invention, they are the energies which animate a social program" (75). However, this sympathy should not be confused with a populist embrace of the wisdom of the people. Lippmann retains his Fabian elitism. For Lippmann, the self-professed aims and methods of agitation are not sufficient for democratic advance; they are rather symptoms of a problem that must still be diagnosed by those capable of constructing a political program: "In actual life, yes, in the moil and toil of propaganda, 'movements,' 'causes' and agitations the statesman-inventor and the political psychologist find the raw material for their work" (75). Sympathy toward agitation "would try to understand the inner feeling which had generated what looks like a silly demand" (76). For instance, Lippmann imagines the case in which a hungry man, ignorant of how to satisfy his hunger, demands an indigestible food. It is a habit of the comfortable classes to ridicule such a demand. But the fact remains that "he isn't any the less hungry because he asks for the wrong food. So with agitations. Their specific plans may be silly, but their demands are real. The hungers and lusts of mankind have produced some stupendous follies, but the desires themselves are no less real and insistent" (76). In short, the true political creator must be a "translator of agitations" (77). Political leaders must perceive the real need behind the public agitation and be able to construct a new political tool to solve the problem without being constrained by inherited political machinery: "The important thing about a social movement is not its stated platform but the source from which it flows. The task of politics is to understand those deeper demands and to find civilized satisfactions for them" (76).

Lastly, political creators must use all the resources of art and science not only to constitute and mobilize public opinion in support of these policies but to create a healthy democratic culture. Lippmann looks with longing to "the close alliance of art, science and politics in Athens, in Florence and Venice at their zenith." For Lippmann, it is evident from history and clear from philosophy that "a lively artistic tradition is essential to the humanizing of politics. It is the soil in which invention flourishes and the organized knowledge of science attains its greatest reality." Artistic works enlarge our moral imagination, which is essential to political judgment. Art, as he finds in the works of Ibsen, "enlarges experience by admitting us to the inner life of others" and "and, therefore, enables us to center our institutions more truly." Science, meanwhile, provides practical frameworks of action based on reliable knowledge that enables us to predict consequences and control effects when allied with the right institutional tools designed to tackle present problems. In sum, "literature refines, science deepens, various devices extend it. . . . And all the while, research studies their results, artists express subtler perceptions, critics refine and adapt the general culture of the times." And the end result is that "those who act on the knowledge at hand are the men of affairs." Here was a philosophy of politics largely consistent with the spirit of the times.

The Later Lippmann: War and Disillusionment

In 1925, Lippmann published *The Phantom Public*. This book jettisoned the idea that public agitations and social movements provided the impetus and raw material for intelligent social reform. Instead, he defended "the theory that what the public does is not to express its opinions but to align itself for or against a proposal."[16] The basis for this theory was a revised understanding of human nature that replaced the active, if impulsive, Freudian organism with the passive spectator of the lonely crowd. Lippmann writes, "We must assume that a public is inexpert in its curiosity, intermittent, that it discerns only gross distinctions, is slow to be aroused and quickly diverted; that, since it acts by aligning itself, it personalizes whatever it considers, and is interested only when events have been melodramatized as a conflict" (65). His early work had portrayed politics as a collaborative drama in which members of the public were central actors who identified conflicts and initiated change; his later work, in contradistinction, adopted the metaphor of a stage play in which the public became distracted spectators. For Lippmann, "the public will arrive in the middle of the third act and leave before the last curtain, having stayed just long enough perhaps to decide who is the hero and who is the villain of the piece" (65). Consequently, democratic politics, to be effective, should thus restrict the role of the public to saying yes or no to policies put before them by political leaders only after they have been formulated and proposed as law. Although this was not a perfect arrangement, it was far superior, the later Lippmann believed, to trusting the public: "For did justice, truth, goodness and beauty depend upon the spasmodic and crude interventions of public opinion there would be little hope for them in this world" (67). So much for the virtue of agitations.

The event that separated early from late Lippmann was World War I. Like many Progressives of his time, including John Dewey, Lippmann grew to be a supporter of American intervention in the war and eventually used his position as editor of the *New Republic* to support President Woodrow Wilson's decision to commit American troops. Unlike Dewey, however, Lippmann became an active participant in developing government policy. Lippmann joined the army intelligence unit of the Committee on Public Information, the propaganda committee organized by George Creel, where he would design pamphlets to be dropped behind enemy lines. Then Wilson appointed him to the "Inquiry," a secret organization tasked with preparing for peace negotiations. Lippmann "organized a research body charged with accumulating relevant geographic, ethnic, and political data," and his work went into preparing "a memorandum which was developed by the president into the substance of the famed Fourteen Points."[17] Yet despite the Allied victory during the war, Lippmann sadly witnessed the utter collapse of Wilson's proposals, the forcing through of the disastrous Treaty of Versailles, and the eventual defeat of Wilson's public campaign for America to join the League of Nations.

The whole experience would leave a lasting impression on Lippmann and transform his view of the public for the rest of his life. Charles Wellborn describes the transformation of his political philosophy before and after the war. During the years leading up to the publication of *A Preface to Politics*, Lippmann had argued "that the impulses and the desires of the public, though often crude and in need of refinement, were generally to be trusted for the direction of basic political policy," at least insofar as political leaders could interpret and direct these impulses.[18] But the war and its aftermath in American politics had destroyed his confidence in this belief:

> Now Lippmann was disturbed by the fact that it was exactly this unrefined public opinion which appeared to have been the main villain in the drama of Wilson's failure. He had observed the consequences of what seemed to be Wilson's naïve confidence in the character of popular support. Furthermore, during his war service he had studied the alarming potential of propaganda. . . . Discouraged by public misunderstanding and ignorance of what actually went on at the Paris Peace Conference, he was inclined to put primary blame on the newspapers who supplied their readers not with clearly interpreted facts but with twisted propaganda.[19]

The war, in other words, had expanded the scene of action to such an extent Lippmann no longer had faith that their immediate experience had any substantial contribution to make to politics. Ordinary individuals now had to rely so heavily on pictures of the world produced by others (namely for-profit newspapers or state propaganda) that there was little difference between their opinions and those of movie spectators. The years that followed his experience of the war thus saw him wavering "between a lingering romantic idealism and a growing intellectual detachment," until by the 1920s "he would resolve that conflict. He would choose a self-protective intellectualism."[20] But this meant that Lippmann now joined the ranks of routineers.

As a point of contrast, for John Dewey the war had the opposite effect. Although Dewey had thrown early support behind American intervention, he soon discovered that the war meant the spread not of democracy but of the "cultivated propaganda of the irrational" that used every technique at their disposal to "detach the volume of passionate energy from its original end and to turn the emotion itself from a means into an end."[21] Yet rather than blame the public for its failure to understand the war, Dewey diagnosed the problem rather as the intentional effort by imperial powers to undermine democratic methods and turned the public precisely into the spectator-crowd described by Lippmann. The solution was not to bypass the public but to find ways to strengthen their interconnections, develop their intelligence, and empower their capacity for collective action. Dewey defended this position most explicitly in his introduction to the 1945 republication of *Peace and Bread in Time of War* by Jane Addams. This book tells how Addams led a pacifist social movement called the Women's International League for Peace and Freedom before, during, and after World War I. What Addams tried to accomplish, Dewey argued, was a rejection of the method of coercive politics by which concentrated authority simply imposes its will on a people with a method that allowed public opinion to form through the use of democratic institutions and methods. Dewey wrote, "Miss Addams repeatedly called attention to the fact that all social movements *outside* of traditional diplomacy and 'international law' had been drawing the peoples of different countries together in ever closer bonds, while war, under modern conditions, was affecting civilian populations as it had never done before."[22] Addams, wrote Dewey, believed that lasting organization would thus have to cut both "*across* nationalistic lines" as well as "*under* those lines," thus putting her "faith in extension of the democratic process to the still wider world of peoples."[23] Leaders had a role to play in this process, but as "trustees for the interests of the common people. Theirs was the duty and the task of giving articulate and effective form to the common impulses she summed up in the word 'Fellowship.'"[24] Dewey thus threw himself behind efforts like those of Addams, who sought to meet the global challenges of the world through mobilizing social movements that cut across and under nationalistic lines. In other words, Addams was the very exemplar of early Lippmann's concept of creative political leadership.

For all his vaunted realism, therefore, it was the later Lippmann who succumbed to idealism. Disenchanted with political leadership and dismissive of public opinion, Lippmann put his faith in the power of ideas themselves to change the world. Of course, faith in intelligence to make a difference is not by itself utopian; without intelligence, action is blind. What was idealistic was his utopian belief that the public and its political leaders would simply adopt these recommendations having neither understood nor assented to them. As Dewey remarked of the public's role in this idealistic plan, "the very ignorance, bias, frivolity, jealousy, instability, which are alleged to incapacitate them from share in public affairs, unfit them still more for passive submission to rule by intellectuals."[25] But one need not just look to Dewey; the early Lippmann already recognized its impossibility. In *A Preface to Politics*, Lippmann had argued that "it is puerile to say that institutions must be changed from top to bottom and then assume that their victims are prepared to make the change." The reality of democratic politics, for young Lippmann, is that "the politics of reconstruction require a nation vastly better educated, a nation freed from its slovenly ways of thinking, stimulated by wider interests, and jacked up constantly by the sharpest kind of criticism."[26]

This reality is precisely why in *A Preface to Politics* he had recommended that the foundation for democratic politics was built slowly over time by publicists, educators, scientists, artists, and preachers. In short, "it is out of culture that the substance of real revolutions is made."[27] The later Lippmann rejected this claim because of a collapse of trust following the war and thereby ended up with a theory of democracy without citizens—or more accurately without living human beings. But early Lippmann had believed, with Dewey, that the challenge of democracy could not be met simply by redefining individuals as machines; it required a renewed sense of communication and cooperation among social movements, political creators, scientists, and artists. Lippmann in his later years accurately diagnosed the enormous challenges facing democracy in the twentieth and now the twenty-first century. *Public Opinion* remains a foundational teaching text to debunk the enduring myth of the omnicompetent citizen. But his retreat into cynically driven idealistic fantasy seems to succumb to the very temptations his younger self had warned against. Yet the question remains open as to which Lippmann we find more persuasive today.

Notes

1. Lippmann, *Phantom Public*, 155.
2. Lippmann, *Preface to Morals*, 283.
3. Lippmann, *Phantom Public*, 155.
4. Dewey, *Public and Its Problems*, 184.
5. Lippmann, *Preface to Politics*, 53. Further citations of this work in this paragraph are given in the text.
6. Wright, *Five Public Philosophies*, 153.
7. Carey, *Communication as Culture*, 70. Further citations of this work in this paragraph are given in the text.
8. Tell, "Reinventing Walter Lippmann," 114.
9. Steel, *Walter Lippmann*, 9. Further citations of this work in this section are given in the text.
10. Quoted in Riccio, *Walter Lippmann*, 3.
11. Dam, *Intellectual Odyssey*, 38.
12. Riccio, *Walter Lippmann*, 11.
13. Dam, *Intellectual Odyssey*, 44.
14. Wellborn, *Twentieth Century Pilgrimage*, 53.
15. Lippmann, *Preface to Politics*, 1–2. Further citations of this work in this section are given in the text.
16. Lippmann, *Phantom Public*, 61. Further citations of this work in this paragraph are given in the text.
17. Wellborn, *Twentieth Century Pilgrimage*, 31.
18. Wellborn, 33.
19. Wellborn, 33–34.
20. Steel, *Walter Lippmann*, 184.
21. Dewey, "Cult of Irrationality," 108.
22. Dewey, "Democratic Versus Coercive International Organization," 194.
23. Dewey, 196.
24. Dewey, 198.

25. Dewey, *Public and Its Problems*, 205.
26. Lippmann, *Preface to Politics*, 228.
27. Lippmann, 229.

Bibliography

Carey, James. *Communication as Culture: Essays on Media and Society.* New York: Routledge, 1988.
Dam, Hari N. *The Intellectual Odyssey of Walter Lippmann: A Study of his Protean Thought, 1910—1960.* New York: Gordon Press, 1973.
Dewey, John. "The Cult of Irrationality" (1918). In *The Middle Works of John Dewey*, vol. 11, *1918–1919*, edited by Jo Ann Boydston, 107–11. Carbondale: Southern Illinois University Press, 1982.
———. "Democratic Versus Coercive International Organization: The Realism of Jane Addams" (1945). In *The Later Works of John Dewey*, vol. 15, *1942–1948*, edited by Jo Ann Boydston, 192–98. Carbondale: Southern Illinois University Press, 1989.
———. *The Public and Its Problems* (1927). Athens: Ohio University Press, 1954.
Lippmann, Water. *The Phantom Public.* New York: Harcourt, Brace, 1925.
———. *A Preface to Morals* (1929). New York: Routledge, 2017.
———. *A Preface to Politics* (1913). Ann Arbor: University of Michigan Press, 1969.
Riccio, Barry D. *Walter Lippmann: Odyssey of a Liberal.* New Brunswick, NJ: Transaction, 1994.
Steel, Ronald. *Walter Lippmann and the American Century.* New Brunswick, NJ: Transaction, 1999.
Tell, Dave. "Reinventing Walter Lippmann: Communication and Cultural Studies." *Review of Communication* 13, no. 2 (2013): 108–26.
Wellborn, Charles. *Twentieth Century Pilgrimage: Walter Lippmann and the Public Philosophy.* Baton Rouge: Louisiana State University Press, 1969.
Wright, Benjamin F. *Five Public Philosophies of Walter Lippmann.* Austin: University of Texas Press, 1973.

3

FROM THE ILLUSIONS OF DEMOCRACY TO THE REALITIES OF ITS APPEARANCES

Bruno Latour
Abridged translation by Catherine Porter

The crisis of representation? What crisis of representation? If you despair of politics, it is because you've asked for more than it can give. You've imprudently burdened it with moral, religious, legal, and/or artistic tasks that it is powerless to fulfill. Ask for the impossible, and you'll harvest something atrocious or grotesque. If you want people to regain confidence in democracy, you first have to relieve it of the illusions that have transformed the dream of harmonious public life into a nightmare.

This was the lesson of Machiavelli's *Prince*: it was cruel for those who lulled themselves with illusions, liberating for true friends of the republican idea. It is also the lesson of Walter Lippmann's *The Phantom Public*: more than eighty years after it was first published, Lippmann's book invites us to rediscover the public spirit, but only after first dissolving the phantoms of politics. From phantom to spirit there is perhaps just a breath, but this breath is, for us, infinitely beneficial. If reading Machiavelli was hard for those who sought virtue not in force, fortune, and cunning but elsewhere, reading Lippmann will be even more painful, for he attacks the very ideas of representation, of people, and of a public. Nevertheless, if many readers are being invited to shed their most cherished beliefs, it is because those beliefs are precisely, in Lippmann's eyes, what has reduced the public spirit to a spectral role. Just as Machiavelli, as a true republican, revealed the power of princes only to allow citizens to counter them, it was as a passionate democrat that Lippmann, ten years after the end of the Great War, inflicted this lesson of "severe realism" on his readers. Democracy had to be saved from the hands of the democrats. Politics had to be freed from bewitchment at last.

If Walter Lippmann, who was born in 1889 and died in 1974, had written the twentieth-century *Prince*, people would know about it, wouldn't they? Not necessarily. Nothing is more unjust than the intellectual history of that century of fire, blood, and ash. If it is true that for science and technology wars are formidable accelerators, for thought they are powerful brakes. Consider how slowly we are still extracting from their ruins the great philosophies of William James, Alfred North Whitehead, or John Dewey. "When an epoch is out of joint," Lippmann writes so aptly, "some take the barricades, others retreat to a monastery. Which explains why most texts in our epoch are either revolutionary in inspiration or belong to escapist literature—and most often it is impossible to tell the difference."[1]

It is not impossible, then, that, owing to the violence of its conflicts, the twentieth century has turned us into complete idiots in politics, and that Lippmann's book, like certain yeasts that can remain quiescent indefinitely until the external conditions become favorable, will finally find its readers. When everything has to be restarted from scratch, it hardly matters whether the inspiration comes from yesterday or has waited nearly a century. If *The Phantom Public* is another *Prince*, it's probably addressed to the twenty-*first* century. [. . .]

And this is a good thing, for, since it appeared in 1925, *The Phantom Public* has only become more contemporary. What Lippmann called the Great Society (and what we call globalization today) has only multiplied the challenges posed to political theory by the prodigious extension of affairs that citizens are led to deal with.[2] From another standpoint, the practical means that allow citizens to become familiar with these matters have never appeared more fragile, more distant, more flawed. The problems have only grown larger, and the remedies have deteriorated. To such an extent that the political realm is in danger of disappearing altogether, that subtle fluid as precious as water, gas, or electricity but whose stock could ultimately dry up if its networks are not produced, distributed, and maintained.[3] *The Phantom Public* invites us to call into question the very premises of all our political reasoning: What, at bottom, do we expect of public life? What can public life offer that is actually achievable?

Citizens with Narrow Outlooks?

Lippmann starts with an observation that has been the basis for all critiques of the democratic idea through the ages: citizens are asked to concern themselves with matters that they lack the mental equipment to handle. If citizens really had to participate in public affairs, as the theory of representation anticipates, each one would have to have the brain of a thousand Demostheneses, a thousand Aristotles, a thousand Einsteins. But, contrary to the reactionaries of all stripes, Lippmann does not conclude from this that the tiller must be handed to princes, learned men, experts, specialists in public matters. His argument on the weakness of our mental equipment applies to *everyone*, philosophers, politicians, journalists, and experts included. The phantom public is first of all the profound darkness in which we find ourselves plunged. No one knows, no one sees, no one foresees. Everyone gropes blindly according to the circumstances. No political theory is plausible if it supposes that there is, *above* this obscurity, some superior knowledge that would make it possible to arbitrate positions *in advance* by detecting with certainty and without tests those that are rational or irrational, enlightened or partisan, progressive or reactionary. Above politics there is nothing more assured on which we could count, no court of appeals to which we could turn in order to abdicate the tasks of experimentation and blind groping. The "problem of the public," to adapt the title of the book John Dewey wrote a few years later in reaction to Lippmann's, is that the public is a blind person led by blind people.[4] All those who believed they were doing better have done worse. Without this darkness, this radical immanence, this preliminary deception, no political reflection will be realistic.

A somber, pessimistic vision that does not square with the ideals of democracy? Wait. We have to enter into this argument the way we might spend a bright sunny day in a dark cave. Our eyes, blinded at first, have to adjust gradually to the darkness—the dim lights that will soon be discerned may be fragile, but they are the only ones we will ever have. The sun may be shining outside—except that there is no outside! [. . .]

One can scorn journalists, criticize the press, make fun of politicians, mock bureaucrats and their dossiers, be indignant at the coldness of economists, but in the cave, inside the political arena where this deep and irremediable obscurity reigns, we have only Ariadne's slender threads with which to order our opinions somewhat. All those who tell you that they have a better view, more direct access, a more immediate grasp, are liars—or rather, they are other journalists, other politicians, other militants, other economists, other bureaucrats who *add* their productions, their revelations, to the ambient confusion—thus tangling even further the threads that we must learn to untangle. [. . .]

In this labyrinth, Lippmann's solution is to suppose, by considering the best of cases, that the actors will be people of average intelligence, constantly agitated by other concerns, who will have no way to untangle affairs but the fragile recourse of the intellectual techniques at their disposal. "When we remember that the public consists of busy men reading newspapers for half an hour a day or so, it is not heartless but merely prudent to deny that it can do detailed justice."[5] Replace the intellectual technologies of his day—newspapers—with ours—the web—and the argument doesn't change: what Lippmann brings to the fore is the fact that any theory of democracy needs to be connected with the cognitive equipment available to the visually impaired people we all are.[6] It is this equipment that we must maintain first and foremost. To deprive citizens of the instruments needed to equip a matter that concerns them is to ask blind persons to throw their white canes. There is no alternate solution.

Once our eyes are used to the dark and we can discern the fragile artificial light that communication techniques can shed, Lippmann draws our attention to another limit on all political discussion: we handle with some degree of assurance only matters that we master fully. As for all the others, we shall never see them up close, we shall never grasp them except as a block and in rough outline; for all the details, we shall have to trust other persons who we hope will be closer, more competent, more "on the ball," as one might say. Lippmann's whole book is built around this distinction. There are indeed those who know and those who do not know, but this distinction does not coincide with the distinction between the governed and those who govern: we are all competent in our own trades, ignorant about all the rest. "The fundamental difference which matters is that between insiders and outsiders" (150).

However, theories of democracy have trouble with this distinction. These theories are most often based on an entirely impossible *political optic* according to which we discern directly, with no fuzziness or confusion, both what we see up close and what we see from a distance, what concerns us primarily and what touches us incidentally, things of which we have firsthand knowledge and things about which we can only have secondhand opinions. If there is a phantom public, it is first of all because of this effect of optics, which reverses the most assured self-evidence: whereas we grasp with good visual acuity only things in which we are somewhat specialized (in fact, things to which we are accustomed), we believe we can discern the remotest affairs even *more clearly* than our own. [. . .]

Lippmann's originality lies in his effort to reconstruct the theory of democracy without losing that idea and without forgetting its cognitive cost, either: "The problems that vex democracy seem to be unmanageable by democratic methods" (189–90). Machiavelli sought to found the republican spirit without wasting any words on the organic, spiritual, and miraculous aspect of the city-state; Lippmann, as a true democrat, seeks to resolve the following aporia: say yes to democracy, but in flesh and blood, not in an illusion.[7] He does not want to take the easy way out by ignoring the practical, cognitive, material impossibility of a public composed of citizens who, like eagles, could see from far away and from close up with the same visual acuity. Where everyone else just sighs and skips over the congenital weakness of democracies, without modifying their goal for all that, Lippmann wants an ideal that belongs to this world, not another.

If he wants to forget neither democracy's exigency nor its impossibility, something has to give. But what? He approaches this daunting question with complete seriousness. All those who have abandoned the idea have become reactionaries, placing their trust in a Sovereign (religious, moral, juridical, economic, it hardly matters) that is no longer accountable to anyone. All those who have forgotten democracy's practical and moral limitations have made a farce of it, leaving the most generous souls in despair and tilting finally into revolutionary evasion or into consumerism. Owing to the refusal to think through the aporia, no one has accomplished anything except making people despair of politics.

Courageously, like the mathematician he admits he would have liked to be had he not been a journalist, Lippmann stubbornly pursues his quest to the end, back to the very source of the aporia: what has to give way, what must be abandoned, is the very idea of a Public. Something has to yield, something we rightly believe that we cherish but that we have wrongly put at the heart of the democratic ideal, whereas it is in fact the principal obstacle to that ideal. The Public with an uppercase *P*, which would be represented by a government wrongly called "representative": this is the premise that must be abandoned in order to establish democracy on a realistic basis at last.[8] The Public is the childhood disease of democracy, the phantom that frightens democracy and forbids it to grow up. There is no Public. Lippmann's is the only solution that no longer skips over the practical realization of democracy—and allows us finally to entertain the material bases of progressive thought. We shall never understand the problems of the public if we do not understand that the Public is a problem.

And yet there are *publics*. When? When the rulers have failed in their duties; when the usual institutions are incapable of functioning; when controversies rage; when the darkness of the political is even more profound than usual. Lippmann does not credit the Public with any sort of happy prehistory; it was not born of some fiery empyrean accessible to selfless souls; it is not, for him, a refreshing bath in which busy citizens, as in the waters of Lethe, would forget their personal interests and become suddenly "impartial," capable of coinciding at last with the General Will. The publics are mobilized in a rush, in all their fundamental incompetence, when catastrophe strikes, because the institutions no longer respond, because the experts have demonstrated their incompetence, because the rulers are incapable of applying the rules they are charged with instituting.[9] The appearance of the public does not mark the rosy-fingered Dawn of democracy; it is first of all the mark of democracy's failure, and only then of its necessary resumption: "Yet it is controversies of this kind, the hardest controversies to disentangle, that the public is called in to judge. Where the facts are most obscure, where precedents are lacking, where novelty and confusion pervade everything, the public in all its unfitness is compelled to make its most important decisions. The hardest problems are those which institutions cannot handle. They are the public's problems" (131). This statement gives the key to Lippmann's book. It is its most decisive moment. Lippmann does not despair of the public, but he does not idealize it, either. He firmly maintains both branches of the aporia: Yes, it is indeed the public that has to grapple with the problems, since all the others have failed; yes, the public has to settle the matter despite all its incompetence, its fragility, and its amateurism. But it is both useless and dangerous to credit it with virtues that it will never have: To do so would be to prevent it from playing its role of judge of last resort.

The full harshness of Lippmann's book arises from this point: nothing will make the public competent and yet no one will come in to replace it; it is the last resort *and* it is incapable. This is literally the moment of exception. The phantom public is first of all, for Lippmann, this harsh reality, this Gorgon's head that most political thinkers do everything possible to avoid looking at directly. They usually cover over the hiatus, the break, the fault line, with a vast cloak of good feeling. True political thinkers—and they are not legion—are recognized by this sign, which they put all their energy into resisting, to the point of vertigo: above politics there is nothing, and yet there are not politics except at the decisive moment when an authority takes things in hand to cross the abyss of indecision. For Machiavelli, it is fortune; for Carl Schmitt, it is decision. But what those two authors attribute to the power of the Prince or Sovereign, Lippmann, who as a good American has never stopped believing in the popular ideal, attributes this authority to the publics in all their fragile incompetence. If there is something beyond the political, the political disappears; if there is no resumption, at moments of rupture, the political disappears even more surely. Whereas Schmitt makes the resumption of control by the Sovereign the moment of extreme strength, one that must by definition escape all justification,[10] Lippmann sees this as a moment of extreme weakness, one that must *increase*, for everyone, the requirement of justification. One could almost say that Lippmann is a democratic Schmitt. [. . .] For democracy to appear, the phantom of the Public has to dissolve.

Publics for Want of Something Better

To understand this radical breach in the notion of representation, to get a good grasp of the distinction between the Public and the publics, we need to follow the rhythm that Lippmann gives to the unfolding of affairs. Let us forget, first of all, the crazy idea according to which there are blinkered individuals preoccupied solely with their shops, and other particularly enlightened individuals through whom the public spirit speaks because these latter individuals have degrees from certain schools and belong to certain state bodies. There are no impartial people. This is the very consequence of the cognitive limitation noted above. We are competent only to address the affairs that interest us directly, whether this entails baking little bread loaves, saving lives in Darfur, operating econometric models, voting in a law, or managing a wastewater treatment plant. "A political theory based on the expectation of self-denial and sacrifice by the run of men in any community would not be worth considering" (111–12).

But our affairs are never only our own affairs, our problems are never just *our* problems, our solutions are never simply *our* solutions. If there are no selfless people, there are no strictly private questions, either. We are tied to one another not by the prior existence of some community or other—not even of a society, as we shall see below—but by the fact that our affairs, our "issues," never stop intermingling. Lippmann starts neither from the fictive individuals of the economic theories of his day nor from an already-constituted global society. We are forced to enter into politics only through the intertwining of our affairs, whose consequences escape us. For Lippmann as for Dewey, politics is resolutely object-oriented: first there are objects of dispute, imbroglios, and only then come the positions taken by the various parties.[11] It is not for nothing that both men are called pragmatists: let us start first with affairs, with things, with *pragmata*, so as to understand later what humans may think of them.[12] And if we start with objects of dispute, there are no two ways about it: those who occupy themselves with these objects will necessarily have contradictory positions. No horizon of agreement, no unanimity to hope for. Pluralism is there from the outset. Not as a defect that has to be corrected first and foremost, but because it is the very nature of this particular ecology: We are forever in contradiction, in always-intermingled affairs. [. . .]

Relativism is not a moral failing, but the simple description of the contradictory ecosystem in which we live.[13] The best we can do is reach a *modus vivendi* thanks to what Lippmann calls adjustments—a term to which he attaches a very strong meaning and in which the reader must relearn to hear the root "just." Those who think they are doing better will achieve only *modus moriendi*: no matter what they claim, they are killers.

To understand the appearance of publics, we have to bring in two new characters, rulers and "activists" or "militants," whose role, in Lippmann's work, is indispensable.

Let us make no mistake about them: rulers are obviously not the custodians of the Public Good by virtue of their impartiality and their vision of the future. Lippmann shares with all his fellow citizens a fundamental distrust of any exaggeration of the role of the State. Rulers are specialists delegated and paid to try their best to ensure application of the rules that have emerged in the wake of preceding crises—for of course we only go stumbling from one crisis to the next.

The word *rule* must not mislead us either. Lippmann takes from pragmatic philosophy an immanent definition of the rule of law as a rule of behavior: a rule is a habit initially imposed by force and followed afterward without too many recriminations.[14] "But, whether the system is obsolete or not, in its naked origin, a right is a claim somebody was able to assert, and a duty is an obligation somebody was able to fulfill" (100). But of course one cannot imagine, in a necessarily pluralistic common life, that the rules will be followed for long. They end up breaking down owing to the very fact of the contradictory affairs in which we find ourselves entangled. Doubt about them settles in. Then a third party intervenes, the activists, who take it upon themselves to criticize a rule, and, to make themselves heard, they all invoke the public spirit: "There is no question for the public unless there is doubt as to the validity of the rule—doubt, that is to say, about its meaning, its soundness or the method of its application" (108).

Political fluidity is manifested by breaks in the course of action: as the concerned parties cannot reach agreement, the rulers intervene; when the rulers do not succeed in maintaining the rules, the activists intervene. And when the activists begin to cause a commotion? This is when the publics, convoked to the scene like rubberneckers attracted by an accident, must begin to be involved, but only for a time and for a very specific function. "When the parties directly responsible do not work out an adjustment, public officials intervene. When the officials fail, public opinion is brought to bear on the issue" (72–73). Instead of basing public life on agreement, continuity, unanimity, and an appeal to the common good, Lippmann rebuilds it on disagreements, ruptures, adjustments, and an appeal to a *modus vivendi*.

Let us take care not to project our own habits onto this scenario. Neither the parties who first imposed the rule nor the rulers who followed its establishment nor the activists who contest its legitimacy represent anything but themselves. They all pursue personal interests, they are all prey to individual passions, they all lack any certitude except through their own expertise, specialized in each instance. No one has a view of the whole. No one can leap directly away from their own personal attachments to fill pitchers from the General Will.

But then how could the publics succeed where the knowledge of experts and the commitment of militants have been powerless? Why demand of the least well informed what the best informed have not been able to maintain? We have to acknowledge that the portrait of the public—with a lowercase *p*—is at first glance hardly flattering: "The public will arrive in the middle of the third act and will leave before the last curtain, having stayed just long enough perhaps to decide who is the hero and who is the villain of the piece. Yet usually that judgment will necessarily be made apart from the intrinsic merits, on the basis of a sample of behavior, an aspect of a situation by very rough external evidence" (65). [. . .]

Some will object that it is impossible to base the entire theory of democracy on such fragile grounds; that democracy can hold up only provided that the whole pyramid is seated on the immense, assured, reassuring pedestal of the uppercase *P* Public and the People. [. . .] It is precisely this illusion, this phantom, that Lippmann is asking us to give up. What was possible for the small Greek city-states, even perhaps for the nation-states, is no longer possible in the era of globalization (or of the Great Society). Political theory continues to dress globalized citizens in the now-outgrown outfits of their childhood or adolescence. They must be offered clothing that fits.

But how can these citizens be made to shed their Phrygian caps, their Roman togas, their Mao jackets? Not by attributing to them some quality that they cannot have, but by asking them to carry out in their entirety the tasks they are capable of accomplishing. Let us recall that the public is always in a position of exteriority and thus of ignorance; that its interest is fleeting, its attention discontinuous, that it can only appreciate things in broad terms without going into the details of the case in point; and that it depends entirely, for its judgments, on the cognitive apparatus made available to it. All the more so in that the public is always ad hoc, convoked on a case-by-case basis as crises and affairs arise. There is not One Public for all questions, but only publics in relation to the more or less numerous and always different ruptures in the application of the rules of behavior. The pluralism of positions is thus compounded by the pluralism of the publics. No Great One to whom to appeal:

> These conclusions are sharply at variance with the accepted theory of popular government. That theory rests upon the belief that there is a public which directs the course of events. I hold that this public is a mere phantom. It is an abstraction. The public in respect to a railroad strike may be the farmers whom the railroad serves; the public in respect to an agricultural tariff may include the very railroad men who were on strike. The public is not, as I see it, a fixed body of individuals. It is merely those persons who are interested in an affair and can affect it only by supporting or opposing the actors. (77)

It will be argued that Lippmann can never succeed, that he has made democracy's task impossible, that he is only putting its pure intentions on display so as to undermine the republican ideal; no one can lay claim to a just order while entrusting the final decision to a public endowed with so little heroic virtue. This is what was said about Machiavelli, too: he would never be able to hold a lasting order together with the slender threads of Fortune.

Signs for Spotting Partisans

Lippmann's novel solution rests entirely on a previously neglected property of the poor public of whom so much competence is demanded but from whom the practical means to exercise it are withheld: this public must be able to discern, even from the outside, and very quickly, which of the parties involved is *the most partisan* in order to put its full weight on the side of the party that appears less so. This is a small thing? It is everything. "Since these random publics cannot be expected to deal with the merits of a controversy, they can give support with reasonable assurance that it will do good only if there are easily recognizable and yet pertinent signs which they can follow.

Are there such signs? Can they be discovered? Can they be formulated so they might be learned and used?" (77–78).

This is the other key to the book, the one that will open its entire second half. Can our public life be organized in such a way as to facilitate, thanks to simple, robust signals, the detection of those who, engaged in inevitable controversies, are the most capable of justifying their positions or, conversely, those who require that we turn ourselves over to their arbitrariness alone? If these signals exist, can we multiply them, make them more salient, familiarize ourselves with them, learn to foster them? We have no other choice: if these signals fade, diminish, or disappear, there will be no more public life. Democracy will be impossible. The very sense of the political will have disappeared for good. It is on this minuscule point that Lippmann, between two wars (the first, in which he played an important role, as we shall see, and the second, which he never stopped predicting), based all his hopes. Since his day, globalization has multiplied the difficulties, while at the same time we have failed to maintain the signaling system that we ought to have been expanding in order to move beyond our difficulties. If we turn to Lippmann's book, it is with despair: everything has gotten worse, and yet this is perhaps the only solution—one that has become still less familiar, alas, still harder to implement.

The capital role attributed by Lippman to the publics is defined by two seemingly banal terms, "alignment" and "meddling," the one positive and the other negative, the one indicating the *impulse* thanks to which the publics can provisionally put an end to a crisis, and the other indicating the *restraint* that they will have to learn to exercise if they do not want to become partisans in their turn. Two quotations allow us to spot the solution:

> The signs are relevant when they reveal by coarse, simple and objective tests which side in a controversy upholds a workable social rule, or which is attacking an unworkable rule, or which proposes a promising new rule. By following such signs the public might know where to align itself. In such an alignment, it does not, let us remember, pass judgment on the intrinsic merits. It merely places its force at the disposal of the side which, according to objective signs, seems to be standing for human adjustments according to a clear rule of behavior and against the side which appears to stand for settlement in accordance with its own unaccountable will. (68–69)

The experts, the militants, the activists, the journalists, the public employees, the elected officials, all have multiplied, for the hastily assembled public, offers of positions to be taken: it is up to the public to detect the position that will allow it to favor not the best solution, but that of the party that "appears" (and this is the key to everything) ready for an adjustment. And that requires signs, proofs, tests, which Lippmann does not hesitate to call "objective." But then the public must be prevented from interfering in vain: "When there is doubt, the public requires simple, objective tests to help it decide where it will enlist. These tests must, therefore, answer two questions: First, Is the rule defective? Second, How shall the agency be recognized which is most likely to mend it? . . . They are the only questions which a member of the public can usefully concern himself with if he wishes to avoid ignorant meddling" (108). Putting one's weight on the scale without interfering is the exact opposite of the mobilized immobility and the detached engagement of those who see themselves as political because they are moved, without budging, by the frightful scenes on television. Clearly, the public requires totally different virtues from the Public.[15]

But for the publics, always ad hoc, to succeed in mobilizing and then in restraining themselves, they must be dealing with parties that agree to make their own actions *detectable* in the eyes of third parties. Here is the heart of the problem. As we have understood, the publics will never judge except in broad terms, from afar, and quickly, on the basis of crude signs. Citizens will never be made competent to take charge of the affairs of others, but recognition of those objective signs can be improved. This is why it is all the more important that *all* the parties responsible for the crisis (who have thus failed to maintain the common rules) agree to multiply, as it were, the signs that allow the public to spot which ones are ready for adjustment and which ones are concealed behind their will, which Lippmann deems *unaccountable*. [. . .]

It will have become clear that Lippmann is by no means abandoning the democratic idea, but he rids it of what has made it unrealizable: the idea that it would suffice to display one's impartiality and to call on a represented people or a higher principle to shed the constraints of justification before third parties. One cannot render the parties involved "accountable for their acts" unless one has, everywhere, *only* people whose interests lie in their own affairs (rulers, judges, militants, and "committed intellectuals" included), but who, by entering into a rich trade in emitting and detecting signals, have made themselves capable of fighting *under their own colors*. Be interested, but display your interests, and then we may be able to reach agreement. [. . .]

It is precisely because there are only power relations that adjustments are possible. It is in this sense that Lippmann can be said, ultimately, to be secularizing politics. Believing that democracy rests on the People is like believing in the power of divine right: "I have conceived public opinion to be, not the voice of God, nor the voice of society, but the voice of the interested spectators of action" (197). What you hold to most firmly is exactly what forbids you to preserve the treasure that you ought to hold, at bottom, most dear: *truth in politics,* that is, the distinction between true and false arrangements. A true arrangement can only be, here, the power relations of one group adjusted to those of another, which will make it lasting. In politics one can lie twice: if one forgets the power relations *and* if one forgets the fairness of the arrangement. We are in the cavern: don't expect anything better, don't confuse this sort of truth with other sorts (scientific, literary, religious, legal), but still, don't give up—whether out of cynicism or idealism—the quest for the truth proper to common life in the democratic tradition. Those who want to do better will always do worse.

We can now better understand the extreme exigency of Lippmann's solution and why people always prefer to indulge in dreams of the Phantom Public rather than to put that solution to work. For one would have to dream of a whole moral economy of democratic speech instead of political "position-taking." Without detection, there is no public, and without a public there is no requirement to make oneself detectable: such is the virtuous or vicious circle of public life. Between the one and the other there is all the difference between regimes of tyranny and regimes of freedom. We can imagine Lippmann's shock, had he had to witness the American press during the run-up to the Iraq war! If there is something tragic in *The Phantom Public*, it is that the solution it envisaged, with the same lucid faith that Machiavelli had manifested in his day, seems to us even more difficult to achieve, eighty years later, as though we were even less lucid and even less confident. This is because, instead of taking every care to maintain and develop *a signaling system for justifications,* we have only poisoned the patient by remedies worse than the disease. We have believed that by developing a critical spirit, by advocating commitment, by clinging to the idea of a people represented by its government, the latter in charge of the Public Good, by preaching impartiality, by seeking from as far away as possible the most fundamental and most indisputable principles, we would manage to resolve the crisis of representation. In fact, we have only amplified it. Doubt about democracy itself has set in, at the very moment when the tasks to be accomplished exceed in every way what the most ardent revolutionaries did not dare even imagine: at stake is nothing less than redrawing the details of the existence of an entire globe of billions of humans. [. . .] If Lippmann did not lose heart before the crimes he saw coming, we must not lose heart before tasks that are infinitely greater—and perhaps, alas, before other atrocities. [. . .]

Despite its tragic dimension, the solution proposed in *The Phantom Public* is the very opposite of commitment. Let us not forget its principal premise: the public is called to intervene only because all the others, the officials, the enthusiasts, the meddlers, have failed. The irruption of the public is the indispensable solution, to be sure, but it is a matter of making do; it is always a case of settling for the lesser of two evils. In this sense, Lippmann shares the very American mistrust of the State. Unbelievably to our French, Continental, Hegelian, Rousseauean, Marxist, Marxian, or simply republican ears, the idea persists, as an ideal, that the public should not interest itself in the *res publica*! And this is fine, this is the default solution, when there is no crisis. This means that the rules are applied and everything is cool. This is so rare that we needn't protest.

If there is anything Lippmann hates, it is that citizens are made to feel ashamed of the lack of interest they take in the *res publica*. He finds it entirely normal to anticipate that, after we have been mobilized for an affair, the time will necessarily come when we must *demobilize*. While he does not believe in the impartiality of public actors, he believes that it is good to detach ourselves from an affair once it has been resolved—and entrusted to those who are the best situated to handle it. Lippmann is probably the only political thinker to envisage our demobilization as a public in a positive way. Why? Well, so we can return to our own affairs, to those that we have abandoned only under pressure and constraint, and only for a limited period of time; moreover, these are the only functions we know how to carry out more or less correctly. We always forget this, but the exceptional moment, as its name indicates, has to remain exceptional. Let's quit assigning guilt to citizens because they are incapable of reaching an ideal that makes no sense whatsoever. Nothing is more absurd than the image of a people up in arms, constantly mobilized, tugged by countless commitments impossible to fulfill, always being scolded for their lack of involvement, their ignorance, their flightiness, for not turning their attention away from their own affairs to become indignant at everything, interested in everything, involved in everything. It is this "everything," as we shall see, that is Lippmann's chief target, the very idea of an Everything, the root of totalitarianisms, this Everything that is not only the source of an unrealistic picture of the cognitive capacities of citizens but is also a defect in social theory and, ultimately, a crime against democracy.

What can Lippmann's public do better? Break up. Let everyone go home! And this is how the book ends: "It is a theory which economizes the attention of men as members of the public, and asks them to do as little as possible in matters where they can do nothing very well. It confines the effort of men, when they are a public, to a part they might fulfill, to a part which corresponds to their own greatest interest in any social disturbance; that is, to an intervention which may help to allay the disturbance, and thus allow them to return to their own affairs" (199).

Lippmann would never have shared today's grand narrative according to which the end of the twentieth century saw the "victory" of neoliberalism over totalitarianism. History has not ended, for the excellent reason that it never began according to the three-act drama imagined by those who thought they were assigning history the meaning that it had tragically lost. Lippmann always applied his conception of liberty, the publics, and the struggle against partisans equally to the *private* schemes of rulers and the *private* schemes of capitalists. If he were writing now, it would be on the joint failure of socialisms and neoliberalisms, of supporters of the State and supporters of the Market, of sectarians of the Visible Hand and worshippers of the Invisible Hand; none of them has ever taken into account the new dimensions that the second globalization has given to the problems of the public. Just as, in his day, the reactionaries, the socialists, and the fascists tried, from the very heart of the Great Society, to return to the phantom of the Public Spirit, today, despite the vastly magnified scale of the stakes, both progressives and their enemies are still attached to the same ideal of totality and organicity. Far from maintaining the democratic system of signalization, they have abandoned it in favor of a dream of totality that is even more implausible in the early twenty-first century than it was at the dawn of the twentieth. It is almost as if adults had been condemned to live in the doll's house of their childhood.

In other words, the great battle between the phantom of democracy and its appearances is still going on exactly as in Lippmann's day—but it has gotten worse. The real obstacle is what he calls "the phantom of identity" (166). And yet we shall no longer be able to confine pluralism within any definitive boundaries:

> Against this deep pluralism thinkers have argued in vain. They have invented social organisms and national souls, and oversouls, and collective souls; they have gone for hopeful analogies to the beehive and the anthill, to the solar system, to the human body; they have gone to Hegel for higher unities and to Rousseau for a general will in an effort to find some basis for union.... We, however, no longer expect to find a unity which absorbs diversity. For us the conflicts and differences are

so real that we cannot deny them and instead of looking for identity of purpose we look simply for an accommodation of purposes. (97–98)

From our perspective, this is an odd position. On the one hand, he accepts radical pluralism; on the other, he proposes as a horizon only accommodation, conciliation, and the adjustment of interests. Isn't this asking at once too little and too much of politics? We cannot help but find the potion too bitter: there must surely be a way to limit pluralism by confining it within narrower boundaries; but it must also be possible to propose much more to public life than a simple *modus vivendi*. Here is where Lippmann is striking at the heart of the European—and, in his terms, "Hegelian"—political tradition. He presses where it hurts: if we want to survive globalization without abandoning the democratic ideal, we must be at once much more radical and much more modest.[16]

Above all, we have to give up the idea that there could be something *better* than the moral economy of detecting signs that Lippmann sought to define in his book, something that would govern politics and that would serve simultaneously as its foundation, its guarantee, its explanation, and its court of appeal. Lippmann has identified with maximum precision what is paralyzing the apprenticeship of liberty: the very idea of society. Liberalism, he says, "was frustrated over the ancient problem of the One and the Many. Yet the problem is not so insoluble once we cease to personify society. It is only when we are compelled to personify society that we are puzzled as to how many separate organic individuals can be united in one homogeneous organic individual. This logical underbrush is cleared away if we think of society not as the name of a thing but as the name of all the adjustments between individuals and their things" (171–72).

Society does not exist. Or rather, there exist adjustments between people and their affairs (their "things"),[17] but these adjustments must never be subsumed under the idea of a macro-actor. Like Gabriel Tarde before him,[18] Lippmann perceived very clearly the strange collaboration between what we would call neoliberal thought today, a way of thinking that sees only individuals, and sociology, which sees only societies: Both forms of thought *delegate to a Great Other the task of reaching an agreement*. And it hardly matters whether this Other is the Market or the State, since in both cases the adjustment of interests no longer needs the help of a particular intellectual technology. It is because of the miracle of pre- or post-established harmony that we think we can get along without politics, which is always relegated to a subaltern function, subjected to derision and cynicism. It is in this sense that Lippmann truly secularizes democracy. The miraculous accord of the Market or the State presupposes a realm beyond or above politics, a real backstage world, the last transcendence to which are attached those who, moreover, no longer believe in anything except their own critical spirit: the totality that is always already mysteriously constituted (the State) or that is going to equilibrate interests miraculously (the Market). Society is the opium of the people. Which makes it forget to maintain the subtle networks that alone would have made it possible to spot the partisans and increase the dosage of public intelligence.

> The democratic ideal has never defined the function of the public. It has treated the public as an immature, shadowy executive of all things. The confusion is deep-seated in a mystical notion of society. "The people" were regarded as a person; their wills as a will; their ideas as a mind; their mass as an organism with an organic unity of which the individual was a cell. Thus the voter identified himself with the officials. He tried to think that his thoughts were their thoughts, that their deeds were his deeds, and even that in some mysterious way they were a part of him. All this confusion of identities led naturally to the theory that everybody was doing everything. It prevented democracy from arriving at a clear idea of its own limits and attainable ends. (147–48)

Those who have not measured the limits of democracy are ill placed to achieve it. Lippmann's lesson is the same as Machiavelli's. That he is accused of being "Machiavellian" or "neoliberal" just proves that people always prefer to hide their faces before the originality of political truth while blinding even more those who are thereby deprived of the only light on which they could rely in order to be a little less deceived. Either you believe in phantoms— and you refer agreement to the beyond—or else you see the appearances of democracy—and you give yourself the means to obtain the necessary adjustments.[19] By believing in the phantoms of identity, one misses the prey for the shadows: the prey may be deceptive, but less so than the shadow. We have to choose: *modus moriendi* or *modus vivendi*; this is the only ecology that counts.

The Eclipse of the Public, or the Renewal of the Lippmann/Dewey Debate

There is reason to fear, alas, that Lippmann's book will be judged according to a system of coordinates in which all political thought is identified by a cursor that slides from timid reform to total revolution (the positive and negative signs vary with the preferences of one's party). It is true that the word *pragmatism* is afflicted with the same ambiguity as the word *liberalism*. One thinks one sees in it a weakening of the will to change, whereas what is really at stake is a powerful amplification of the requirements of democracy. Lippmann is still less reformist than he is revolutionary—and this is saying a great deal. Reformism, for him, would be acceptance of the world as it is; but the world is not, is no longer, has never been "as it is." [. . .] The interweaving of affairs and interests makes it critical through and through—always in the physical, material sense of critical situations. To understand what can be radical about such a refusal of reform or revolution, we must make no mistake about the importance of the political signaling system that Lippmann calls for: A public life that ceases to be maintained would be like an economy gradually deprived of all means of transport or communication: no more paved roads, no more telephones, no more laptops. It is not likely that we would reach agreement more often.

The accommodation of interests and the adjustments of power relations demand much greater energy than the cowardly complacency of those who see themselves as "realists" because they have simply tossed their ideal out the window. The reformists, from Lippmann's standpoint, are even more lost in the clouds than the revolutionaries: The latter believe in a totality that can be overturned, the former concern themselves with details and leave the whole aside. Whereas Lippmann's enemy is precisely the Whole. Some seek to overturn it, others to leave it intact; either way, it is the same illusion, the same phantom. There is no Whole.

This is particularly clear in the combined critique Lippmann makes of capitalism and of his socialist ex-fellow travelers:

> The people as a whole supporting a centralized government cannot tame capitalism as a whole. For the powers which are summed in the term capitalism are many. They bear separately upon different groups of people. The nation as a unit does not encounter them all, and cannot deal with them all. It is to the different groups of people concerned that we must look for the power which shall offset the arbitrary power that bears upon them. The reduction of capitalism to workable law is no matter of striking at it wholesale by general enactments. It is a matter of defeating its arbitrary power in detail, in every factory, in every office, in every market, and of turning the whole network of relations under which industry operates from the dominion of arbitrary forces into those of settled rules. (194–95)

These are not the statements of a reformer who has accepted the indisputable rules of the Market. As if those rules existed! As if there were a beyond of politics! When will we stop bringing piety to politics? If we have to worship civic gods, let us at least erect temples to Jupiter and the god of the Stock Market; that would be more honest, more amusing, more kitsch. The paradoxical divide between reformists and revolutionaries prevails at the very moment when the global ecological crises require such a complete restructuring of the material conditions of our existence that even the most furious revolutionaries would never have dared to imagine it. The hope of "total revolution" whose dizzying genealogy Bernard Yack has traced so well may have meaning right now—after it has been abandoned![20] It is true that there is something truly new about this hope: it is based entirely in details, and not in a totality. There is indeed a pragmatic revolution, but it is a revolution in care, attention, experience, in the stubborn conquest of details, in adjustment, precaution, in what Isabelle Stengers has called the "ecology of practices."[21] Here are two visions of politics, two aesthetics, that are very hard to reconcile. Either you believe that we can only reach agreement because there is an external guarantor somewhere, a deux ex machina, that will bring us into harmony, or else you think, as Lippmann does, that the belief in a God of politics is what makes the adjustment impossible. Chairman Mao was decidedly right, one must always revolutionize the revolution. [. . .]

If there was anyone who did grasp Lippman's importance and originality, it was John Dewey. He reacted at once to the shock of *The Phantom Public* with a vigorous analysis in the *New Republic* (to which he was also a contributor).[22] Dewey was a philosopher of science and education, "America's educator," as he was called then. He was at once seduced, shaken, and shocked by Lippmann's arguments—so much so that less than two years later he published his own response by adopting the entire critical section but rejecting the solution. As Joëlle Zask has noted, what separates them is once again a story of phantoms: "If Lippmann and Dewey agree on the one hand that 'the omnicompetence of the citizen' is a now-empty presupposition, they diverge considerably, on the other hand, as to the remedies that they envisage. For Lippmann, the public is a 'phantom,' a mirage of liberal thought, a 'myth.' For Dewey, the public is 'dispersed,' 'chaotic,' and 'eclipsed.' Now, between a 'phantom' and an 'eclipse' there is all the distance that separates an illusion from a disappearance."[23]

Dewey never resigned himself to the loss of what he calls the Great Community, which was in his eyes the necessary pendant to the Great Society: globalization requires a Globe. Everything Lippmann says is true: we shall never return to communes, to communism, to communities. But he lacks imagination, and he does not dare invent a common good that would be commensurate with the new stakes. The greater the problems, the greater the solutions must be. As accurate as is his devastating critique of the State, Lippmann does not see that, behind the illusions of totality, the State also entails a function of *composition*.[24] For Dewey, Lippmann's adjustments will never suffice to compose a viable world. Dewey cannot bring himself to believe that one can be satisfied with a public that is so little engaged and whose only objective is to go back home! For Dewey is much more interested in the sciences than Lippmann and has a much more pronounced taste for grasping the political importance of the arts.[25]

Lippmann in fact manifested a profound distrust of the new communication technologies—of which he nevertheless provided the first detailed analysis. He did not believe that the democratic signaling system could ever profoundly modify the distribution between "insiders" and "outsiders." Indeed, he continued to think that "insiders" truly existed, specialists who were effectively minding their own business because they held both ends of the continuous chain of what they knew best. In contrast, Dewey saw clearly that that distribution was untenable: the "outsiders" were less "outside" than they were thought to be, while the "insiders" had long since ceased to be "inside," since the very development of technologies had blinded them, too, had left them ill-equipped to deal with large swatches of "what they knew best." What surgeon, what deputy, what computer specialist, what hairdresser can say that he or she has achieved mastery of everything needed in order to act? Lippmann neglected the capacity of the public to learn because he did not see that technological equipment was both less favorable to insiders and much more favorable to outsiders. Dewey thus accepted the problem as posed by Lippmann (this is the title of his book), but he explored an entirely different solution, well summarized in the term *experience*.[26] Can we imagine a political life that is finally concerned with contemporary technologies of representation? Can we reinvent representative government and rediscover the State? Can we retool the very notion of representation so as to bring the crisis of representation to an end?

Who is right, Lippmann or Dewey? One may well hesitate between the two. Lippmann is darker, more realistic, a much better writer, more concrete, much better informed about the affairs of his day, co-opted by the powerful. Dewey is more generous, more ample, more precise in his concepts, more ambitious in the last analysis, but a more ponderous and abstract writer, more radical, too. Both are on the trail of a political truth infinitely livelier than the traditions Europeans have inherited, because that truth has discovered in the details of human affairs—the famous *pragmata*—the secret of its possible *verification*.

Notes

1. Cited by Steel, *Walter Lippmann*, 26.
2. The term Great Society, which we also find in Dewey, comes from the great English socialist Graham Wallas (1858–1932), who became a friend and mentor to the young Lippmann. Like the term globalization today, Wallas's term designates at once the hopes and the threats of a politics that no longer remains within the narrow confines of the past.
3. There are commonplaces that end up being verified; see d'Allones, *Le dépérissement de la politique*.
4. Dewey, *Public and Its Problems*.
5. Lippmann, *Phantom Public*, 119. Further citations of this work in this chapter are given in the text. We are in 1925: "men" must include, implicitly, "women." We shall have to wait for the feminist movements to remedy the sexism of language.
6. Marres, "No Issue, No Public," "Tracing the Trajectories," and "Issues Deserve More Credit."
7. In his *Public Opinion*, Lippmann praised Machiavelli as "a man most mercilessly maligned, because he happened to be the first naturalist who used plain language in a field hitherto preempted by supernaturalists" (168).
8. The history of the many solutions proposed for this aporia can be found in Manin, *Principles of Representative Government*.
9. Critics often claim that Lippmann wanted to entrust the task of ruling to experts, but those critics must never really have read him: the experts may have good eyesight, but they are too narrowly focused not to be partisan for their part too. As Dewey puts it marvelously, "They are persons of a specialized infrequent habit" (*Public and Its Problems*, 160).
10. Schmitt, *Concept of the Political* and *Theory of the Partisan*. Whereas for Schmitt the partisan is an ideal of politics, for Lippmann the partisan is only a necessary evil, and one must do everything possible to channel partisan anger.
11. "The public consists of all those who are affected by the indirect consequences of transactions to such an extent that it is deemed necessary to have those consequences systematically cared for. Officials are those who look out for and take care of the interests thus affected" (Dewey, *Public and Its Problems*, 15–16).
12. See Zask, *John Dewey, philosophe du public*.
13. Hence the strange chapter 7 on the definition of the "problems" and the basis, in some sense ecological, of pluralism. The best we can do is to reach a *modus vivendi*.
14. Lippmann was a friend of Oliver Wendell Holmes (author of *Common Law*, 1885), one of the great pragmatics of law. See Menand, *Metaphysical Club*. Lippmann again: "When a rule is broken not occasionally but very often the rule is defective. It simply does not define the conduct which normally may be expected by men who live under it. It may sound noble. But it does not work. It does not adjust relations. It does not actually organize society" (*Phantom Public*, 123–24).
15. In practice, of course, as Dominique Reynié has shown in *Le triomphe de l'opinion publique*, the uppercase P Public was never produced by anything other than a multitude of lowercase p publics.

16. We find the same critique of totality, in a totally different spirit but with the same attention to *modus vivendi* taken in its literal, ecological sense, in the work of Sloterdijk, especially *Foams* and *In the World Interior of Capital*.

17. Let us recall that one very strong and eminently pragmatic meaning of the English word *thing*: like the German *Ding*, it can refer to an ancient form of political gathering. See Latour and Weibel, *Making Things Public*, especially Marres, "Issues Spark a Public."

18. See Latour and Lépinay, *Introduction*.

19. Visitors to the *Making Things Public* exhibit can attest to the difficulty they had visualizing the "phantom public" that the exhibit's organizers had requested of Michel Jaffrennou and Thierry Coduys. See Jaffrennou and Coduys, "Mission Impossible."

20. Yack, *Longing for Total Revolution*.
21. Stengers, *La Vierge et le neutrino*.
22. Dewey, "Practical Democracy."
23. Zask, *L'opinion publique et son double*.
24. See Linhardt, "L'état et ses épreuves."
25. Dewey, *Art as Experience*.

26. It is this experience that all those who are interested in decoding what is called by the very un-Lippmannian term *participation of the public* in technological debates. See Callon, Lascoumes, and Barthe, *Agir dans un monde incertain*; in the hope that, for some, certain of the technologies available thanks to the web will make it possible to identify Lippmann's political signaling system, see Rogers, *Information Politics on the Web*, and especially concerning the MACOSPOL (Mapping Controversies on Science for Politics), https://medialab.sciencespo.fr/en/activities/macospol/.

Bibliography

Boltanski, Luc, and Laurent Thévenot. *On Justification* (1991). Princeton, NJ: Princeton University Press, 2006.
Callon, Michel, Pierre Lascoumes, and Yannick Barthe. *Agir dans un monde incertain: Essai sur la démocratie technique*. Paris: Seuil, 2001.
d'Allones, Myriam Revault. *Le dépérissement de la politique: Généalogie d'un lieu commun*. Paris: Aubier, 1999.
Dewey, John. *Art as Experience*. New York: Perigee Books, 1934.
———. "Practical Democracy." *New Republic*, December 2, 1925.
———. *The Public and Its Problems* (1927). Athens, OH: Swallow Press, 1976.
Jaffrennou, Michel, and Thierry Coduys. "Mission Impossible: Giving Flesh to the Phantom Public." In *Making Things Public: Atmospheres of Democracy*, edited by Bruno Latour and Peter Weibel, 218–23. Cambridge, MA: MIT Press, 2005.
Latour, Bruno, and Vincent Lépinay. *Introduction à l'anthropologie économique de Gabriel Tarde*. Paris: La Découverte, 2008.
Latour, Bruno, and Peter Weibel, eds. *Making Things Public: Atmospheres of Democracy*. Cambridge, MA: MIT Press, 2005.
Linhardt, Dominique. "L'état et ses épreuves: Éléments d'une sociologie des agencements étatiques." *Clio / Themis* (2009): https://doi.org/10.35562/cliothemis.
Lippmann, Walter. *The Phantom Public*. New York: Harcourt, Brace, 1925.
———. *Public Opinion* (1922). New York: The Free Press, 1925.
Manin, Bernard. *The Principles of Representative Government* (1995). Cambridge: Cambridge University Press, 1997.

Marres, Noortje. "The Issues Deserve More Credit: Pragmatic Contributions to the Study of Public Involvement in Controversy," *Social Studies of Science* 37, no. 2 (2007): 759–80.

———. "Issues Spark a Public into Being." In *Making Things Public: Atmospheres of Democracy*, edited by Bruno Latour and Peter Weibel, 208–17. Cambridge, MA: MIT Press, 2005.

———. "No Issue, No Public: Democratic Deficits After the Displacement of Politics." PhD diss., University of Amsterdam, 2005.

———. "Tracing the Trajectories of Issues and Their Democratic Deficit on the Web," *Information Technology and People* 17, no. 2 (2004): 124–49.

Menand, Louis. *The Metaphysical Club: A Story of Ideas in America*. New York: Farrar, Straus and Giroux, 2001.

Reynié, Dominique. *Le triomphe de l'opinion publique: L'espace public, du XVIe au XXe siècle*. Paris: Odile Jacob, 1998.

Rogers, Richard. *Information Politics on the Web*. Cambridge, MA: MIT Press, 2004.

Schmitt, Carl. *The Concept of the Political* (1932). Chicago: University of Chicago Press, 2007.

———. *Theory of the Partisan: Intermediate Commentary on the Concept of the Political* (1963). New York: Telos, 2007.

Sloterdijk, Peter. *Foams* (2004). Cambridge, MA: MIT Press, 2016.

———. *In the World Interior of Capital: For a Philosophical Theory of Globalization* (2005). Cambridge: Polity, 2013.

Steel, Ronald. *Walter Lippman and the American Century*. New Brunswick, NJ: Transaction, 1999.

Stengers, Isabelle. *La Vierge et le neutrino*. Paris: La Découverte, 2005.

Yack, Bernard. *The Longing for Total Revolution: Philosophic Sources of Social Discontent from Rousseau to Marx and Nietzsche*. Berkeley: University of California Press, 1992.

Zask, Joëlle. *L'opinion publique et son double*, vol. 2, *John Dewey, philosophe du public*. Paris: L'Harmattan, 2000.

4

DEBATES CONJURED, DEBATES FORGOTTEN

Anna Shechtman and John Durham Peters

For more than three decades, the intellectual capital of the "Dewey/Lippmann debate" has undergone a series of inflations and deflations. Conceived by James W. Carey in the mid-1980s as a paradigm for communication studies and democratic theory, Walter Lippmann and John Dewey's post–Progressive Era "debate"—call it a "disagreement," "a "shared investment," if you'd prefer—was, throughout the 1990s and early 2000s, hypostasized by polemicists and scholars into a defining "set piece of American political thought."[1] According to Carey, Lippmann set the debate stage with his 1922 *Public Opinion* and its 1925 sequel *The Phantom Public*, two withering critiques of American democracy in an increasingly urban and mass-mediated age. Dewey reviewed Lippmann's publications, rather glowingly, in the *New Republic*, and his own book *The Public and Its Problems* (1927) is explicitly indebted to Lippmann's work, engaging with many of its themes. After all, on many of the perils of modern democracy, the two men agreed: the scale of American life had far outpaced the agrarian communities on which the founders framed the nation; the burgeoning field of public relations intensified and made transparent the extent to which politicians and journalists served private interests, not the voting public. What Lippmann called the "phantom public"—the inability of American citizens to participate meaningfully under these new conditions, despite propaganda to the contrary—Dewey deemed the "eclipse of the public."

According to strict followers of Carey, however, Dewey and Lippmann's responses to this apparent impasse offered two paths forward for modern American democracy and its study.[2] Lippmann carved the path of the wonk: his is the "administrative tradition" in communication studies—one that privileges technocratic expertise and social science over the cultivation of the voice of the demos. As Carey has it, "Lippmann endorsed the notion that it was possible to have a science of society such that scientists might constitute a new priesthood: the possessors of truth as a result of having an agreed-upon method for its determination."[3] Carey's Dewey, meanwhile, was a humanist, consolidating the "critical tradition," which, scaling up from the small town meeting, aimed to transform the industrial Great Society into a "Great Community" through democratic educational reforms and a vibrant, aesthetically engaged press.

Even as Carey's schema found its way into textbooks and trade books alike, scholars were quick to point out that not only did the "debate" between Lippmann and Dewey never happen as such (Lippmann never *responded* to Dewey's book reviews or his *The Public and Its Problems*), Carey's Lippmann and Dewey are straw men, not faithful to either writer's ideological and methodological complexity. Carey's Lippmann is the elitist and his Dewey the populist; they are the sinner and saint of democratic theory.[4] They are, as Lippmann would have it, stereotypes.[5] Indeed, by 2010, the "debate" was effectively debunked in these terms. Chief among its vanquishers were Sue Curry Jansen and Michael Schudson, who respectively demonstrated that communication studies' mythologization of Dewey and Lippmann was symptomatic of its ahistorical tendency—and its need, in the late 1980s and early '90s, for a new, post–Cold War *modus operandi*.[6] Both scholars called for renewed attention to the historical texture of the field's Progressive Era origins—and the Reagan-Clinton Era of its most seductive origin myth. This chapter—our chapter—heeds both calls.

Carey was right to locate in these figures and this moment important precedents for the problems we continue to face around media and democracy. Dewey and Lippmann's questions foreshadow ours: Can democracy thrive under industrialism (and postindustrial globalism), when the spread and scale of information eclipses that of the Aristotelian polis and the Jeffersonian township? Is there even a "public" to speak of, to justify democratic practice, under these material conditions? What is the role of the press, commercial by design and ever altered by new technologies and social pressures, in shaping, channeling, and trumpeting public opinion? Dewey and Lippmann provided still provocative answers to these questions, but during the interwar period, the rough time frame of their debated debate, these questions were not theirs alone. Unsurprisingly, they were posed and discussed by a generation of social scientists, philosophers, and critics of their milieu. We add their roles to the dramatis personae, their voices to this conversation. A more varied cast makes the conversation, a vague term of Careyan vintage that we prefer to his too-pointed "debate," both more complicated and more relevant.[7] Moreover, recovering the extent of this conversation sheds light on the '80s–'90s scene of disciplinary mythmaking: who was forgotten to make "the Dewey/Lippmann debate"?

In our telling, Dewey is the quilting point—the intellectual suture holding together the threads of questions concerning democracy and publicity in the interwar period. His investment in the conversation is perhaps most clearly articulated in *The Public and Its Problems*, but Dewey's instrumentalist approach to these questions (elaborated in *The Public*, as well as his *New Republic* articles [1914–21], *Experience and Nature* [1925] and *Art as Experience* [1934]), excited response from social psychologist Floyd Allport, political critic Randolph Bourne, polymorphic intellectual Lewis Mumford, theologian Reinhold Niebuhr, and critical sociologist Max Horkheimer. And unlike Lippmann—whose theory of mass-mediated democracy was shaped by his practice as a reporter and political adviser during World War I and not any exchange with Dewey—many of these other figures went into print combat with the philosopher to signal a break from their mentor. If not explicitly trained by Dewey, they were shaped by two burgeoning areas of inquiry indelibly marked by his influence: American philosophy and social science. Deweyan pragmatism influenced the development of both intellectual modes into the twentieth century, but only through intensive, sometimes agonistic debate with Dewey's works.

Neither formally rigorous enough for the social scientist nor metaphysically deep enough for the humanists, Dewey's philosophy caught him between a rock and a soft place—between new forms of quantitative social science and radical humanistic critique. Ironically, then, in mapping the foundational rift in communication studies (the administrative and critical traditions) onto Lippmann and Dewey, Carey sketched two different historical criticisms of Dewey himself. As we will see, Allport, Bourne, Mumford, Niebuhr, and Horkheimer all partially invented the Dewey with whom they sparred. Two generations later, Carey fell into the distinguished tradition of turning Dewey into a straw man against (or with) which to build a new paradigm for American democracy—for intellectuals and for the masses, for the humanities and the sciences. We return to the conversation—the milieu in which Dewey and Lippmann thought, wrote, and maybe even debated—to rediscover how.

The Problem of Reading Dewey

Interpreting John Dewey, even during his lifetime, has long been a vexing business. His student and critic Randolph Bourne spoke of Dewey's "protective coloration," his tendency to adopt the colors of his environment like a chameleon.[8] Since his death in 1952, his works have been read (or misread or not read) in numerous, often-contradictory ways. His faith in science and modernity is, depending on how you take it, a stumbling block or a source of inspiration. So inconsistent he sometimes appears in our intellectual landscape—radical-democratic visionary or scientistic technocrat—that it is tempting to follow Morton White's classic description of "two John Deweys."[9] Dewey's response to the role of scientific method in resolving the "eclipse of the public" and resuscitating democracy is a case in point.

Dewey wrote *The Public and Its Problems* in an intellectual climate prone to "democratic realism." The pendulum of American political thought in the 1920s had swung far to the right. A new breed of realists on the American social science scene took from pragmatist and progressive sources a zealous faith in scientific method and, from European crowd psychology, a deep suspicion of democratic masses.[10] The state's intensified management of American sentiment during World War I and the spell (as some saw it) of the temperance movement heightened the anti-populist suspicions of political scientists, sociologists, and psychologists of the realist ilk.[11] (We might also speculate that high hopes around the Nineteenth Amendment—the widely bruited notion that women would bring new kinds of enlightenment to the voting booth—were dashed by the election of one of the most ineffectual and corrupt presidents in American history, Warren G. Harding.) Democratic realists bolstered their concerns about this state of affairs with empirical methods to "give scientific confirmation to the old Aristotelian dogma that some men are born to rule and others to serve," as Harry Elmer Barnes wrote.[12] Using science to test and verify the irrationality of mass psychology, they advocated a "new paternalism," as Dewey called it, or, more encouragingly, a new "politics of prevention," per Harold Lasswell, in which experts and statisticians advised leaders on how to "reorient minds" and protect the national interest.[13]

These were not Dewey's values, but they were his methods. He decried anti-democratic thought just as he renounced the anti-scientific, metaphysical speculations on which much existing democratic theory relied. His prose reflects these values—to a fault. It neither swells with inspiring abstractions ("we the people!"), nor does it have the precision of a specialized professional discourse. He maintained that the problems facing modern democracy were compounded by empty, anti-scientific rhetoric and demanded rigorous methods and standards to manage its risks: "Democracy," he wrote, "cannot obtain either adequate recognition of its own meaning or coherent practical realization as long as anti-naturalism operates to delay and frustrate the use of methods by which alone understanding of, and consequent ability to guide, social relationships can be attained."[14] In keeping with pragmatist tenets,

Dewey insisted on abandoning a priori theories about the nature of society and the individual, approaching democratic theory and practice experimentally instead. The truth of democracy was found in a mode of life that enabled all to partake in world-building; its end came into being from the means.

In *The Public and Its Problems*, however, Dewey conceded that the application of scientific method to the social and humanistic questions of democratic theory would be an imperfect fit. He wrote, "When we say that thinking and beliefs should be experimental, not absolutistic, we have then in mind a certain logic of method, *not, primarily, the carrying on of experimentation like that of laboratories*. . . . They will be experimental in the sense that they will be entertained subject to constant and well-equipped observation of the consequences they entail when acted upon, and subject to ready and flexible revision in the light of observed consequences."[15] Unlike the natural and physical sciences, then, the study of society would never settle into immutable principles: there would be no "social law" to complement "natural law." It is for this reason that many champions of Dewey revise his theory of the public in *The Public and Its Problems* into a tacit theory of *publics*, always evolving, plural, and contingent on various instrumentalities—acts and their "observed consequences."

Dewey began his theory of the public with a local distinction between private and public activity. In his terms, *private* activity is that which has no observed consequences outside its immediate actors. By contrast, *public* activity emerges when a transaction extends beyond those directly concerned. (Though he didn't use the term, his "public" is precisely characterized by what economists call "externalities.") "Those indirectly and seriously affected [by an action] for good or for evil," he wrote, "form a group distinctive enough to require recognition and a name. The name selected is The Public." From here, Dewey built up to the watchdogs of the public's interests—the government and the state—which, he insisted, are as mutable and experimentally derived as the publics they serve. Methodologically, in other words, Dewey wanted to have it both ways: he wanted to retain the explanatory nature of the natural sciences (i.e., the ability to analyze behavior in terms of its "consequences") and the anti-absolutist, case-by-case sensitivity of humanistic inquiry.

Administrators on Dewey: The Case of Floyd Allport

But consequences can only be assessed as such if *causation* is known, and causation can only be known by means of social laws or, at least, deterministic norms. This was a principal criticism of Dewey's pragmatic democratic theory launched by Floyd Allport—his most sophisticated critic from the social sciences. "When it comes to the actual work of conducting experiments," Allport wrote of Dewey's social scientific method in *Public*, "it is to be feared that the solutions offered will not be of much avail."[16] In an otherwise largely sympathetic reading of *The Public*, he continued, "In the absence of laws or generalizations affording a prediction of the consequences of proposed adjustments, there can be but little intelligent pre-direction. A failure, moreover, to secure the expected result cannot in social phenomena as in the natural sciences, lead to the discovery of a more general law heretofore unnoticed. Each exception must be regarded as a 'law' unto itself and hence scarcely as a law at all. Hence little social knowledge can be acquired in these experimental efforts, which will help us to predict the results of applying our techniques to new situations" (95).

Allport commended Dewey for attempting to replace absolutism with experimentalism, but he conceded that scientific experiments require a bit of the absolute in order to posit and test generalizations for future scholars to employ. "Does not," he asked, "the notion of a causal nexus, upon which [Dewey's observable] 'consequences' depend, imply a certain universality of occurrence, comparable, at least, to the universality of the laws of physical science?" (93). Dewey might counter that his entire pragmatist or "instrumentalist" method was designed to rescue the study of consequences from causal determinism, but such philosophical revisions didn't do a lot to help the practicing social scientist disentangle rival hypotheses.

In addition to questioning the validity of Dewey's social scientific method, Allport also criticized the philosopher for failing to account for the psychological complexity of social activity. He thought Dewey misguided for making "the full social expression of an integrated personality" the "criterion of successful citizenship" (95–96). We can act in public and political affairs, argued Allport, only as partial beings. In a political party, for instance, the full range of one's individuality is irrelevant. Other sorts of groups, generally less explicitly political ones, invite the fuller expression of the personality, such as families or friendship, for instance. Dewey's mistake was to suppose that public life could express whole selves: "The very existence of the public tends to produce an insoluble problem so far as complete individual self-expression is concerned" (132). Here Allport's criticism anticipates later public sphere theorists who articulated the pragmatics of partial inclusion— the political and technical processes by which some belong to "the public" under certain conditions.[17] In Dewey's sunny vision of the Great Community, spontaneous and "totally inclusive" communication offered *everyone* a platform for self-expression in and as "the public." But the dream of participatory democracy as authentic self-actualization was not only a historical impossibility (based on the realities of class, race, gender, sexuality, and ability), it was, per Allport, a logical fallacy.

Critiques of the Critical Tradition: From Randolph Bourne to Max Horkheimer

If Dewey's pragmatist approach to public opinion was not instrumental enough for Allport—not, in other words, practically useful to the scientific community studying civic life—it was *too* instrumental for many left intellectuals between World War I and World War II. At his ninetieth birthday celebration at Columbia University in 1950, Dewey confessed that "the word pragmatism was perhaps unfortunate, though Mr. Peirce, who originated it, gave it a very specific meaning. But it became identified with a very narrow view of practical utility . . . which (from my point of view) is a complete misunderstanding."[18] Over the second half of his career (and the first half of the twentieth century), Dewey suffered a string of attacks from critics to his left who, often unfairly, collapsed his pragmatic method into the very forms of for-profit utilitarianism that had created the conditions for the "eclipse of the public" in the first place.

Like many American intellectuals of the generation following Dewey's, these writers (Randolph Bourne, Lewis Mumford, Waldo Frank, Reinhold Niebuhr) can be difficult to pin down politically, as they traversed the ideological spectrum between and after the wars. It is, however, fair to classify their critiques of Dewey as forms of "left critique," if only because they consistently identified his pragmatic method with an affirmation of power—military power, industry, capital, and the incumbent power of a political elite. Most damning because most persuasive were the criticisms of Bourne, who, in his blistering essay "Twilight of the Idols" of 1917, took Dewey to task for his complicity in the country's (in his mind, brutal and unjustified) intervention in World War I.[19]

Far from a jingoist, Dewey did ultimately advocate American intervention in World War I, hoping to use instrumentalism to avoid war's prevailing logic in which victory for victory's sake was justified at any cost. Instead, war could function as a means to a worthy end: freedom of the seas, disarmament, racial equality, anti-colonialism, and, most importantly, the establishment of an international governing body that could work to outlaw war. In this way, Dewey came close to arguing for "a war to end all wars." He wrote, "As a pacifist, Mars has not been a success. But a war to establish an international order and by that means to outlaw war is something hitherto unknown. In the degree to which the American conception of the war gains force and *this* war becomes a war for a new type of social organization, it will be a war of compelling moral import."[20]

Perhaps due to naïve optimism or hubris, Dewey overinvested in Wilsonian democracy, presuming the president's fidelity to his own worldview. It's easy, a bloody century later, to note how quixotic entertaining war as an occasion for progressive social reconstruction is (even if wars have been inadvertently transformative); and by the signing of the Treaty of Versailles in 1919, Wilson had surely disappointed Dewey and his fellow interventionist editors at *The Dial*: among the ends meant to justify the Great War as means, Wilson had sacrificed all but a League of Nations. "America has won the war; America has lost the peace, the object for which she fought," the editors ruefully wrote in a fundamentally Deweyan construction.[21]

A year earlier, Bourne seemed to have anticipated this state of affairs, condemning Dewey and his pro-war followers for imagining a hyperrational military offense without the "mob-fanaticisms, the injustices and hatreds, that are organically bound up with it."[22] Using Dewey's own method against the philosopher's war support, Bourne contended that Dewey had invoked democracy to justify the war, but that democracy remained, in Dewey's work, "an unanalyzed term, useful as a call to battle, but not an intellectual tool, turning up fresh sod for the changing future" (688). He continued:

> I search Professor Dewey's articles in vain for clues as to the specific working-out of our democratic desires, either nationally or internationally, either in the present or in the reconstruction after the war. No program is suggested, nor is there feeling for present vague popular movements and revolts. Rather are the latter chided, for their own vagueness and impracticalities. . . . In the application of their philosophy to politics, our pragmatists are sliding over this crucial question of ends. Dewey says our ends must be intelligently international rather than chauvinistic. But this gets us little distance along our way. (688)

According to Bourne, then, Dewey compromised his pacifist ideals for the sake of an undefined end. This was not only a failure of pragmatic method—in which means and ends are explicit, mutually constitutive moral collaborators—it demonstrated the method's fundamental pitfall: a lack of ideals to begin with. "It is now bumming plain," Bourne wrote, "that unless you start with the vividest kind of poetic vision, your instrumentalism is likely to land you just where it has landed this younger intelligentsia which is so happily and busily engaged in the national enterprise of war" (688). If one's means are to justify one's ends, one must have a vision of the end in sight—and a poetic vision at that! Instead, Bourne suggested, pragmatists had fallen in love with technique for its own sake and had an untenable aversion to ugly feelings: "Impossibilism, apathy . . . any attitude that is not a cheerful and brisk setting to work to use the emergency to consolidate the gains of democracy" (688) were anathema to Dewey and his followers. This was "scientific method applied to 'uplift'" (688)—intellectualized jingoism and grist for the war machine.

After the Treaty of Versailles, even as Dewey repudiated his interventionist platform, committing himself to the outlawry of war and the expansion of civil liberties that had contracted in wartime, Bourne's criticisms trailed him.[23] Dewey's putative lack of ideals, lack of poetry, and his unfounded faith in progress were seen, by his critics on the left, as naive, at best, and, at worst, as complicit with the agendas of American imperialism and rapacious capitalism.

Mumford built on Bourne, noting the aesthetic emptiness of Dewey's instrumentalism. Dewey's language is "as fuzzy and formless as lint," he wrote; his pages are "as depressing as a subway ride—they take one to one's destination, but a little the worse for wear."[24] Homing in on the philosopher's lack of poetry, Mumford couldn't help but draw a contrast to his own sparkling wit. Further, Dewey's philosophy was a "one-sided idealization of practical contrivance"; "a philosophy of adjustment"; "the mere apotheosis of actualities: all dressed up with nowhere to go."[25] These were just a handful of Mumford's epithets for pragmatism in *The Golden Day*, his 1927 intellectual history of American life and encomium for American transcendentalism, to which pragmatism was the ungrateful heir. Dewey's social philosophy paints, Mumford complained, with a restricted palate: he knew no madness, terror, or sublimity. Like Bourne, Mumford contended that Dewey's focus on "uplift" blinded him to evil, corruption, and suffering. For them he was insufficiently acquainted with the night.

When Niebuhr added to this critique in 1934 and again in 1944, the Marxian politics of his position were more explicit. Dewey—whose commitment to democratic socialism, the rights of labor to the means of production, and income equality were unwavering throughout his career—was painted by default as a "bourgeois liberal."[26] Dewey's healthy-mindedness, Niebuhr contended, made him an accommodationist to power; focusing on uplift and education, Dewey ignored power's clear-eyed, corrupt accumulation under capitalism: "In spite of Professor Dewey's great interest in and understanding of the modern social problem . . . the real cause of social inertia, 'our predatory self-interest,' is mentioned only in passing without influencing his reasoning, and with no indication that he understands how much social conservatism is due to the economic interests of the owning classes. On the whole, social conservatism is ascribed to ignorance, a viewpoint which states only part of the truth and reveals the natural bias of the educator."[27]

Dewey's unflappable optimism and lack of metaphysical gravitas—as in Bourne, as in Mumford—was, for Niebuhr, neither benign nor democratic. It denied him a tough-eyed grasp of "predatory self-interest"—a notion that for Niebuhr nicely combined a critique of capitalism and a theology of fallen human nature. As much as with Lippmann or Allport, but from a different point on the intellectual compass, Niebuhr's critique of Dewey was in the name of realism. Dewey's secular philosophy turned the pursuit of progress into what the Christian theologian called a "covert religion, which believes that it has ultimate answers to life's ultimate problems."[28] But if pragmatism was the covert religion of the secular, he wrote, it was also a "pathetic" religion, a "sorry affair," and a "dangerous," albeit "less vicious, version of the Nazi creed."[29]

With this reproof, Niebuhr produced an argument cannily similar to that of Theodor Adorno and Max Horkheimer in *Dialectic of Enlightenment* (1944, translated into English in 1972), in which the Frankfurt School critics saw in rationalist bourgeois ideology a reversion to myth that facilitated the barbarism of the Third Reich. In 1947, Horkheimer elaborated this history of "reason"—its glorification and paradoxical mystification of value—in a series of essays, two of which take Deweyan pragmatism to task. He wrote:

> Pragmatism, in trying to turn experimental physics into a prototype of all science and to model all spheres of intellectual life after the techniques of the laboratory, is the counterpart of modern industrialism, for which the factory is the prototype of human existence, and which models all branches of culture after production on the conveyor belt, or after the rationalized front office. . . . Thought must be gauged by something that is not thought, by its effect on production or its impact on social conduct, as art today is being ultimately gauged in every detail by something that is not art, be it box-office or propaganda value.[30]

At its extreme, Horkheimer contended, Dewey's liquidation of ideals in the name of technique signaled the abasement of real value under capitalism. Readers of *Dialectic of Enlightenment* will recognize images of the conveyor belt, the box-office, and the propaganda machine as Frankfurt School icons of instrumental reason. What is interesting here is not the fairness of the account—in saying that experimental physics was his model for all science, it seems Horkheimer had briefly mistaken Dewey for a member of the Vienna Circle—but the ways that Dewey, despite his Progressivism, could present a target for a variety of radical critiques.

Contrary to this hysterical vision of the fruits of Dewey's method, however, the philosopher spent the first years of World War II cajoling American politicians to avoid fighting at any cost. He also spent the war years reiterating his critique of German idealism that he had first outlined in 1915, with which Horkheimer and Adorno would partly agree. Arguing that the moral absolutism of Germany's philosophical tradition was directly responsible for its history of militarism and nationalism, Dewey's critique was in striking harmony with much coming out of the Frankfurt School during World War II.[31] In contrast to Dewey's complete dismissal of German idealism, the Frankfurters saw it as the remnant of an ever-potent philosophical and political program of critical liberation whose speculative powers could save it from its own abused and abusive history. Nonetheless, the pragmatists and the critical theorists were like long-lost cousins who had trouble recognizing each other at the family reunion. Both were hostile to abstract metaphysics, irrationalism, and absolutism (Dewey's term) or positivism (Horkheimer's); both were looking for a middle ground between subjectivism and materialism; both rejected dialectical materialism and its Soviet application; both saw in capitalism a strong anti-democratic force.[32]

Despite these important caveats, it is impossible to overlook the fact that Horkheimer's Dewey—close kin to Niebuhr, Mumford, and Bourne's Dewey before him—seems far more emblematic of an "administrative tradition" in American thought than one that privileges critique. How did Dewey come to represent critique in the historiography of communication studies?

Triangulating the Conversation

"Only a prepared soil and a highly favorable climate of opinion could have brought to fruition the seeds which Hitler sowed," Dewey wrote in his 1942 introduction to the reprint of *German Philosophy and Politics*.[33] So what prepared the soil for Dewey's own growth in the culture of the 1980s and '90s as the champion of "critique" and the foe of anti-democratic elites? Why, for example, did Christopher Lasch seize onto the images of Lippmann as anti-democrat and Dewey as the great communicator in his 1995 polemic *The Revolt of the Elites and the Betrayal of Democracy*?[34] Why did scholarly histories of American democratic theory reproduce these stereotypes, too?[35] In his myth-busting article "The 'Lippmann-Dewey Debate' and the Invention of Walter Lippmann as an Anti-Democrat, 1985–1996," Michael Schudson speculated that Reagan's second election and the defeat of Soviet Communism contributed to the appeal of Carey's Lippmann/Dewey schema in these years. Schudson wrote, "I suspect that for Carey and Lasch and others, a Reagan-dominated America was incomprehensible and the loss of a sense of the public that they mourned was in some measure an effort to make sense of a federal government run by people who claimed to want to remove the government from people's lives."[36] He continued: "In the absence of a believable Marxism, the vocabulary of the Frankfurt school, already sounding archaic, began to appear an increasingly poor fit with the American scene of ethnic, racial, and gender identity politics. Meanwhile, some thinkers, Carey among them, comfortable in American thought, convinced that there was a native intellectual tradition worth every bit as much, and more than the latest European imports, rejected the 'sludge' of postmodernism, as Carey called it . . . and sought to reclaim an intellectual heritage appropriate to the study of media in a democracy."[37]

Schudson identified the right components of the "debate's" 1990s cultural fertilizer—American conservatism, Marxism, cultural heritage—though we would want to add that if Frankfurt notions of a dominant culture industry and infantilizing propaganda, for instance, once sounded antiquated, they do not, to our ears, today.

But reading the balance of political tendency here is tricky: it's as hard to say that Carey and Lasch's uptake of Dewey was a vigorous *defense* of the American left as it is to pin down the politics of Dewey and his critics. Take Lasch. Earlier in his career, he was an avowed socialist. But by the time he wrote *The Revolt of the Elites*, Lasch was a full-throated social conservative, rejecting the left's cultural elitism, which he considered the principal symptom of its fixation on "identity politics." Though we find it hard to dismiss feminist, queer, and Black studies as only "elite" discourses, given their long vernacular histories, Lasch thought he was protecting the left from itself, rather than betraying it. He thought you could be a cultural conservative, a political democrat, and an economic socialist all at the same time. He was sympathetic to communitarianism, a name for a loose collection of political tendencies that offered a vision of a political life that was missing, in his view, from both Reaganite rollbacks of the welfare state on the right and fissiparous discord on the left. His communitarianism could look both radical and neoconservative all at once.

Reading Carey's case is delicate for the same reasons. He was an enduring advocate and host for cultural studies, including the British Marxist version. He was a working-class Catholic who loved both poetic flights and tough-minded fights. Indeed, one of us once found ourselves the target of his argumentative ferocity, when he suggested that an essay was "an open invitation to the destructive denominationalism and factionalism that is endemic to progressive politics, intellectual or otherwise."[38] Like Lasch, he offered a critique of the left in the name of the left that left other leftists aghast. He thought the left had to take seriously notions of common culture and shared ideals. He was a maverick social critic and a constant thorn in the side of the professional (scientific) pretensions of journalism educators. He took heat from many directions and seemed to enjoy the warmth it generated.

Perhaps what we need to make sense of this fertile invention, this Dewey/Lippmann debate, of Carey's is a properly Deweyan analysis. For Dewey, ideas emerge from circumstances. Philosophy is just an elaborated symptom, a sometimes nacreous and sometimes nauseous outpouring of deeper social troubles. Carey's myth arose from his situation, just as Dewey would have predicted. His politics and intellectual positions were subject to the exact same kind of critiques as Dewey's. He was finding a distinguished ancestor for his own position—giving birth to his parents, as Elihu Katz likes to say, or what sociologist Charles Camic calls "strategic predecessor selection."[39] For his more behaviorist colleagues, Carey was both obscurantist and politically misguided in missing the kingdom-building opportunities that came with quantitative research. For his Marxist colleagues at the Institute of Communications Research at the University of Illinois, where he spent most of his career before moving to Columbia University in 1988, he was the leader of "idealist" cultural studies. (This was not a compliment. His colleagues claimed the honorific of "materialist.") Carey, rightly in our view, would always defend himself as not ignoring questions of power, even if he was not a Marxist.[40]

An eerily similar alignment of critics, in other words, rose up in battle array against both Dewey and Carey. Both men were progressive democrats who believed in thick notions of culture and robust, critical, and participatory investigation into social life; both were caught in the pincer movement between technicist professionalizers on the one hand and Marxian or other radicals on the other. In inventing his Dewey, Carey was, like Richard Rorty, forging an Americanist narrative of a path not taken, an intellectual tradition unjustly neglected. It's too bad that he didn't pick the right enemy in Lippmann and truncated the fuller story (which we barely begin to tell).[41] By lopping off the extreme ends of the political and methodological spectrum—by ignoring the most conservative and left-critical positions in the conversation in which Lippmann and Dewey participated between 1917 and 1947—Carey triangulates communications history. That he missed the real debates Dewey had with critics just shows that his aim was not a proper reckoning with the history of ideas; it was the making of a usable past and the forging of an elective genealogy. He invents a long American tradition that is both culturally conservative ("ritual" was his famous notion) and democratically progressive, one in which humanism and grassroots participation prevail over scientism and technocracy. It's a valiant end, but it doesn't justify his ahistorical means.

Prospects

In returning to the larger conversation out of which Carey plucked the "Dewey/Lippmann debate," we find that its common chord is crisis. A crisis of humanity—World War I, the Great Depression, World War II—that was necessarily a crisis of the humanities: a time to reimagine the role of intellectuals in shaping the "ends" that are fought for and tested under duress. Despite their historical and positional differences, however, Dewey, Lippmann, and Carey would agree that the work of intellectuals across traditions is to shape and maintain such goals without letting them harden into rigid norms, laws, or stereotypes. This is especially true in periods of crisis, when high-minded goals can so easily ossify into dogma and propaganda—and when expedient means can sabotage righteous ends.

Lippmann, "the man with the flashlight mind," was there at every crisis in the twentieth century from World War I to Vietnam as a political commentator and actor, but Dewey is no less useful for reassessing the social crises of our past in order to approach those of our present—perhaps because his relevance didn't get used up in the heat of each moment. His legacy, to be sure, has often been one to take distance from. He has long provided a convenient intellectual wrestling partner. There's something for everyone. Too naive about corporate power? Check. Too in love with a rhetoric of modernization and progress? Check. Not critical enough of science as the model of all inquiry? Check. Too wedded to liberal notions of pluralism and personhood without recognizing the structural barriers to access and participation? Check. So in love with the language of means that he fails to present a vibrant vision of ends? Check. Too squishy about what counts as truth? Check. In addition to the figures treated in this chapter, more recent Marxists, postmodernists, hermeneuts, race and gender theorists, positivists, and even fundamentalists have also all found him a useful target.[42]

How fair are these attacks? We agree that these are essential pressure points in Dewey's writings and that his critics have clarified his legacy—perhaps more so than his fans. But in a very different world and moment from the one we sketch in this chapter, we also find something inspiring in his work for navigating current troubles. Dewey's gift was to see threats to thought and action in crisis and to muster courage, not cynicism. The political settlement that emerged from the public sphere of 1980s and '90s has failed the stress tests of the new millennium: first with neoliberal deregulation and then with the triangulations of the so-called third way of Clinton and Blair—in which business-friendly centrism prevailed over equity, racist crime bills shored up electoral support, and global overreach took precedent over justice at home. This was, to be sure, a moment ideologically sold as a step forward in democratic life, and one in which Dewey's intellectual stock rose, thanks to thinkers like Carey, Lasch, and Rorty.

What would a Deweyan response look like in a time of pandemic, global economic crisis, the unceasing slow burn of climate change, and the grief and rage at the open wound of anti-Black racism in the United States and elsewhere? One of Dewey's greatest legacies was faith in critical intelligence and his ever-ready call for "reconstruction," to use one of his favorite words. To be clear, his use of this term had nothing to do with the troubled Northern efforts to reform the former Confederate states after the Civil War: it was a concept of ultimately Hegelian lineage standing for the possibility that everything as we know it could change, and change intelligently. The beauty and danger of philosophy, he liked to quip, is that it puts the world in jeopardy.

Like Carey before us, then, we turn to Deweyan instrumentalism as an antidote to cynicism. There is so much in our moment that deprives us of hope—and with good reason. In the United States, we've seen the civil rights progress narrative—one that solidified in the wake of *Brown v. Board of Education* (1954) and the Civil Rights Act (1965)—dispelled as liberal fantasy, turned back into the story of four hundred years of racist violence, a trauma not yet reckoned with, a nightmare repetition of yet another Black life stolen. We've seen the institutions of epistemic legitimacy—the press, the university, centers for disease control, even intelligence services—undermined by feckless social media companies that can't quite figure out how to reconcile open and rational debate with pleasing their sponsors. You might, with fairness, call Dewey naive in his hope for a public realm of active participation. He didn't imagine trolls, doxxing, or viral rumors feeding conspiracy theories. But Dewey possessed an abundance of a rare quality—animal spirits, we might call it, following John Maynard Keynes—an energy and faith in inquiry. Hope is, perhaps, always structurally naive, in that it does not see the world as it is. That can also make it radical.

What would a world look like without billionaires and with a universal basic income? Without prisons and with restorative justice? With a media system designed to enhance a society-wide debate about truth? What steps can be taken to achieve these goals without sacrificing others like safety, privacy, and freedom? What would a world look like in which the arts, broadly understood, were the educational birthright for all, in which schools would genuinely teach their students the act of critical intelligence, the work of putting the world in jeopardy? These are Deweyan questions fit for our age. We take his hint to fight the temptation—and believe us, we have felt it—of demoralization and resignation.

But our hope is restored and radicalized by "our Dewey," who we confess is slightly different from Carey's, Lasch's, or Rorty's. Our Dewey is a democratic socialist, allergic to doctrine and committed to humanistic inquiry. His goal was the expansion of human rights, chief among them the right to educated critique, experimentation, and debate. His vision of democracy would not only secure voting rights for all and limit the electoral power of money but would envision democracy as a way of collective world-making that extends from everyday life to the structure of the economy. Democracy is an ongoing project of liberating humanity. It is therefore also a socializing of the means of communication. Our Dewey has been tested (if sometimes unfairly) by generations of philosophers, social scientists, political theorists, and educators to articulate new ends for modern democracy and the experimental means with which to reach them. He asked for that kind of testing, and he is worthy of it. His liberated humanity went together with liberated humanities. And perhaps it is his own example of endless openness to debate and inquiry, even when it is bruising, that we can most use in a moment when we are all feeling bruised.

Notes

1. MacGilvray, "Experience as Experiment," 545; quoted in Jansen, "Phantom Conflict," 222.
2. On Carey's fondness for darkness-and-light stories, his habit of ventriloquizing his thinking via others, and his lifelong engagement with Dewey, see the excellent analysis in Pooley, *James W. Carey and Communication Research*, 97–104, 130–50, and passim.
3. Carey, "Reconceiving 'Mass' and 'Media,'" 59–60.
4. Peters, "Public Journalism and Democratic Theory." See also Arnold-Forster, "Democracy and Expertise," a persuasive article that finds, in the exchange between Lippmann and Lewis Terman about the ability of science to measure intelligence, a reversal of Carey's Lippmann stereotype.
5. Lippmann was famously the first to redefine "stereotype" figuratively—not as a printing plate cast—but as a "picture in one's head," a "way of substituting order for the great blooming, buzzing confusion of reality." (In this he built on the psychological theories of both William James and Dewey.) Indeed, it was because humans process information by way of stereotypes and other cognitive shortcuts through a mediated environment that he advocated a new, less romantic approach to understanding public opinion. Lippmann, *Public Opinion*, 96.
6. Jansen, "Phantom Conflict," 224; Schudson, "'Lippmann-Dewey Debate.'"
7. Carey probably took the term *conversation of mankind* from Rorty, *Philosophy and the Mirror of Nature*, who in turn borrowed it from Michael Oakeshott. Like Carey, Rorty forwarded a tendentiously rosy portrait of Dewey for field-reforming purposes.
8. Bourne, "John Dewey's Philosophy," 154.
9. White, *Social Thought in America*, 244.
10. For a classic treatment, see Purcell, *Crisis of Democratic Theory*.
11. Prohibition plays a surprising consistent role in the conversation around the role of the public in modern democracy in these years. It is Dewey's principal example of public opinion run amok and the "unwisdom" of the average voter in his review of *Phantom Public* ("Practical Democracy," 52). It is Floyd Allport's example of the same in "Toward a Science of Public Opinion."
12. Barnes, "Some Contributions of Sociology," 373; quoted in Westbrook, *John Dewey and American Democracy*, 283.
13. Dewey, "The Paternalism," 216–17; Lasswell, *Propaganda Technique in World War I*, 4–5.
14. Dewey, "Anti-naturalism in Extremis," 27.
15. Dewey, *Public and Its Problems*, 151. Emphasis added.
16. Allport, *Institutional Behavior*, 95. Further citations of this work in this section are given in the text.
17. Habermas, *Structural Transformation of the Public Sphere*. For the most complete analysis of the necessarily partial, self-abstracting process by which a subject enters the public sphere, see Warner, "Mass Public and the Mass Subject"; see also, Warner, *Publics and Counterpublics*.
18. N. N., "Reminiscences of John Dewey: Oral History, 1949."
19. For more on Dewey's interventionist turn in World War I and Bourne's response, see Westbrook, *John Dewey and American Democracy*, 195–227.
20. Dewey, "Morals and the Conducts of States," 233.
21. "Reconstruction Editorial"; quoted in Westbrook, *John Dewey and American Democracy*, 238.

22. Bourne, "Twilight of Idols," 688. Further citations of this work in this section are given in the text.

23. Lippmann opposed Dewey's outlawry platform on technical and political grounds. For a smart reading of that interaction, the "other" Dewey/Lippmann debate, see Trudel, "'Outlawry of War.'" Obviously, our argument here is that there are several other Dewey debates.

24. Mumford, *Golden Day*, 255–56.
25. Mumford, 267, 268, 266.
26. Niebuhr, *Children of Light*, 129.
27. Niebuhr, *Moral Man and Immoral Society*, xiv.
28. Niebuhr, *Children of Light*, 131.
29. Niebuhr, 133.
30. Horkheimer, *Eclipse of Reason*, 35.
31. Dewey, *German Philosophy and Politics*.
32. For a cogent analysis of the "narcissism of small differences" separating the Frankfurt School and American pragmatists between the wars, see Wheatland, *Frankfurt School in Exile*, 97–139.

33. Dewey, *German Philosophy and Politics*, 13.
34. Lasch, *Revolt of the Elites*. Lasch directs readers to Carey's *Communication as Culture* for "shed[ding] much needed light on the Lippmann-Dewey debate" (249). Lasch's first entry into the Dewey/Lippmann business was "Journalism, Publicity and the Lost Art of Argument."

35. See, for example, Auerbach, *Weapons of Democracy*, 93–129; Gary, *Nervous Liberals*, 26–37; Fink, *Progressive Intellectuals*, 30–37; Lebovic, *Free Speech and Unfree News*, 25–36; and Mattson, *Creating a Democratic Public*, 118–20.

36. Schudson, "'Lippmann-Dewey Debate,'" 1039–40.
37. Schudson, 1039–40.
38. Carey, "*Commentary*," 264.
39. Pooley, *James W. Carey and Communication Research*, 25.
40. See Carey, "Afterword," 315–16; and his illuminating, sometimes undiplomatic comments about his Marxist colleagues at Illinois, in "From New England to Illinois," 23–25.

41. One example would be the case of Columbia sociologist Robert Staughton Lynd, who hired Paul Felix Lazarsfeld and touted Dewey-style applied but progressive social research in his book *Knowledge for What?* According to this lineage, Dewey rather than Lippmann would be the inspiration for the administrative tradition. Our point is not to find the "true" founder but to show how problematic the distinction was in the first place.

42. He was, for example, a villain of the evangelical right in the 1980s. See, for example, Ryan, *John Dewey and the High Tide of American Liberalism*, 353.

Bibliography

Allport, Floyd. *Institutional Behavior*. Chapel Hill: University of North Carolina Press, 1933.
———. "Toward a Science of Public Opinion." *Public Opinion Quarterly* 1 (1937): 7–23.
Arnold-Forster, Tom. "Democracy and Expertise in the Lippmann-Terman Controversy." *Modern Intellectual History* 16, no. 2 (2019): 561–92.

Auerbach, Jonathan. *Weapons of Democracy: Propaganda, Progressivism, and American Public Opinion.* Baltimore: Johns Hopkins University Press, 2015.
Barnes, Harry Elmer. "Some Contributions of Sociology to Modern Political Theory." In *A History of Political Theories*, edited by Charles E. Merriam and Harry E. Barnes, 357–402. New York: Macmillan, 1924.
Bourne, Randolph. "John Dewey's Philosophy." *New Republic*, March 13, 1915.
———. "Twilight of Idols." *Seven Arts* 11 (1917): 688.
Carey, James W. "Afterword / The Culture in Question." In *James W. Carey: A Critical Reader*, edited by Eve Stryker Munson and Catherine A. Warren, 308–39. Minneapolis: University of Minnesota Press, 1997.
———. "*Commentary*: Communications and the Progressives." *Critical Studies in Mass Communication* 6, no. 3 (1989): 264–82.
———. "From New England to Illinois: The Invention of (American) Cultural Studies." In *Thinking with James Carey: Essays on Communications, Transportation, History*, edited by Jeremy Packer and Craig Robertson, 11–28. New York: Peter Lang, 2006.
———. "Reconceiving 'Mass' and 'Media'" (1989). In *Communication as Culture*, 3rd ed., 59–60. New York: Routledge, 2009.
Dewey, John. "Anti-naturalism in Extremis." *Partisan Review* 10, no. 1 (1943): 27.
———. *German Philosophy and Politics* (1915). Rev. ed. New York: Putnam, 1942.
———. "Morals and the Conducts of States." *New Republic*, March 23, 1918.
———. "The New Paternalism." *New Republic*, December 21, 1918.
———. "Practical Democracy." *New Republic*, December 2, 1925.
———. *The Public and Its Problems* (1927). University Park: Penn State University Press, 2012.
Fink, Leon. *Progressive Intellectuals and the Dilemmas of Democratic Commitment.* Cambridge, MA: Harvard University Press, 1997.
Gary, Brett. *The Nervous Liberals: Propaganda Anxieties from World War I to the Cold War.* New York: Columbia University Press, 1999.
Habermas, Jürgen. *The Structural Transformation of the Public Sphere.* Translated by Thomas Burger. Cambridge, MA: MIT Press, 1989.
Horkheimer, Max. *Eclipse of Reason.* Oxford: Oxford University Press, 1947.
Jansen, Sue Curry. "Phantom Conflict: Lippmann, Dewey, and the Fate of the Public in Modern Society." *Communication and Critical/Cultural Studies* 6, no. 3 (2009): 221–45.
Lasch, Christopher. "Journalism, Publicity and the Lost Art of Argument." *Gannett Center Journal* 4 (1990): 1–11.
———. *The Revolt of the Elites and the Betrayal of Democracy* (1995). New York: Norton, 1996.
Lasswell, Harold. *Propaganda Technique in World War I* (1927). Cambridge, MA: MIT Press, 1971.
Lebovic, Sam. *Free Speech and Unfree News: The Paradox of Press Freedom in America.* Cambridge, MA: Harvard University Press, 2016.
Lippmann, Walter. *Public Opinion* (1922). New York: Free Press, 1997.
Lynd, Robert Staughton. *Knowledge for What? The Place of Social Science in American Culture.* Princeton, NJ: Princeton University Press, 1939.
MacGilvray, Eric A. "Experience as Experiment: Some Consequences of Pragmatism for Democratic Theory." *American Journal of Political Science* 43, no. 2 (1999): 542–65.
Mattson, Kevin. *Creating a Democratic Public: The Struggle for Urban Participatory Democracy During the Progressive Era.* University Park: Penn State University Press, 1997.
Mumford, Lewis. *The Golden Day.* New York: Horace Liveright, 1926.

N. N. "Reminiscences of John Dewey: Oral History, 1949." Columbia University Rare Book and Manuscript Library, NXCP87-A1018.

Niebuhr, Reinhold. *The Children of Light and the Children of Darkness*. New York: Charles Scribner's Sons, 1944.

———. *Moral Man and Immoral Society*. New York: Charles Scribner's Sons, 1932.

Peters, John Durham. "Public Journalism and Democratic Theory: Four Challenges." In *The Idea of Public Journalism*, edited by Theodore L. Glasser, 99–117. New York: Guilford Press, 1999.

Pooley, Jefferson. *James W. Carey and Communication Research: Reputation at the University's Margin*. New York: Peter Lang, 2016.

Purcell, Edward A. *The Crisis of Democratic Theory: Scientific Naturalism and the Problem of Value*. Lexington: University Press of Kentucky, 1973.

"Reconstruction Editorial." *The Dial*, December 14, 1918.

Rorty, Richard. *Philosophy and the Mirror of Nature*. Princeton, NJ: Princeton University Press, 1979.

Ryan, Alan. *John Dewey and the High Tide of American Liberalism*. New York: Norton, 1997.

Schudson, Michael. "The 'Lippmann-Dewey Debate' and the Invention of Walter Lippmann as an Anti-Democrat, 1985–1996." *International Journal of Communication* 2 (2008): 1031–42.

Trudel, Dominique. "'The Outlawry of War,' ou l'autre débat DeweyLippmann." *Canadian Journal of Communication* 41 (2016): 135–56.

Warner, Michael. "The Mass Public and the Mass Subject." In *Habermas and the Public Sphere*, edited by Craig J. Calhoun, 377–401. Cambridge, MA: MIT Press, 1992.

———. *Publics and Counterpublics*. Brooklyn, NY: Zone Books, 2010.

Westbrook, Robert B. *John Dewey and American Democracy*. Ithaca, NY: Cornell University Press,1991.

Wheatland, Thomas. *The Frankfurt School in Exile*. Minneapolis: University of Minnesota Press, 2009.

White, Morton. *Social Thought in America: The Revolt Against Formalism*. New York: Viking Press, 1949.

5

SOCIETAL EMBEDDING OF THE LIPPMANN/DEWEY DEBATE: FROM OPINION EXPRESSION TO OPINION POLLING AND MINING

Slavko Splichal

Contemporary controversies around the relationship between the digital communication infrastructure and possibilities for participation in public communication committed to the public good, which is essential for democratic governance, remind us of a comparable discourse staged by John Dewey and Walter Lippmann a century ago. They both published significant works discussing the role of "the public" and "public opinion" in democracy, thus recognizing the relevance of the concepts for the social sciences—against the prevailing belief of the time in the United States that the term public opinion should be avoided whenever possible, as argued at the roundtable of American political scientists held in 1924.[1]

After being exposed to several attempts of transformation, relativization, and negation, and found empirically unreliable and categorically insufficient, the notions of the public and public opinion have been rather compromised in the twentieth century. Nevertheless, differences between Lippmann's and Dewey's conceptualizations discussed almost a hundred years ago remained relevant in the entirely new context of globalization and datafication of public opinion, where conceptually similar concerns of (democratic) governance persist. The continuing and growing need to address socially significant human consequences of technological achievements and the questions of "where the public shall end and the sphere of the private begin," was clearly noted by Dewey in his introduction to the 1946 edition of *The Public and Its Problems*, arguing that after World War II, "relations between nations are taking on the properties that constitute a public, and hence call for some measure of political organization. . . . The matter of the scope or range and of the seriousness of the factual consequences of associated human transactions is the determining factor in affecting social behavior with political properties too evident to be ignored. The problem of discovering and implementing politically areas of common interest is henceforth imperative."[2]

While recognizing the contemporary relevance of the so-called Dewey/Lippmann debate[3] on the role of public opinion, which continuously raises scholarly attention and new controversies about public opinion, an important qualification needs to be added. Contrary to (American) popular beliefs and even some scholarly accounts,[4] the study of publics and public opinion did not spring fully panoplied from the Dewey/Lippmann debate in the 1920s. Rather, the idea of public opinion became widespread in the popular and professional literature from the seventeenth century onward. The first systematic treatises on public opinion can be found in the political-philosophical debates of the Enlightenment and utilitarian philosophers, and later among the social scientists, primarily in France, England, and Germany, culminating with the works of Gabriel Tarde and Ferdinand Tönnies at the turn of the nineteenth and twentieth centuries.

For the founder of the concept, however, we need to look further into history: it was the Italian Enlightenment predecessor Niccolò Machiavelli, who was completely ignored in the later debates on public opinion—although praised by Lippmann for having been "the first naturalist who used plain language in a field hitherto preempted by supernaturalists" to discover "elemental truths [which] confronted the democratic philosophers."[5] Similarly to Dewey and Lippmann (and many others) four centuries later, Machiavelli addressed the question of whether "governments of peoples are better than those of princes."[6] He trusted in "ordinary people" as the most reliable guardians of human freedom and social prosperity and argued that, "if a people hears two orators who incline to different sides, when they are of equal virtue, very few times does one see it not take up the better opinion, and not persuaded of the truth that it hears."[7]

Long after Machiavelli, by the end of the eighteenth century, the notion of public opinion was adopted in the scholarly literature. Among the prominent authors of the nineteenth and early twentieth century, we find representatives of philosophy first (Bentham, Kant, Hegel), followed by political theory (Tocqueville, Bryce), and finally sociology (Tönnies, Tarde). In the twentieth century, public opinion studies moved largely to America, where they continued to develop in traditional disciplines (Park, Dewey, Lippmann, Albig), with significant contributions by (social) psychology (Allport, Cantril), economics (Keynes), market and promotional research (Bernays) and, more recently with polling, by methodology and statistics (Gallup). With the possible exception of polls, Dewey and Lippmann have become and remain by far the most popular public opinion scholars to this day.

In the myriad of different approaches, understandings, and definitions of "the public" and "public opinion," a consensus on their definitions has never been reached. Differences in conceptualizations of public opinion resulted from different disciplinary frameworks and theoretical approaches within disciplines that have adopted public opinion as the subject of their study, as well as specific historical—social, cultural, political—circumstances in which ideas of public opinion emerged (e.g., in France, England, and America, later Germany). Although it is hardly possible to find the smallest common denominator of different conceptualizations, at least three constitutive ideas that are actually implied already in Machiavelli's idea of effective universal opinion could be identified as a kind of minimal "matching points." Public opinion (1) arises in some interaction between objectively unreliable and variable subjective opinions (2) on matters or issues of broader societal importance that (3) collectively affect the behavior and functioning of individuals, groups, organizations, and/or institutions. Within these general matching points, major differences always existed, for example, in terms of (1) the nature of judgments and the mode of social interaction required for "public opinion" to be formed, and the character of the group(s) of individuals who act as the bearers of public opinion; (2) how to conceptualize "broader importance" or "important consequences" that ought to define "public issues" on which opinions are formed and expressed as "public opinion"; and (3) who are or supposed to be direct or indirect addressees of public opinion, and how public opinion is influencing them.

In the history of public opinion theories, the Dewey/Lippmann debate has an undeniable significance. However, this debate should also be viewed in a broader historical and societal perspective, and in the context of the ideas of other key actors of the centuries-old, sometimes fierce debates, in order to assess their comparative historical validity. This, in a nutshell, is also the plan of this chapter. Just before the Dewey/Lippmann debate, public opinion theory was significantly enhanced by Tarde and Tönnies, who aimed at constructing a (sociological) theory of public opinion as a sociocultural phenomenon or a "complex form of societal will," according to Tönnies. On the other hand, substantial social and technological changes also emerged since the debate—including, among other things, the datafication of public opinion initiated by polling—that can help us assess validity and possibly further develop some of the intriguing ideas of the "old" theories.

Public Opinion, Experts, and Masses

Much of Dewey's and Lippmann's work was related to the fate of "public opinion" and its bearer, "the public"—its character, intelligence, legitimacy, and efficacy—as either "human facts" (Dewey) or "phantoms" (Lippmann), although (mass) democracy rather than public opinion and modes of communication was at the core of their intellectual efforts. Both Dewey and Lippmann addressed the logic and assumptions on which democracy rests, particularly the intellectual capacity of ordinary citizens to fulfill their civic rights and obligations, but they differed strongly on what—and how realistic—those assumptions are and need to be. They outlined their arguments for radical reforms of the existing system with the aim to find an autonomous and efficacious role for the citizen, each contributing to a critical and constructive vision of democracy, but having different reforms and versions of democracy in mind. While they largely agreed on the diagnosis of the state of modern democratic systems, they disagreed on the necessary actions and solutions to the pressing problems of democracy, resulting from relatively uninformed and incompetent citizens normatively supposed to make informed decisions on political affairs.

For both Dewey and Lippmann, the paramount question of democracy was how (for Dewey), if at all (for Lippmann), the existing limited intellectual and information capacities of the citizen can (be improved to) reduce the increasing complexity of human environment to be dealt with in the democratic political process.[8] Lippmann, who argued that "democracy in politics is the twin-brother of scientific thinking,"[9] could not resolve the "mystery" of how the average citizen could have the necessary knowledge to pass informed judgments on issues of public policy and to participate intelligently in the formation of public opinion. His technocratic "solution" was to abandon the essence of democracy altogether—to transcend popular participation by creating a "bureau of experts" capable of passing judgments and making informed decisions on issues of public policy on behalf of the public. Subscribing to the long-lasting liberal distrust of the virtues of public opinion, most markedly expressed in J. S. Mill's *On Liberty*, Lippmann believed that the "intelligence work" of professional experts was the only way to reduce the complexity of "the world outside" and make it humanly manageable. Only experts could find effective solutions to problems, thus providing "a way of overcoming the subjectivism of human opinion based on the limitation of individual experience," but not large-scale publics in public debates.[10] Like Mill, Lippmann did not see any possibility for citizens in democracy to perform anything but rather insignificant roles. "What the public does is not to express its opinions but to align itself for or against a proposal. If that theory is accepted, we must abandon the notion that democratic government can be the direct expression of the will of the people. We must abandon the notion that the people govern. We must abandon the notion that by their occasional mobilizations as a majority, people support or oppose the individuals who actually govern. We must say that the popular will does not direct continuously but that it intervenes occasionally."[11]

Lippmann argued that no such thing as "opinion of the public" could exist as "the public" is merely a "phantom," and public opinion(s) a series of individual opinions—"the pictures inside the heads of human beings, the pictures of themselves, of others, of their needs, purposes, and relationship."[12] He cynically compared the public with a "deaf spectator in the back row who ought to keep his mind on the mystery off there, but cannot quite manage to keep awake."[13] With the propagandistic "manufacture of consent," a phrase he coined in *Liberty and the News* (1920), he referred to the management or fabricating public opinion, which he felt was necessary though maybe not desirable for democracy since public opinion was an irrational force.

In contrast to Lippmann, Dewey considered an actively involved public essential for democracy, as it emerges from discussions of important social consequences of transactions among individuals who did not take part in them but were seriously affected by them.[14] He admitted that the actual performance of publics was below normative expectations, which made the public a marginal actor in democracy, but this was not to say that it could not be improved; publics could get much stronger if "secrecy, prejudice, bias, misrepresentation, and propaganda as well as sheer ignorance are replaced by inquiry and publicity." Only in such new conditions, based on "the improvement of the methods and conditions of debate, discussion and persuasion," it would be indeed possible to find out "how apt for judgment of social policies the existing intelligence of the masses may be" (208–9). Dewey agreed with Lippmann that generally "education is the supreme remedy" to improve the validity of decision-making, but he insisted that democracy demands a better education for everyone, not just for the (future) experts, which would require new approaches and methods to the spread, acquisition, and use of knowledge. This would not imply that all citizens should have "the knowledge and skill to carry on the needed investigations; what is required is that they have the ability to judge of the bearing of the knowledge supplied by others upon common concerns" (209).

Yet it is not education and knowledge alone that can bring in democratic changes. Interpersonal communication within publics ought to breathe a spirit of local community and human contiguity into the scientifically managed society: "No government by experts in which the masses do not have the chance to inform the experts as to their needs can be anything but an oligarchy managed in the interest of the few. And the enlightenment must proceed in ways which force the administrative specialists to take account of the needs" (208). As once believed by Machiavelli, Dewey indicted that "the world has suffered more from leaders and authorities than from the masses," which is why the public should not be considered unable to take informed decisions and thus replaced by experts in decision-making; rather, the existing "methods and conditions of debate, discussion and persuasion" have to be improved to empower the public as a key actor in democracy. "The eclipse of the public," as he termed it, did not denote its collapse or utopicity, but rather its inability to "identify and hold itself." The constitutive elements of the public as Dewey defined it (i.e., a "large body of persons having a common interest in the consequences of social transactions . . . which have indirect, serious and enduring consequences") did not disappear. On the contrary, they became so multitudinous, diversified, and complex that—despite the great number of people affected by and interested in these consequences—it became extremely difficult "to hold these different publics together in an integrated whole" (187). Instead of denying any possibility for the public to exist, or the existing, simplistic, and frivolous public opinion to improve and ripen, "a search for the conditions under which the inchoate public now extant may function democratically" (147) would be needed.

Disagreements between Dewey and Lippmann on the role of experts and the nature of education needed for citizens to take part in democratic politics reflect differences in their views on the nature and social role of science and technology. Both Lippmann and Dewey trusted in science and technology as key factors of social progress, but whereas Dewey argued for active public engagement with scientific research, for Lippmann the only way to overcome the drawbacks of democracy was the elite of experts who would develop and apply their expert scientific knowledge to provide the knowledge needed by professional decision-makers. Lippmann believed in scientific objectivity and political neutrality of experts, based on his famous Cartesian separation between the objective "world outside" and the subjective and unreliable "pictures inside our heads," which people—but not experts—generate within their "filter bubbles," to use the modern phrase or, according to Lippmann, "as if on a leash, within a fixed radius of acquaintances according to the law and the gospel of their social set."[15] In contrast, Dewey argued that the more experts are specialized, the more they are alienated from common interests, so that they only have two options: either they become "willing tools of big economic interests" or they "would have to ally themselves with the masses, and that implies . . . a share in government by the latter" (207).

Ignoring the fundamental difference between the natural sciences and the social sciences—"between facts which are what they are independent of human desire and endeavor and facts which are to some extent what they are because of human interest and purpose, and which alter with alteration in the latter" (7)—was the greatest possible delusion of the social sciences and the cause of danger for their transformation into pseudo-science for Dewey. Thus, in principle, experts and publics (can) suffer from the same disease: neither of them is immune to "their prejudice, and capable of overcoming their subjectivism," which Lippmann believed (only) experts are.[16]

This ontological and epistemological difference reveals the core of the controversy between Lippmann and Dewey. It also illuminates differences in identifying the fundamental problem of public/ness and democracy, and in finding solutions to practical problems. For Dewey, this was a plurality of forms of communication that originate in people's interpersonal communication, where the subject/ive and the object/ive are always intertwined. For Lippmann, the fundamental problem to be solved by science (and which could be only solved by science) was the reliability of (scientific) information about facts in the objective world, solipsistically discovered and provided by independent experts.

From two distinct perspectives, Lippmann and Dewey mark the end of the dominance of the normative-political era in studying public opinion. At the same time, a new European sociological tradition was established as part of a more general response to the crisis of Western thought of the time, prominently represented by Gabriel Tarde and Ferdinand Tönnies. Changing economic and political conditions in Western societies at the beginning of the twentieth century have spurred the depoliticization and universalization of public opinion. Tarde and Tönnies offered a more nuanced (sociological) consideration of the dynamics of public opinion, the public, and the masses (crowds), including reflections on controversial issues of education and (un)reasoned actions, and group (class) interests. The relevance of these conceptual changes was demonstrated by the political institutionalization of opinion polls in the 1930s, which raised again the question of the democratic nature and importance of public opinion (and) polling.

The Tarde-Tönnies Paradigmatic Break: Public Opinion as Public Conversation

For normative-political theories of public opinion in the eighteenth and nineteenth centuries, public opinion was a distinctive political phenomenon inextricably linked to the realization of the principle of publicity, freedom of the press, and political rights of citizens. The theoretical turn that originated in the early sociologization of public opinion theories in the twentieth century did not eliminate these postulates of the liberal Enlightenment conceptualization of public opinion altogether, but changed them from normative concepts to more practical concerns rooted in the study of human behavior. French social psychologist Gabriel Tarde and German sociologist Ferdinand Tönnies pioneered the paradigmatic break away from the classical normative tradition in public opinion theories. These academic discussions, which preceded that of Lippmann and Dewey, are by no means marginal.[17]

As Dewey's *The Public and Its Problems* (1927) appeared as a response to Lippmann's *Public Opinion* (1922), Tönnies started to write his *Kritik der öffentlichen Meinung* (Critique of public opinion) after he became familiar with Tarde's book *L'opinion et la foule* (Public opinion and the crowd) of 1901.[18] Still, Tönnies had included public opinion as one of the three complex forms of social will in society already in his comprehensive conceptual scheme for sociological analysis presented in his early and most famous work, *Gemeinschaft und Gesellschaft* (1887), published much before Tarde's book. Tönnies appreciated Tarde's work, and although he disagreed with his (positivistic) "scientific assumptions" he shared some of Tarde's ideas, such as his psychological theorizing of conversation, discussion, and opinion formation, and his view of public opinion as a sociopsychological and cultural rather than a mere political phenomenon.

Contrary to Dewey and Lippmann's conclusive "findings" about the (non) existence of the public, Tarde and Tönnies agreed that the only "solution" was to conduct empirical research on "where the public proceeds from, how it is born, how it develops; its varieties; its relations with its leaders; its relations with the crowd, with corporations, with the States; its power for good or bad, and its ways of feeling or acting."[19] For both Tarde and Tönnies, the primary task was a sociological and empirically viable conceptualization of the public—in opposition to "crowds" and "masses"—and public opinion, to "replace" the former conceptually dominant relationship of the public to authority and critique of majority rule. Their conceptualizations of the public and its opposites, the mass and the crowd, were influenced by the rising significance of the masses at the turn of the century, associated particularly with the mass (popular) press and propaganda. They considered the public a kind of dispersed, "spiritualized crowd," whose members are capable of clearly articulating opinions and mutually influencing one another "on the level of ideas" at a distance, which is growing ever larger due to technological developments. The public is a "transient social formation" in the sense that it is easily dissolved or transformed into its opposite—the crowd or the mass—and vice versa, but it is also substantially different from the crowd in its ability to articulate opinions clearly. Nevertheless, this ability does not prevent public opinion from being biased and even prejudiced, mainly due to differences in education and property of its actors or on racial or ethnic grounds.

In various ways, the issues posed by the new tradition—from (inter)personal "imitative propagation" and "reciprocal awareness" (Tarde) to public opinion as a "complex form of social will" (Tönnies)—were echoed in theoretical and methodological disputes about the concept and meaning of public opinion after the invention of polling. The emerging European sociological tradition in studying public opinion was a blind spot for Dewey and Lippmann; there is also little evidence that Anglo-American scholars have read their scholarship at all. The difficulty in accessing their works was largely due to the fact that they were written in French and German, languages that were not sufficiently mastered by most American scholars.

In contrast to Lippmann and Dewey, Tarde and Tönnies have devoted a major part of their lifework to empirical research, including surveys, in such diverse but also related fields as studying suicides, criminality, socioeconomic situations of lower classes, and marriages. They also paid special attention to statistical analysis: both Tarde and Tönnies discussed quantification and empirical foundations of social sciences, and Tönnies has even developed a statistical measure of association for ordinal variables.[20] Tarde introduced the "crowd-public" dichotomy in his 1898 article "Le public et la foule" (The public and the crowd), which was republished as chapter 1 of his book *L'opinion et la foule* (Public opinion and the crowd, 1901). This conceptual differentiation epitomizes the transition from the former normative-political to the new sociological paradigm in studying publics and public opinion in the first half of the twentieth century.

The newly emerging tradition, which both Dewey and Lippmann failed to recognize, "depoliticized" the public and public opinion and restored the tradition beginning with Milton's assertion in *Areopagitica* that "opinion in good men is but knowledge in the making"—a tradition of understanding opinion in general and public opinion in particular as contributing to the recognition of truth and the common good. Tönnies emphasized rationality, discursivity, and morality, but also volatility of public opinion, which is "a common way of thought, the corporate spirit of any group or association, in so far as its opinion formation is built upon *reasoning and knowledge, rather than on unproved impressions, beliefs, or authority*."[21] His understanding of "opinion" was based on the ancient Greeks' distinction between *doxa* (opinion) and *episteme* (knowledge), and Kant's differentiation between three levels of "holding for true" (*Fürwahrhalten*) determined by subjective and objective validity of judgments—with one significant modification. For Kant, *opining* is the lowest level of "holding for true" as it is both subjectively and objectively insufficient; *believing* is sufficient subjectively but lacks objectivity; only *knowing* is sufficient on both accounts. Following Milton, Tönnies no longer regarded opining as the opposite of knowing, but as the opposite of believing. He rationalized Kant's "opining" and placed it above affective believing, since opining always incorporates elements of knowledge and is based on them, which does not apply to believing. Believing is "a matter of mood and heart," whereas opining is "a matter of thought and reason," whose progress "is primarily a consequence of the influence of advances in scientific knowledge" (121). Thus, Tönnies considered public opinion a manifestation of human reasoning or, in Kant's words, public use of reason, and similarly to Dewey related the concept of the public and its historical ascent to "the scientific way of thinking," knowledge, and education, "particularly scientific education, on whose nature and strength all other types of education depend to a certain extent" (85–86).

For Tönnies, the formation of public opinion is historically determined by the spread of knowledge and education, which he conceived of as an explanatory variable in a version of the theory of "cognitive dissonance" he developed: "The lower the level of education, the more a man listens only to what suits his ideas, opinions, feelings, strengthens and promotes them, the less able and inclined he is to let reasons and motivations opposed to his 'prejudices' affect him" (319). At the same time, the prevalence of education in the formation of public opinion brings social stratification to the public, since the bearers of public opinion are, above all, "the ruling class, the townspeople and the men, as the more educated on average." The result is "that the more education, especially political education, is extended and spread to wider circles, the more it also embraces women, the rural population and the lower people, especially the working class, the greater the participation of these layers in public opinion, and the more general it becomes, but at the same time it becomes all the more improbable as a unity, as unanimous public opinion" (229).

Like Tönnies, Tarde was not primarily concerned with the workings of deliberative democracy but with the more general task of conceptualizing public opinion in the general theory of society. For Tarde, "a forefather of actor network theory,"[22] the principal task was to conceptualize "any [social] fact whatsoever under three aspects, corresponding, respectively, to the repetitions, oppositions, and adaptations which it contains, and which are obscured by a mass of variations, dissymmetries, and disharmonies,"[23] and public opinion was such a "social fact."

Tarde's sociopsychological paradigm is based on his idea of imitation as an elementary and universal social fact, together with invention and opposition. He recognized the pressure to imitate and he acknowledged that "the need to agree with the public of which one is a part, to think and act in agreement with opinion, becomes all the more strong and irresistible as the public becomes more numerous, the opinion more imposing, and the need itself more often satisfied."[24]

Tarde distinguished between the crowd and the public, and considered the latter a particular form of crowd, creating, as he called it, "cette grande foule appelée l'Opinion,"[25] "social opinion," "the opinion," or "the Opinion." The mass and the public are temporary entities that are similar in that they are both created by imitation and therefore easily transformed into one another. The crowds are highly suggestive and easily manageable, whereas publics are constituted by reflexive communication. The public-mass dichotomy is an ideal-type dichotomy, whereas in the empirical world neither the public nor the mass exists in its "pure form."

In addition to imitation, *opposition* is constitutive of public opinion, its main "factors" being *conversation* and its main source, in modern times, *the press*. Conversation—"this elementary social relation, quite neglected by sociologists"[26]—is not only the strongest and most universal "agent of imitation" identified by Tarde, but also an "agent of opposition" resulting from internal (i.e., between different tendencies within a given person) and external oppositions to imitation, which continuously bring about innovations. Tarde identified three principal forms of opposition: (1) war in the sphere of politics, (2) competition in economy, and (3) verbal discussion or conversation.

The dual character of conversation—being both an "agent" of imitation and opposition—makes it the most important action by which public opinion is generated. As for Dewey, for Tarde and Tönnies the role of conversation ("with strangers," as Tönnies emphasized) is even more important than the press in constituting public opinion, because "if no one conversed, the newspapers would appear to no avail . . . because they would exercise no profound influence on any minds" (297).

In addition to conversation, Tarde and Tönnies saw newspapers as playing a central role in the process of public opinion formation—transmitting information to the public and constituting the public as its major "means of expression." Yet the press was also considered closely connected with interpersonal conversation as it "unifies and vivifies conversations, standardizes them in space and diversifies them in time."[27] Both Tarde and Tönnies commented on the dangers of "the secret surrender of the newspaper to business interests"[28] and the threats to freedom of expression for journalists and independence of newspapers, which—as also Lippmann[29] argued—the loyalty of newspaper readers could protect. Tönnies was strongly convinced that only legal- and self-regulation and socialization of the press could protect its freedom and independence more effectively. Unfortunately, as Tarde and Tönnies realized, "it is hard to make a good press law. It is as if we wanted to regulate the sovereignty of the Great King or Napoleon."[30]

The press reformers advocated for newspapers as "organs of the public" and for the elimination of their dependence on owners, political parties, and advertisers by regulating the press as a public service that would restrict monopolies and ensure plurality, so that "the voices of the people in the newspaper would find a direct expression."[31] These efforts were unsuccessful, as they had no affect on the development of the press or the subsequent development of radio and television (with the partial exception of Europe until the end of the last century). Instead, a new but more controversial "organ" of public opinion was born—opinion polls.

Polling: "Machinery for Measuring the Popular Will"[32]

Part of the bleak picture of the "phantom public" painted by Lippmann were individuals confronted with the puzzle of too much space, too much time, and too many entities (people, actions, issues) to be considered when forming their "public opinions." To solve the problem of (over)complexity of the "world outside," people have to "summarize and generalize . . . to pick out samples, and treat them as typical."[33] For an ordinary citizen, this cognitive process would be impossible without creating and using mental "stereotypes," because "we cannot send out a questionnaire to 816 random samples every time we wish to estimate a probability . . . that a certain thing ought to be true."[34]

The idea of a "machinery" "sending questionnaires to random samples" to increase the reliability of individual "public opinions" and to test them on "typical samples" seemed utopian to Lippmann. His mistrust in the "quasi-statistical organ" (to borrow Elisabeth Noelle-Neumann's term) that people would use to monitor their environment is remindful of James Bryce's disbelief that science would ever invent "machinery for weighing or measuring the popular will from week to week or month to month . . . without the need of its passing through a body of representatives, possibly even without the need of voting machinery at all."[35] Yet both Lippmann and Bryce, to whom Lippmann often referred, underestimated the power of social and scientific changes and innovations. Only a decade after Lippmann's skeptical argument against "typical samples," a "machinery" using random sampling to measure popular will was invented in the form of public opinion polls.

The concept of public opinion as an aggregate of individual opinions championed by Bryce and Lippmann represented the theoretical underpinning of public opinion polling. By pluralizing "public opinion" as an aggregate of individuals "who are treated as consumers by politicians and who respond as such, giving 'yes' or 'no' answers to the questions they are asked,"[36] Lippmann paved the way for the operational concept of public opinion represented by surveys and later consolidated by opinion polls. Not referring directly to Lippmann but rather to Bryce, Gallup defended an aggregative operational definition of "public opinion" suggested by Lippmann, against those who "regard public opinion as a mysterious force which manifested itself in unknown ways. . . . To us, as to James Bryce, public opinion was 'the aggregate of the views men hold regarding matters that affect or interest the community.'"[37] Polls made Gallup believe that with this revolutionary social-scientific technology, "the final stage of democracy," of which Bryce was dreaming half a century earlier, "is rapidly being reached."[38]

With polls, the debates over public opinion have almost ended. They did not decline because the attitude of the American political scientists' roundtable would have been generally approved or, unexpectedly, a "definite theoretical conclusion" would have been found. Rather, it was a consequence of the "datafication" of public opinion in polling, which soon became a routine and often commercial procedure, and partly at least resulting from the outbreak of World War II, which shifted researchers' attention from public opinion to propaganda and its attitudinal and behavioral effects.[39]

In polling, public opinion has been reduced to "the uniformities observed in opinions," which promised to provide "a sound theory of opinion formation, and only because of the riches and variety of empirical research"[40] and a "homogenized definition" of public opinion.[41] In contrast, for the opponents of polls following Dewey's search for ways to empower the immature public, public opinion does not correspond to what pollsters want to measure in public opinion polls at all. They criticized opinion polls as either a mere reproduction of public ignorance and prejudice, or a conceptual negation of the genuine public opinion altogether and practical tool to destroy it.

Polling has radically marked (re)conceptualizations of "the public" and "public opinion,"[42] as it is often the case with scientific paradigm shifts due to new or improved ways of acquiring data about well-examined phenomena. This could also be said of polling as it proliferated due to the increasing importance of quantification in many research fields of social sciences and the ease of questionnaire design and statistical analysis of data.[43] Like academic surveys, polls were worked out in the interwar United States to satisfy interests in the prevailing opinions in society, but the differences between public opinion polls and academic surveys are instructive. Academic researchers were not interested in "superficial expressions of opinion" in polls; rather, they performed much of the work themselves or used graduate students with some research experience to make survey responses "a genuine expression of beliefs or feelings." In contrast, polls were "conducted by poorly paid assistants, such as housewives, who were not initiated into the arcana of the craft," to make "the relatively rigid and objective form of the multiple-choice questionnaire ... de rigueur."[44]

Like quantification in many other research fields, public opinion polling was not only about identifying and describing "social facts." By directing and managing people and society through data management, polling itself has become a "social fact" sui generis, a new version of—or an opposition to— public opinion. In polling, a large variety of topics identified by Tarde and Tönnies as critical for sociological analysis of public opinion dropped off the map entirely. Knowledge and education of respondents, a key topic in the Dewey/Lippmann "debate," only matters in polls as a possible explanatory variable for variations in responses and nonresponses, and criterion variable for testing the representativeness of the sample. Quantitative "objectification" of people reduced the study of people to classes and social categories, which results in the loss of their individuality at the expense of their "belonging" to a particular statistical category. Polling is a clear example of how quantification has not only changed the nature of social sciences; by turning people into "manipulative objects" of study, it also effectively contributed to systemic control and management of people in economy and politics. In the absence of any discussion in polls, relatively poorly informed and unmotivated respondents answer the questions asked with improvised and unreliable answers, rarely admitting that they "do not know" or "have no opinion" and thus generate "phantom opinions."[45]

Public Opinion Mining and Fabricating

Theoretical critiques of opinion polling have never really undermined its social—commercial, political, and partly academic—dominance and its apparent validity of "measuring public opinion(s)." However, the primacy of the systematic "measurement of opinions" with the interview response data was challenged in the era of big data by the development of data mining in social media, which made all human online activities easily traceable, quantifiable, and thus potentially instrumentalized, with the potential for supplementing or even replacing the established polling methods.[46]

Polling requires large financial investments and unpaid labor of respondents to generate the data needed for analysis. In contrast, data mining or "semantic polling" enables continuous and automated identification and prediction of opinion and behavioral patterns of individuals from (meta)data mined from or found in social media, which users (often unintentionally and unknowingly) generate—at no cost to researchers. Quantitative analyses of big data generated independently of researchers' data-collection efforts go beyond responses collected in polls and surveys to include data about behavioral phenomena that polls cannot deal with; they focus on social interaction and conversation rather than simple preferences and include the temporal dimension, which enables researchers to study human behavior in a much more complex way. Moreover, by systematically collecting and analyzing information about individuals' online communication in conjunction with offline activity data, both can be effectively influenced.

The rise of quantification in public opinion management, first by polling and now by data mining, makes the issues discussed in the two prominent "debates" in Europe and the United States at the beginning of the twentieth century as relevant today as they were at that time. They are now primarily related to the internet, which emerged in the time of a global crisis of trust in governments, political parties, traditional media—including newspapers considered the main organs of public opinion a century ago—and other national and transnational institutions. Despite an immense potential to entice social changes attributed to the internet, concerns about the democratic potential of publicness and publics that dominated in the former century do not cease to persist. In principle, new communication technologies corroborate Dewey's idea of creating a "Great Community" based on interactive communication or "conversation" that Tarde and Tönnies so strongly favored, which the internet technically enables without any time-space constraint. Nevertheless, concerns remain that, as before the internet, the public "cannot quite manage to keep awake" when faced with complex and specialized policy issues or that it is constrained by the commercial and political interests of those in power.

While the development of new communication technologies removes the existing obstacles and constraints, new types of problems and constraints are emerging. The development of information technologies and activities enable people to reduce, in principle, the excessive complexity of the world, but at the same time they themselves create an ever-increasing complexity of the world. Thus we are continually confronted with the problem that Lippmann characterized as that of the temporal distance between cause and effect and the spatial distance "between the centers where decisions are taken and the places where the main work of the world is done,"[47] which publics are not able competently and effectively to address.

Dewey's "Great Community, in the sense of free and full intercommunication," is easily empirically conceived as a "virtual community" created in the virtual space of the internet. Convergence integrating powerful digital technologies of print, telecommunications, and broadcasting toward the development of a single integrated platform that meets all communication needs can, in principle, solve the problem of the missing "local community as the medium of an immense intelligence."[48] New technologies allow people to read, listen, and watch at the same time, which, as Dewey believed, would allow dialogue to expand beyond the boundaries of the local community, but the technology alone does not solve the question of who has an interest and is qualified to engage in such discussion. It was precisely because of the lack of a clear answer to this question that Lippmann rejected the thesis of "participatory publics" and put an expert "organized intelligence" in the place of participation of all, and his argumentation in this sense still seems valid. Even the rapid and revolutionary technological development cannot eliminate the limitation of conversation to a relatively small number of active citizens, since this limitation is not only due to the limited capacity and user-unfriendliness of technical means of communication (which can, of course, be improved), but also to the limited human capacity of listening and reading, which, however, cannot be radically abolished by any technological revolution (yet). The crux of the contemporary discomfort still caused by Lippmann's critique of the tyranny of the ignorant majority is that the increase in complexity resulting from the same technological development that reduces complexity still implies that, more than ever, "the world that we have to deal with politically is out of reach, out of sight, out of mind. It has to be explored, reported and imagined."[49]

Numerous pre-internet experiments and case studies were designed to explore the possibility of using communication technologies to increase people's political engagement and develop participatory forms of political democracy.[50] They included community radio, telephone conferencing, televoting, and two-way cable TV, which are now all part of the integrated public-private communication network based on the internet. The common thread running through those studies in the 1970s and 1980s was the expectation that new forms of political participation could emerge from an imaginative use of (new) communication technologies. In essence, they followed Dewey's claim that "the idea of democracy is a wider and fuller idea than can be exemplified in the state even at its best,"[51] which is why we have to return constantly to the idea of democracy itself to "criticize and re-make its political manifestations."[52] Ideas are decisive, but only as long as they are connected with, and validated against, specific, given, and potential historical circumstances, material resources, technological developments, and existing social and political actors and movements.

Many studies advanced Dewey's idea of "the public" through an empirical analysis of how and where citizens talk, discuss, and deliberate with one another "on public issues that affect the communities in which they live."[53] In 1988, Fishkin designed the famed "deliberative polling experiment"—a social science experiment combined with elements of public education— which has been conducted over seventy times in twenty-four countries by now.[54] These studies were primarily interested in whether citizens are in a position to make informed judgments and how they come to their preferences and opinions.[55] Findings of those studies echo Dewey's conclusion of 1927 that "the democratic public is still inchoate and not organized." At present, the internet's emancipatory power of creating new democratic platforms and fostering reflexive publicity or the Kantian "public use of reason" seems (still) questionable. When addressing the question of what steps can and should be taken to bring down the "deliberative deficit," which would enhance legitimacy and, hopefully, effectiveness of democratic process, Dewey's "intellectual instrumentalities for the formation of an organized public"—better education, distribution of knowledge, and interpersonal communication—are widely recognized as potentially the most effective remedies. There is hardly any discussion, however, of how and where to get those "remedies," which is in sharp contrast to the extent of business-minded discussions of "the entrepreneurial abilities, skills, competencies and perspectives that are essential pre-requisites for success in the new global economy."[56] More information and education alone will not make people better citizens. As, for example, from the point of view of an individual voter, their vote will not affect the outcome of the election, participation in the election does not seem to be a sufficient incentive to invest in information. Nevertheless, experiments with the organization of group discussions suggest that learning through discussion can reduce civic apathy. Several democratic incentives have emerged in political theory and practice to organize political institutions promoting a communicative-rational or deliberative form of democracy, including Dahl's idea of a minipopulus, Fishkin's deliberative opinion polls, and Goodin and Dryzek's mini-publics.[57] However, it is unrealistic to expect leading political forces, such as political parties, to systematically support such incentives that challenge the power of elites.

The continuation of the Dewey/Lippmann debate—as well as Tönnies's concerns about how more education can have the side effect of reducing the power of public opinion—can also be seen in encouraging citizens to take control of their personal data transmitted over the internet, including opinions expressed online, and to establish their algorithmic sovereignty. These initiatives are crucial since most users are already aware of the far-reaching (potentially) negative consequences of datafication, but are less interested in who collects their data, how they do it, for what purposes, and what personal data they collect and analyze. The disinterest is largely due to the lack of relevant information and knowledge among internet users. However, this is not the "natural state of affairs," but the consequence of (1) an increasingly complex division of labor in the data creation, collection, and analysis chains, and the complexity of the technologies involved in data production;[58] (2) the fact that datafication and data analysis algorithms are not made visible to users; and (3) the absence of applicable knowledge. The resulting lack of interest points to the importance of initiatives for the algorithmic literacy of citizens in order to identify opportunities and threats of communication datafication, as well as their algorithmic sovereignty to move algorithmic accountability efforts out of the realm of experts and ensure personal data ownership and public control over data(fication).

Conclusion: From Public Opinion to Public Knowledge

For both Dewey and Lippmann, the principal question of democracy was whether and/or how citizens' (in)ability to make informed judgments and decisions could be made commensurate with an increasingly complex world, in which they had to act. Neither of them found a solution to this "mystery," as Lippmann called it.

In *Social Laws*, Tarde argued that the growth of education, which is an instance of imitation, should not be confused with the progress of science—a phenomenon of invention and adaptation. Nevertheless, Tarde emphasized that social expansion of education is not merely an imitative repetition; it is "something more than mere addition; for the community of intellect that results from the similarity of *the education given to different children increases the confidence of each in his own knowledge, and this also is a social adaptation, and not one of the least precious.*"[59] Not only is science, by virtue of its democratic nature, as Dewey argued, compatible with the principle of publicity and thus of the public; scientific progress can only be expanded and strengthened through the rise of education and increase in general knowledge in society. Without this "imitative repetition," invention as the fundamental social adaptation would itself be hampered.

Tarde thus paved the way for a settlement between Dewey and Lippmann. Improving citizens' education to enable them to participate in the (political) decision-making advocated and called for by Dewey is not merely an end in itself. It is a prerequisite for the continued development of science, and thus a condition for the functioning of "organized intelligence" that Lippmann would entrust with responsibility for finding the way "to overcome the central difficulty of self-government, the difficulty of dealing with an unseen reality."[60] Failure to increase continuously the level of education of citizens would eventually halt scientific progress itself.

Moreover, contemporary societies are characterized by a global popularization, extensive diffusion, and increased accessibility of expert knowledge that can no longer be controlled by professional expert groups. Citizens have instant online access to information and knowledge sources on the internet, share information, and influence one another independently of professional intermediaries. Yet although the demonopolization of professional knowledge and "self-regulated learning" have some democratic components, it is likely that only privileged groups will be able to act in such an enhanced way and new forms of monopolization of expert knowledge by authoritarian powers and/or commercial corporations like Google and Facebook will be established. To prevent this, a continuous expansion of general education is needed not only for citizens to participate in a decentralized online environment—despite the "contradictory" consequences of educational expansion for public opinion formation, as pointed out by Tönnies—but also to establish a democratic internet governance system.[61] In the long run, as Dewey noted, it always turns out that no expertise is interest neutral, so that experts have only two options: to support either the interests of the ruling elites or the interests of the citizens.

Without "adaptation" through general education, both of Lippmann's "twin-brothers"—democracy in politics and scientific thinking—can be severely compromised, as contemporary right-wing populism and its powerful leaders demonstrate.[62] By developing mobile and web-based citizen science platforms, contemporary citizen science movements successfully promote citizen-led scientific work in collaboration with, or under the supervision of, professional scientists, motivating citizens to not only use the existing expert knowledge but also contribute to it. If citizens can be close friends with one of the Lippmann twins, why should they not be able to bond with the other?

Notes

1. Binkley, "Concept of Public Opinion," 389.
2. Dewey, *Public and Its Problems*, iv, ix–x.
3. According to Jansen, "the cumulative bibliographic evidence strongly suggests that the Dewey-Lippmann exchange transmogrified into a great debate of the twentieth-century several decades after it took place" ("Phantom Conflict," 229). See also Rakow, "Family Feud."
4. See, for example, Burawoy, "For Public Sociology."
5. Lippmann, *Public Opinion*, 264, 266.
6. Machiavelli, *Discourses on Livy*, 118.
7. Machiavelli, 117–18.
8. Lippmann, *Public Opinion*, 68; Dewey, "Creative Democracy," 164.
9. Lippmann, *Drift and Mastery*, 275.
10. Lippmann, *Public Opinion*, 397.
11. Lippmann, *Phantom Public*, 51–52.
12. Lippmann, *Public Opinion*, 29.
13. Lippmann, *Phantom Public*, 3.

14. Dewey, *Public and Its Problems*, 35. Further citations of this work in this section are given in the text.
15. Lippmann, *Public Opinion*, 50.
16. Lippmann, 396.
17. Keane, "Elements of a Radical Theory"; Splichal, *Public Opinion*.
18. Tönnies, *Kritik der öffentlichen Meinung*, v.
19. Tönnies, 9.
20. Heberle, "Sociology of Ferdinand Tönnies," 11; Deflem, "Ferdinand Tönnies on Crime and Society."
21. Tönnies, *Kritik der öffentlichen Meinung*, 78. Emphasis added. Further citations of this work in this section are given in the text.
22. Latour, "Gabriel Tarde," 117.
23. Tarde, *Social Laws*, 9.
24. Tarde, *L'opinion et la foule*, 318.
25. "This great crowd called the Opinion."
26. Tarde, *L'opinion et la foule*, 7.
27. Tarde, 58.
28. Tönnies, *Kritik der öffentlichen Meinung*, 186.
29. Lippmann, *Liberty and the News*, 326.
30. Tarde, *L'opinion et la foule*, 17.
31. Tönnies, *Kritik der öffentlichen Meinung*, 575.
32. Bryce, *American Commonwealth*, 919.
33. Lippmann, *Public Opinion*, 148.
34. Lippmann, 153.
35. Bryce, *American Commonwealth*, 919.
36. Di Mascio, "Dewey's Democratic Individualism."
37. Gallup, "Changing Climate for Public Opinion Research," 23.
38. Gallup, "Testing Public Opinion," 9.
39. Splichal, *Datafication of Public Opinion*.
40. Hyman, "Toward a Theory of Public Opinion," 59.
41. Converse, "Changing Conceptions of Public Opinion," S13.
42. Splichal, *Datafication of Public Opinion*.
43. Albig, *Modern Public Opinion*, 156–57.
44. Porter, *Trust in Numbers*, 34–35.
45. Fishkin, "Virtual Public Consultation," 33.
46. Schober et al., "Social Media Analyses for Social Measurement."
47. Lippmann, *Phantom Public*, 171.
48. Dewey, *Public and Its Problems*, 211, 219.
49. Lippmann, *Public Opinion*, 29.
50. Coleman, *Can the Internet Strengthen Democracy?*, 49–51.
51. Dewey, *Public and Its Problems*, 143.
52. Dewey, 144.
53. Jacobs, Cook, and Delli Carpini, *Talking Together*, 3.
54. Fishkin, "Virtual Public Consultation."
55. Chambers, "Deliberation and Mass Democracy."
56. Passaris, "Business of Globalization."
57. Dahl, *Democracy and Its Critics*; Fishkin, "Virtual Public Consultation"; Goodin and Dryzek, "Deliberative Impacts."
58. Diaz-Bone, "Statistical Panopticism and Its Critique," 78.
59. Tarde, *Social Laws*, 81. Emphasis added.
60. Lippmann, *Public Opinion*, 395–96.
61. Splichal, "Deprofessionalization."

62. *New York Times*, "How Trump Reshaped the Presidency."

Bibliography

Albig, William. *Modern Public Opinion*. New York: McGraw Hill, 1956.
Binkley, Robert C. "The Concept of Public Opinion in the Social Sciences." *Social Forces* 6 (1928): 389–96.
Bryce, James. *The American Commonwealth* (1888). Vol. 2. Indianapolis: Liberty Fund, 1995.
Burawoy, Michael. "For Public Sociology." *American Sociological Review* 70, no. 1 (2005): 4–28.
Chambers, Simone. "Deliberation and Mass Democracy." In *Deliberative Systems*, edited by J. Parkinson and J. Mansbridge, 52–71. Cambridge: Cambridge University Press, 2012.
Coleman, Stephen. *Can the Internet Strengthen Democracy?* Cambridge: Polity, 2017.
Converse, Philip E. "Changing Conceptions of Public Opinion in the Political Process." *Public Opinion Quarterly* 51, no. 4, pt. 2 (1987): S12–S24.
Dahl, Robert A. *Democracy and Its Critics*. New Haven, CT: Yale University Press, 1989.
Deflem, Mathieu. "Ferdinand Tönnies on Crime and Society: An Unexplored Contribution to Criminological Sociology." *History of the Human Sciences* 12, no. 3 (1999): 87–116.
Dewey, John, "Creative Democracy: The Task Before Us" (1939). In *Teachers, Leaders, and Schools: Essays by John Dewey*, edited by D. J. Simpson and S. F. Stack Jr., 163–65. Carbondale: Southern Illinois University Press, 2010.
———. *The Public and Its Problems. An Essay in Political Inquiry* (1927). Chicago: Gateway Books, 1946.
Diaz-Bone, Rainer. "Statistical Panopticism and Its Critique." *Historical Social Research* 44, no. 2 (2019): 77–102.
Di Mascio, Patrick. "Dewey's Democratic Individualism." *E-rea: Revue électronique d'études sur le monde anglophone* 9, no. 2 (2012): http://www.doi.org/10.4000/erea.2558.
Fishkin, James S. "Virtual Public Consultation: Prospects for Internet Deliberative Democracy." In *Online Deliberation: Design, Research, and Practice*, edited by Todd Davies and Seeta Peña Gangadharan, 23–36. Stanford, CA: CSLI Publications, 2009.
Gallup, George. "The Changing Climate for Public Opinion Research." *Public Opinion Quarterly* 21, no. 1 (1957): 23–27.
———. "Testing Public Opinion." In "Public Opinion in a Democracy," special issue, *Public Opinion Quarterly* 2 (1938): 8–14.
Goodin, Robert E., and John S. Dryzek. "Deliberative Impacts: The Macro-Political Uptake of Mini-Publics." *Politics and Society* 34, no. 2 (2006): 219–44.
Heberle, Rudolf. "The Sociology of Ferdinand Tönnies." *American Sociological Review* 2, no. 1 (1937): 9–25.
Hyman, Herbert H. "Toward a Theory of Public Opinion." *Public Opinion Quarterly* 21, no. 1 (1957): 54–59.
Jacobs, Lawrence R., Fay Lomax Cook, and Michael X. Delli Carpini, eds. *Talking Together: Public Deliberation and Political Participation in America*. Chicago: University of Chicago Press, 2009.

Jansen, Sue Curry. "Phantom Conflict: Lippmann, Dewey, and the Fate of the Public in Modern Society." *Communication and Critical/Cultural Studies* 6, no. 3 (2009): 221–45.

Keane, John. "Elements of a Radical Theory of Public Life: From Tönnies to Habermas and Beyond." *Canadian Journal of Political and Social Theory / Revue canadienne de theorie sociale et politique* 6, no. 3 (1982): 11–49.

Latour, Bruno. "Gabriel Tarde and the End of the Social." In *The Social in Question: New Bearings in History and the Social Sciences*, edited by Patrick Joyce, 117–32. London: Routledge, 2002.

Lippmann, Walter. *Drift and Mastery: An Attempt to Diagnose the Current Unrest*. New York: Mitchell Kennerley, 1914.

———. *Liberty and the News*. New York: Harcourt, Brace and Howe, 1920.

———. *The Phantom Public* (1925). New Brunswick, NJ: Transaction, 1993.

———. *Public Opinion* (1922). New Brunswick, NJ: Transaction, 1998.

Machiavelli, Niccolò. *Discourses on Livy* (1517). Translated by Harvey C. Mansfield and Nathan Tarcov. Chicago: University of Chicago Press, 1996.

Mill, John Stuart. *On Liberty* (1859). Kitchener: Batoche Books, 2001.

Naughton, John. "Smartphones Could Help Us Track the Coronavirus—but at What Cost?" *The Guardian*, March 21, 2020. https://www.theguardian.com/commentisfree/2020/mar/21/smartphones-could-help-track-coronavirus-but-at-what-cost.

New York Times. "How Trump Reshaped the Presidency in Over 11,000 Tweets." November 2, 2019. https://www.nytimes.com/interactive/2019/11/02/us/politics/trump-twitter-presidency.html.

Passaris, Constantine E. "The Business of Globalization and the Globalization of Business." *Journal of Comparative International Management* 9, no. 1 (2006): http://journals.hil.unb.ca/index.php/jcim/article/view/5666/10661.

Porter, Theodore M. *Trust in Numbers: The Pursuit of Objectivity in Science and Public Life*. Princeton, NJ: Princeton University Press, 1995.

Rakow, Lana F. "Family Feud: Who's Still Fighting About Dewey and Lippmann?" *Javnost—the Public* 25, nos. 1–2 (2018): 75–82.

Schober, Michael F., Josh Pasek, Lauren Guggenheim, Cliff Lampe, and Frederick G. Conrad. "Social Media Analyses for Social Measurement." *Public Opinion Quarterly* 80, no. 1 (2016): 180–211.

Snowden, Edward. "If I Happen to Fall Out of a Window, You Can Be Sure I Was Pushed." *Spiegel Online*, September 13, 2019. https://www.spiegel.de/international/world/interview-with-edward-snowden-about-his-story-a-1286605.html.

Splichal, Slavko. *Datafication of Public Opinion and the Public Sphere*. London: Anthem Press, 2022.

———. "Deprofessionalization." In *Wiley Blackwell Encyclopedia of Sociology*. 2nd ed. Oxford: Wiley-Blackwell, forthcoming.

———. *Public Opinion: Developments and Controversies in the Twentieth Century*. Lanham, MD: Rowman & Littlefield, 1999.

Tarde, Gabriel. *On Communication and Social Influence: Selected Papers*. Edited by Terry N. Clark. Chicago: University of Chicago Press, 1969.

———. *L'opinion et la foule*. Paris: Les Presses universitaires de France, 1901.

———. *Social Laws: An Outline of Sociology* (1898). Translated by Howard C. Warren. Kitchener: Batoche Books, 2000.

Tönnies, Ferdinand. *Gemeinschaft und Gesellschaft*. Leipzig: Fues, 1887.

———. *Kritik der öffentlichen Meinung*. Berlin: Julius Springer, 1922.

6

THE LIPPMANN/DEWEY DEBATE IN THE HISTORY OF TWENTIETH-CENTURY PROGRESSIVISM

Steve Fuller

Introduction: A Struggle for the Soul of Progressivism

The Lippmann/Dewey debate was arguably dead on arrival when it first transpired a century ago. Dewey was "always already" defeated, insofar as the positions taken in the debate can be largely explained in terms of a profound cross-generational difference: Dewey was sixty-three and Lippmann thirty-three when it began in 1922. Dewey was born before the US Civil War began. He went to his death in 1952 invoking face-to-face interaction, community spirit, and town hall meetings as the spontaneous wellspring of "the public." In contrast, Lippmann's sense of "the public" was mindful of the volatility of a mass population that was increasingly empowered as decision-making individuals—both as citizens and as consumers. Where Dewey tended to regard "technology" as a capitalist false siren potentially impeding the sorts of "natural" interaction that generate publics, Lippmann took a more neutral view. He accepted that technological mediation in mass democracy was inevitable—regardless of capitalist motives. For Lippmann, that necessitated creative thinking about how to organize people for the greatest overall benefit in the "Great Society," a term that recurs throughout "Progressive" thought in the twentieth century. And both Dewey and Lippmann identified themselves as "Progressives."

Dewey and Lippmann's shared focus on the ontological status of "the public" foreshadows the great division in the Progressive ranks between, respectively, "social democracy" and "neoliberalism." To be sure, they agreed on two key points: an open-ended view of the future and a broadly "Pragmatist" sense of the embedded, in medias res character of the human condition.

Where they differed—quite substantially—was over whether such embedding was largely a liability or a benefit to social progress. Lippmann clearly thought the former, Dewey the latter. Their views on "the public" follow from this difference. Lippmann was very suspicious of "the public" as a reification independent of the individuals who are taken to constitute it. Among the potential agents of reification are the state, pollsters, market researchers, as well as academic social scientists. This explains Lippmann's early stress on the statistical nature of data about "public opinion," underscoring its fluid and malleable character, which in turn posed special problems of governance in a period of mass democracy coupled with mass media, when an unprecedented amount of such data is produced and consumed simultaneously.[1] In contrast, Dewey regarded "the public" as the self-conscious version of connections that organically emerge among people, initially at the local "face to face" level, to which the state then needs to be sensitive in its policies, especially as its sphere of governance both broadens and deepens. His awareness of the mass media shadowed Marxism's in terms of being more about its mode of production than its actual products. Dewey understood the media as an extension of industrial capitalism that generally operates in opposition to some authentic sense of the common good, his gloss on "the public."[2]

The downstream effects of the Lippmann/Dewey debate have been felt and amplified over the past century. They are normally conceived in terms of "collectivism" (Dewey) versus "individualism" (Lippmann). Certainly this works as a first approximation. Indeed, Lippmann was seen by neoliberalism's 1930s founders as someone who supported the capacity of people to "disembed" from their default social (including intellectual) settings in order to be truly free. This tenet provided the philosophical underpinning for Alexander Rüstow's coinage of "neoliberalism" at the Walter Lippmann Colloquium in Paris in 1938. The Colloquium was the crucible that forged that notorious neoliberal club, the Mont Pèlerin Society, whose statement of purpose was drafted by someone who will resurface later in this chapter, Lionel Robbins, the chair of the London School of Economics who hired Friedrich Hayek.[3] Lippmann inspired the original neoliberals to "denaturalize" classical liberalism, which by the end of the nineteenth century—courtesy of Herbert Spencer's brand of social evolutionism—had come to be associated with laissez-faire capitalism.[4] According to these early neoliberals, the "artificial" monopolies of the mercantilist state that had so troubled Adam Smith had been effectively replaced by the monopolies of industrial capitalism in their own time, now in the name of "survival of the fittest." And while the source of the patronage involved had changed, the result was the same: the mutual corruption of the state and the economy.

Lippmann's links to Progressivism threw a lifeline to liberals who were becoming disenchanted that the modern secular democratic state was no better than the old church-authorized absolute monarchy. In this spirit, Rüstow championed a muscular state whose primary business was "liberal interventionism," which is to say, opening the sphere of freedom whenever a default social trajectory might otherwise close it.[5] Nowadays we tend to think of this policy as "deregulation," but it is more accurately seen as "regulation for freedom" in the face of the tendency for power and capital to concentrate, left to their own devices, thereby stifling the prospects for freedom. Indeed, this framing of neoliberalism is more in line with a second strand of classical liberalism concurrent with Smith's, but which did not appeal to the market "naturalistically" in terms of spontaneous self-organization. It came from France, the original home of both mercantilism and the Walter Lippmann Colloquium—and it more explicitly reflected Enlightenment sensibilities. Its champions included, first and foremost, the Marquis de Condorcet and later Charles Comte (no relation to Auguste Comte), the latter known for his coinage of the phrase "permanent revolution" to characterize the 1789 French Revolution as a failed experiment that nevertheless should be tried again in the future.[6]

The basic idea is that markets should *not* be seen as forms of social life that spontaneously emerge once the artificial constraints of state privilege are removed (pace Smith and later Hayek) but rather as themselves state-induced artifices to unblock the natural flow of human talent—as understood against the backdrop of a profoundly imperfect ("sinful") world that required regular disruption. In that case, the prospect of revolution is implied insofar as the people are licensed to take matters into their own hands if the state fails to perform this unblocking function. This version of classical liberalism regards the 1789 French Revolution as simply having been a more violent and less successful version of the 1776 American Revolution. It is worth contrasting the Marxist take on the two events: the American Revolution was an arrested "bourgeois revolution" that stopped short of "total revolution," the prototype of which was the French Revolution.

However, what these classical liberals—not least Lippmann—failed to realize was that liberalism itself might be invoked by one state to intervene in the affairs of another to bring about the desired level of freedom, thereby enacting a "second-order" version of "liberal interventionism." As we shall see below, Lippmann's original realization of this possibility led him to shift his Progressive allegiances from Theodore Roosevelt to Woodrow Wilson in 1912. Nevertheless, more than three decades later, Lippmann would be blindsided by the advent of the "Cold War," even though he was the one who popularized the phrase.[7] Lippmann was alarmed by the "Truman Doctrine," which basically licensed the United States to supply any sort of aid—including military—to prevent the spread of Communism. He committed his thoughts to print after an interestingly misdirected exchange of correspondence with the US State Department's chief policy adviser George Kennan over the latter's signature concept of "containment."[8]

Nevertheless, contrary to both Kennan's and Lippmann's efforts to avoid an arms race, a more hawkish neoliberalism came to the fore, which by the end of the Cold War would become indistinguishable from "Neo-Conservatism." In truth, it was simply liberal interventionism globalized, the mirror image of the Soviet worldwide exportation of Marxist Communism. This exceptionally muscular sense of liberalism was epitomized by such more or less violent external state actions as the 1973 CIA-induced Pinochet coup in Chile, the "shock therapy" approach to post-socialist economies championed by Jeffrey Sachs in the early 1990s, and the 2003 toppling of Iraq's Saddam Hussein.[9] Lippmann avoided this trajectory altogether, ironically resulting in his support of Richard Nixon, who saw a clearer path than did Lyndon Johnson to the withdrawal of US troops from Vietnam, where they probably shouldn't have been in the first place.[10] In the next section, we shall see that Progressivism always contained the hawkish swagger on the world stage, which Lippmann found increasingly problematic.

Lippmann's Progressive Pilgrimage from Roosevelt to Wilson—and Beyond

The definitive expression of US Progressivism occurred in the 1912 presidential election. The two principal candidates, former president Theodore Roosevelt and New Jersey governor Woodrow Wilson, were arguably the most "intellectual" chief executives in US history, although they could not have been further apart in temperament, public image, or political grounding. Nevertheless, their alternative policy horizons—Roosevelt's "New Nationalism" and Wilson's "New Freedom"—were truly visionary, differing in interesting and subtle ways that repay a second look. In contrast, the "New Deal," the catchphrase for the epic post–Great Depression reforms of Theodore's younger cousin, Franklin Delano Roosevelt, began life as a mere campaign slogan, with policies made up as his administration went along. Unlike TR, FDR was no intellectual but a connoisseur of intellectuals, as manifested in the coterie of smart lawyers and economists who constituted his "Brain Trust."

By the time Lippmann debated Dewey, he had migrated from TR to Wilson, only to be disillusioned by Wilson's final act on the world stage, namely, his campaign for a "world government" to end war for all time. Nevertheless, the "intellectualism" that united Roosevelt and Wilson—as well as Dewey and Lippmann—was based on a national self-understanding of the United States in terms of German idealism, which was the nation's leading school of academic philosophy in the nineteenth century. To be sure, it was critiqued, refined, and sublimated, but its presence was always felt, especially in terms of the "big picture" issues. Ralph Waldo Emerson's self-styled "Transcendentalism" can be understood as an American makeover of German idealism, which received clearest academic expression in Lippmann's day by his Harvard teachers, William James, Josiah Royce, and perhaps even George Santayana.[11]

If anyone would have gladly accepted the label "social justice warrior," it was Roosevelt. He was keen to flex the muscle of state power to champion "the little guy," thereby releasing their hidden potential—and the New Nationalism supported women's suffrage. He was about intervening boldly, threatening corporations with breaking up their monopolies if they didn't clean up their act and serve the public interest. He would, however, accept corporate-driven solutions to monopoly capitalism. The legacy of that settlement is an array of influential private foundations officially dedicated to supporting science in the public interest. Thus, the Rockefeller, Carnegie, Ford, and Sloan Foundations have served to save their parent companies enormous tax bills to the federal government for over a century.[12] It would seem that for Progressives, science is the only religion that can absolve capitalism of its sins.

Roosevelt matched his self-styled social justice warrior image with a fiendish ability to infuse the media with his own "crusading" spirit. He welcomed "photo-ops" and even cartoons of his activities. For better or worse, Roosevelt became as familiar as "Uncle Sam" as the face of America on the world stage. Moreover, Roosevelt invited journalists into the White House and encouraged them to investigate political and business dealings that he was thinking about prosecuting for corruption and tax evasion.[13] Echoes of this tactic could still be heard in Trump's innuendo-laden press conferences—but with less efficacy. And that's largely due to Lippmann. He knew the journalists who had done Roosevelt's bidding, now known fondly as "muckrakers." Lippmann's first job was as personal assistant to their intellectual ringleader, Lincoln Steffens. In his day, Steffens was known for the first muckraker book, *The Shame of the Cities* (1904), but is now remembered, perhaps notoriously, for having declared of the early Soviet Russia, "I have seen the future and it works." Lippmann played a decisive role in debunking the muckraking approach to journalism—not in the context of Roosevelt's domestic agenda, which he supported, but a decade later, when muckrakers got matters of fact hopelessly wrong in the 1917 Bolshevik Revolution because they were, as Lenin branded them, "useful idiots."[14]

The Bolshevik leaders Lenin and Trotsky had watched Roosevelt's moves closely and were impressed by his grooming of the press. As for the muckrakers, the restoration of their legacy in the United States required a more adversarial relationship between the media and the presidency, which emerged in the Cold War era, acquired momentum with the Vietnam War, and culminated in the Watergate scandal. Nevertheless, the techniques of what is now called "investigative journalism" remain subject to the same cognitive liabilities of bias, sensationalism, and privileged sourcing that plagued the original muckrakers. Indeed, what ultimately distinguishes Lincoln Steffens and, say, Seymour Hersh is only the latter's greater sense of autonomy from state power. Notwithstanding their cognitive similarities, the contrast in moral psychologies of the two journalists is striking: the naive optimism of the former versus the hard-boiled cynicism of the latter.[15]

Another feature of Roosevelt-style Progressivism that had attracted Lippmann as a Harvard student but from which he later distanced himself was Roosevelt's barely concealed imperialist aspirations for the United States. Lippmann held that imperialism went against the grain of the American people, who as instinctive isolationists entered foreign entanglements only with great reluctance.[16] Nevertheless, Roosevelt's original take on imperialism was influential. For him it marked a rite of passage to adulthood as a nation on the world stage, especially at a time when the other "adults"—Britain and France—were showing signs of fatigue and decline, and the "adolescents"—Germany and Japan—were showing signs of belligerence. Thus, Roosevelt seized the opportunity to broker the peace in the Russo-Japanese War, the first time that the East had defeated the West in military conflict. For his efforts he was awarded the 1906 Nobel Peace Prize. Closer to home, Roosevelt saw imperialism as amplifying the spirit of the Republican Party, at least in the sense that animated Abraham Lincoln, who gave the party its first two presidential victories. In his time in office, Lincoln had deployed an unprecedented level of state power to keep the union together, while abolishing the divisive institution of slavery—albeit at the cost of two million lives in a civil war. Roosevelt understood imperialism in similarly dialectical terms as being about both emancipating and unifying—and if necessary, involving military force. This was the spirit in which Roosevelt easily spoke of the US colonial replacement of a "senescent" Spain in the Philippines, Cuba, and Puerto Rico as a form of "liberation."

Again watching Roosevelt's moves, the Soviet Union adapted its own policy of "limited sovereignty" toward its satellite republics based on what came to be known as the "Roosevelt Corollary" to the Monroe Doctrine.[17] The Monroe Doctrine, reflecting the emergence of Latin American nationalism in the early nineteenth century, had guaranteed that the United States would protect all the countries in that region from European colonization. Roosevelt's Corollary appeared in his 1904 State of the Union address, declaring that the United States would additionally intervene if its own interests were threatened as Latin America started to be more assertive as nation-states. At this point, newspaper cartoons started to depict the United States as the world's police officer, an image that lingered for the rest of the twentieth century—and no doubt set the precedent for Lippmann's refusal to participate in America's second great effort to play that role after World War II. The short-term effect was to shift Lippmann's style of Progressivism in the 1912 presidential election from fellow Harvard man Roosevelt to ex-Princeton president Wilson.

As Lippmann had already seen from the vantage point of a twenty-five-year-old,[18] Wilson represented a shift in leadership style toward the emerging technocratic elites, extending from the federal civil service (aka "state bureaucracy") to the "managerial class" of professional corporate executives, whose competence was largely demonstrated "behind the scenes." It convinced Lippmann to engage in Wilson's pioneering public relations campaign to persuade a reluctant America to enter World War I, which it eventually did in what turned out to be the war's final year. However, Lippmann ended up condemning Wilson for thinking he could end war for all time by persuading America to join the League of Nations. Indeed, Lippmann saw Wilson's hubris on this score as turning the "democratic idealism and optimism about the perfectibility of American society" of the Progressive era into a "spiritual disaster."[19] As a result, the 1920 presidential election swept into office Wilson's antithesis, Warren Harding, someone whose supine attitude to governance—under the guise of "normalcy"—has led to his being ranked among the least competent occupants of the Oval Office.

As for Wilson's contrasting vision of Progressivism, keep in mind that he not only remains the only US president with a PhD—and was among the founders of political science as an academic discipline in the United States—but he was also a staunch Democrat born in the antebellum South.

This means the Democratic Party of Thomas Jefferson and Andrew Jackson, two quite different Southern personalities who were nevertheless joined in their belief in "popular sovereignty," that is, a devolution of power from central government to local authorities, usually understood as the constituent American state legislatures. Thus, prior to the Civil War, the Democratic Party generally regarded slaveholding as a decision for each state to take for itself, which in practice served to accentuate the political and economic differences between the North and South. Nevertheless, antebellum Democrats held that the maintenance of liberty for citizens overrode any concerns about the consequences of how that liberty might be exercised: the union should be based on a principle of maximum tolerance for local practices and not subject to a "one size fits all" imposition from Washington.

Needless to say, slavery provided the ultimate stress test for this principle, resulting in much hypocrisy, not least from Jefferson, who like the other US Founding Fathers explicitly defended hypocrisy as a political principle.[20] Also, as a slaveholder, he believed that a democratic legislature should revisit its mandate every generation. Such radical albeit hypocritical liberalism explains Jefferson's original opposition to the US Constitution as a document designed to bind future generations in perpetuity. But following the Constitution's ratification, he supported the passage of the document's first ten amendments, known as the "Bill of Rights," which has served the "popular sovereignty" agenda to this day. Wilson's own contribution to this trajectory was to complement his own constitutional reforms, which extended the power of the federal government to unprecedented levels, with a new ethic of accountability in government. True to his Presbyterian upbringing, Wilson believed that the state cannot credibly dictate to local authorities unless its own house is in order: no more hypocrisy! Indeed, Wilson's dedication to "professionalism" in politics, which contrasted sharply with Roosevelt's more spontaneous *modus vivendi*, inspired Lippmann to extend the same spirit to journalism, arguably his most enduring legacy.

More generally, Wilson's professionalism was consistent with his adaptation of Hegel to lead the world by example rather than by force. To be sure, "example" may mean propaganda while precluding outright invasion. Lippmann turned out to be a more consistent Wilsonian than Wilson himself, who was not content simply with brokering the Treaty of Versailles, which concluded World War I by breaking up Europe's internal empires into autonomous states. In addition, Wilson promoted the idea of a "League of Nations" invested with superordinate authority over what these states do, with the specific aim of "outlawing" war. Lippmann found the proposal unfeasible, especially if this "world government" was meant to function as a kind of second-order representative democracy: how could such a body have substantial binding force yet remain subject to the political vicissitudes of the member states, whose interests might suddenly change with a new electoral cycle?[21] Even before their famous exchanges, Lippmann had singled out Dewey's enthusiasm for the League of Nations in the pages of Lippmann's own *New Republic* as the height of political naivete.[22]

Dewey Versus Lippmann on the State: Society's Amplifier or Lens?

Dewey's *The Public and Its Problems* is not simply a response to Lippmann's views on public opinion but the definitive statement of his philosophy of "politics," understood in the broad sense of both political practice and political science. In this context, Dewey's signature use of the vague word *inquiry* makes sense. His basic thesis is that if politics is, as Aristotle held, the collective workings of humanity as *zoon politikon*, then its theory and practice will develop simultaneously. As with many of Dewey's works, this book began as an invited set of lectures delivered in his self-styled scholasticism. Nevertheless, it provides a clear sense of his "first principles," admittedly a phrase that its author would be loath to use, given that a general feature of Dewey's philosophical method is to start in medias res and then define. This is in contrast to what he calls "absolutistic" philosophies, which define from outside the phenomena under study. Dewey means here to cover a broad range of philosophers, including Plato, Hegel, and Mill. For Dewey, such "absolutists" create a false sense of transcendence by detaching the conduct of science from the business of living, which is manifested in abstract, "value-free" language. Dewey's allergy to absolutism, a hallmark of his self-styled "naturalism," was his version of William James's "anti-intellectualist" approach to inquiry, which embraced a relaxed approach to "introspection" in experimental psychology to include various forms of pre-theoretical awareness. All of this put Lippmann in Dewey's line of fire, as his younger contemporary appeared to argue that just such an "absolutistic" and "intellectualist" science of statecraft was the only way forward in mass democracies.

Dewey's main objection to what he regarded broadly as the "intellectualist" and "absolutistic" conception of political inquiry that has dominated Western thought is the image of the state as a superordinate entity that somehow constrains and channels the natural state of individuals, understood as atomic essences. Indeed, he quotes John Stuart Mill's use of the phrase "the social state" as indicative of this pernicious residual Platonism.[23] However, read in context, it becomes clear that for Mill "the social state" is analogous to the positivist conception of boundary conditions in the application of physical laws. The underlying idea is that an organizational principle is needed for matter to take some sort of stable albeit dynamic form, given the indefinite number of ways in which it might combine. A similar spirit had informed the drafting of the US Constitution, with its Newton-inspired idea of "separation of powers" and "checks and balances" to structure the countervailing forces driving factional interests in society, themselves understood as the reflection of deep-seated features of human nature.[24]

In contrast, Dewey, who never considered the US Constitution with the same care as Mill—or, for that matter, Lippmann[25]—dealt with the state in the exact opposite way. Instead of seeing it as a formal constraint on spontaneous human activity, he regarded it as the emergent product of such activity. More specifically, the state emerges from what Dewey calls the "public," which is the self-conscious expression of "social life," which he understood as the matrix out of which such foundational political distinctions as "individual" versus "collective" emerge. His preferred term for social life was "community," another vague word that resonates of the primordial interconnectedness of the human condition. Dewey's account of the state epitomizes his brand of "naturalism," a blended normative/empirical narrative that is closer in spirit to Montesquieu and Hume than to the more positivistic style of theorizing emerging from the nascent social sciences in whose direction Lippmann tended to lean.

Taken as a rhetorical strategy, Dewey's interpolation of the "public" between community and the state was meant to provide an organic grounding for an entity that Lippmann had provocatively claimed in *Public Opinion* to be largely "fictional" in the strict sense of being alternatively constructible. It is worth dwelling on this difference. For Dewey, the state is the natural outgrowth of people realizing the externalities of their interactions, with geographical boundaries providing the outer limit of concern—that is, barring a world government, which Dewey also favored. In this respect, Dewey's sense of the state appears quite "minimalist," in that its ends extend no further than managing the consequences of the totality of a population's consensual transactions. Moreover, Dewey suggests that a truly Progressive democracy would regularly involve the population deliberating and setting the terms of such management, mindful of the demands of liberty, equality, and community. He envisaged "political evolution" as moving from the sort of representative democracy that preoccupied Mill and the US Founding

Fathers to the sort of direct and participatory democracy championed by, say, Rousseau. Indeed, the 1920s witnessed the rise of a largely Dewey-inspired "Forum Movement," which boomed once it became a sounding board for the New Deal's reconstruction of American society after the Great Depression. At its peak in 1937 the Forum Movement consisted of five hundred forums in forty-three of the forty-eight states, involving up to 2.5 million people, or 2 percent of the entire US population. However, federal sponsorship turned out to be the kiss of death for the movement, as it was increasingly suspected by the New Deal's critics of being a propaganda vehicle.[26]

Such an outcome would not have surprised Lippmann. He regarded Dewey as suffering from at least two major misapprehensions about the nature of mass democracy. The first was to presume that the governance structure of democracy is either scalable from or reducible to the proverbial New England town hall meeting, on which the Forum Movement was modeled. Moreover, whatever nostalgia had remained for such meetings was bound to disappear in the wake of "mass media," which replaced face-to-face interaction with a "broadcast" style of communication, in which an elite can transmit to the many, all of whom would be in their homes or workplaces, where the radios (later televisions) are located to receive the media's messages—and at most a telephone with which to reply to those messages with the requisite speed. Of course, *we* don't live in such a world anymore, but at least Lippmann—unlike Dewey—realized that *he* did. However, since Lippmann accepted Mill's "social state," he would regard the Forum Movement's propaganda potential as less an indictment of its legitimacy than an indicator of its efficacy, assuming its "spontaneous" results were widely reported as synchronized with government thinking. Dewey's second misapprehension was to suppose that people have clear interests on the basis of which they could deliberate rationally. To be sure, Dewey's own view is nuanced: he conceded that many of those interests might only become evident in the process of collective deliberation—which for him constituted an argument for the process, understood as a means by which people *discover* their interests. But Lippmann's trump to this entire line of thought is that those "interests" are only stable for the period that the people are in the room deliberating. Once they go home or back to work, they are faced with different problems and their interests will shift accordingly.

Public Opinion is full of skepticism that humans possess *any* sort of stable interests. Lippmann took aim at both instinct- and class-based theories, including Freud and Marx by name. Dewey would also be in the line of fire, notwithstanding his own rejection of instinct, as he accepted class as a "habitualized" response to one's role in society's mode of production. Dewey agreed with Marx that capitalist social relations repressed humanity's potential for full self-expression, something he had hoped to remedy with the sort of innovative pedagogy that first brought him widespread notice and arguably made him the most influential figure in teacher education in the twentieth century. Moreover, Lippmann's intuitions about the plasticity of people's interests were probably also molded by his participation in Wilson's public relations campaign to persuade Americans to join World War I five years earlier. He effectively helped to persuade a nation whose self-understanding was mainly predicated on its independence from Europe to entwine its fate with the continent once again—indeed, in the context of an overseas war that was already beginning to look pointless to its European combatants.

Lippmann's approach to the plasticity of interests was originally striking for his focus on the government's greater gathering and use of statistical data for legislative and administrative purposes. He picked up this idea from Graham Wallas's "Great Society," a future state that was in the business of harmonizing—"organizing" was Wallas's word—an array of mass tendencies, each of which sliced social life from a different angle.[27] The statistical data on which those tendencies are based would need to be gathered on a regular basis because they would eventually become obsolete, even if accurate at the time of collection. Indeed, Lippmann smartly recognized that the epistemic quality of these data streams would degrade at varying rates, which statisticians would need to monitor to advise the state on when to change policy.[28] Whereas in true Fabian style Wallas explicitly discussed this battery of indicators as a tool for domesticating a nation's febrile collective psychology, Lippmann backpedaled any metaphysical implications of a "mass mind" in favor of a more basic pitch that aspiring American leaders should cultivate and refine the state's statistical functions to monitor how individual minds changed under changing conditions.

Nevertheless, Lippmann seriously underestimated the extent to which the commercial sphere might make use of the very same data for its own purposes—and moreover invest heavily in the collection and analysis of such data, potentially competing with government. To be sure, Lippmann's neoliberal followers have been relatively relaxed about this prospect as it unfolded in the twentieth century. Lippmann himself wrote at the dawn of private firms devoted to market research, public opinion surveys, and public relations, more generally. Indeed, his own words may have unwittingly inspired a fellow traveler in Wilson's campaign to get the United States into World War I, Edward Bernays. Bernays rephrased the ambiguous moral valence of Lippmann's reference to the "manufacture of consent" to characterize public relations, the field he founded, as positively engaged in the "engineering of consent."[29] Stripped of any state imperatives, public relations would be less about focusing diverse passions in a unified direction than creating opportunities for people to see things anew and thereby revise their self-understanding in a potentially boundless space of consumer choice. Bernays's diabolical genius lay in the ease with which he could rhetorically convert what Lippmann had identified as the indeterminacy of human judgment into displays of individual freedom that could then be redeployed for commercial profit.

The "Melting Pot" as a Test Case for Progressivism

As we have seen, Dewey's *modus operandi* is to tease out distinctions as emerging features of some previously undifferentiated mass, which he believes tracks "human social evolution," in a robust sense that incorporates bioecological factors but not necessarily what we would now call "genetic" ones. Thus, Dewey makes great play of the morphological features, technological infrastructure, and geographical localization of humans as shaping the characteristics of persons and institutions, but he repeatedly rejects the appeal to "instincts," which he regards as empty metaphysics that typically serves to prop up prejudices. In this respect, Dewey is on the side of today's social justice warriors, though he is much more sanguine than they are about our overcoming such prejudices.

Indeed, conspicuously absent from *The Public and Its Problems* is any discussion of the relevance of human genetic variation ("race"), even though that was a significant component of US democratic discourse of the 1920s—and, for that matter, the 2020s. But this is not to say that Dewey was oblivious to racial prejudice. On the contrary, he recognizes and opposes it, but he explains racism as a matter of "habit" that results in revulsion toward the unfamiliar, which is then exacerbated under the competitive conditions of the labor market.[30] In contrast, Lippmann's perspective in *Public Opinion* is sharp and interesting: he discusses race as a stereotype that various sides deploy to their political advantage, all of which aim to hold hostage the future prospects of some group to past events involving them or their ancestors.[31] Lippmann shrewdly sees racism as a struggle over control of time, which is especially threatening to a "liberal" society that aspires to enable everyone to be all they can be—which is presumably more, and certainly other, than their forefathers were. It is here that racism reveals its truly "unprogressive" character.

While the problem of race was incidental to both Lippmann's and Dewey's thinking, their divergent assessments suggest radically different orientations to the social world. Dewey treated racism as a first-order phenomenon that is jointly experienced by its sources and targets. We would now say that he saw racism as a "social construction" that requires the mutual recognition of its perpetrators and victims. This move affiliates Dewey with the "symbolic interactionist" school of sociology inspired by his Chicago colleague, George Herbert Mead. A signature feature is the appeal to a restricted sense of "context" to cover only the shared lifeworld that is presupposed by the relevant social transactions. It is against this backdrop that Dewey could imagine that the habitual character of racism would dissolve over time as people became accustomed to the diversity of peoples in their midst, as ameliorated by a more cooperative postcapitalist social ethic, ideally in the manner of his experimental school for children. In the historiography of psychology, Dewey's self-styled "functionalism" is often presented as a prelude to behaviorism, and here it's easy to see why. For him, *racism as thought* is a function of *racism as experienced*, so if one changes the conditions under which ethnic diversity is experienced, racism as a "bad habit" will be eventually extinguished.

In contrast, Lippmann did not regard such a widespread social problem as racism in straightforwardly empirical terms. He adopted a second-order perspective, which he identified alternatively with political expertise or scientific objectivity. From this perspective, things acquire a new look: their significance is no longer as they appear to those experiencing them firsthand. Moreover, this new look is proposed as better explaining the fault lines in the phenomena that result in social conflict. Thus, racism is not really about, say, a visceral aversion to non-white peoples but a struggle over how the past is deployed to go forward into the future. Critics of Lippmann, including Dewey, are right to regard this perspective as "intellectualist" and even "Platonic." Whether the perspective is wrong is another matter entirely. For his own part, Lippmann's detachment may reflect his having been among the first generation to overcome the anti-Semitism that had prevented Jews from attending Harvard, as well as having witnessed the various forms of race-like prejudice facing southern and eastern European immigrants to the United States in the early twentieth century.

For Lippmann, racists were less reacting to alien morphological features than projecting a "theory" based on a backstory that makes it natural to speak of Jewish and other recent European immigrants as "false whites." This is how to understand the centrality of "symbols" to Lippmann's influential coinage of "stereotypes." In this rendering, racists see "others" as specimens of a type of person that has meaning in the context of their larger theory. Readers of Harper Lee's *To Kill a Mockingbird* will understand this point in light of how Tom Robinson, the Black man on trial, is understood by both the prosecution and the defense. Robinson is a pure projection of either people's fears or hopes for the racialized "other." This makes Lippmann's appeal to "context" orthogonal to Dewey's. It is not about a shared physical space that results in common experiences for its multiple inhabitants, aka "lifeworld." Rather it is about a shared mental space in which multiple strands of thought need to be synthesized for each person to constitute themselves as a coherent self.

Lippmann might have picked up this way of looking at things at Harvard from William James, whom he "love[d] more than any very great man I ever saw."[32] The formative Jamesian idea would be that of "conceptual scheme," which presents the mind as a sieve that filters the world's content. However, the metaphor of the sieve is ambiguous. In James's original presentation, what remains on the sieve corresponds to what is known and what passes through it corresponds to what is ignored, very much in the spirit of a Kuhnian paradigm.[33] But of course the metaphor may be flipped, in which case what remains on the sieve is simply redundant on the scheme's mesh, or what is nowadays called "confirmation bias," and what passes through the scheme provides the true reality check as "anomalous experience." Lippmann's "stereotypes" appear to be based on the flipped interpretation, in which case racism is to overcome so to speak, loosening the mesh on the conceptual scheme so that it is no longer serviceable.

The sort of "backstory" that informs racist stereotypes involves a certain systematic (mis)understanding of causal factors in history. It selects a few isolated facts and events—often unproblematic in their own right—and then weaves an insidious narrative around them. In its most sophisticated form, the backstory may take the form of a conspiracy theory. This *modus operandi* is true to the metaphor of the "stereotype," which derives from the stereoscope, a late nineteenth-century device popular in both laboratories and drawing rooms, which involved viewing two images of the same thing simultaneously depicted at slightly different angles to create the illusion of depth, as the mind backfilled the missing visual information. By implication, racism is unlikely to be defeated simply by racists becoming accustomed to different-looking people in their midst but rather by the relevant backstory losing its salience in the racist mind.

There are at least two ways that might happen. One is that the backstory doesn't fit easily with other backstories that come to inform one's worldview, especially if the state promotes a change in society's collective self-understanding. The relevant precedent is Lippmann's own involvement in Wilson's pro-war propaganda campaign, which persuaded Americans to identify much more strongly with Europeans than they were otherwise inclined. The second way is that a backstory might lose salience because its purported targets become harder to identify over time due to assimilation. I refer here to the famed US "melting pot," a metaphor central to US Progressive ideology, which was just as much about building a distinct national identity without lingering ties to ancestral lands as about relieving social injustice in the immigrant population.

Lippmann's and Dewey's contrasting responses to the "melting pot" metaphor epitomize their different attitudes. Again in the spirit of today's social justice warriors, Dewey was a celebrant of diversity who suspected the "melting pot" metaphor of promoting a stealth "Anglo-Saxonism" in the name of "Americanization." Indeed, Dewey welcomed the prospect of "hyphenated Americans," as in the case of "Jewish-Americans" or "Negro-Americans."[34] For his part, Lippmann dealt with one of Dewey's most brilliant Columbia students, fellow *New Republic* writer Randolph Bourne, a complex "disabled" figure who promoted the idea of a "trans-national America" in which the United States would be unique among the world's nations in rejecting homogenization in favor of the explicit cultivation of diversity, including the homelands of its immigrant populations. Historic US support for Irish Republicanism and Zionism can be easily understood in this light.

Nevertheless, Lippmann could not have been more adamantly opposed to this line of thinking.[35] With specific reference to Zionism, he held that it made more sense for Jewish influence to be diluted worldwide than to be concentrated in one place (i.e., a prospective "Israel") for which the United States would then serve as its global underwriter. As Lippmann saw matters, and keep in mind that this was 1918 not 1948, at stake was the meaning of "cosmopolitanism." Bourne envisaged the concept in terms of the United States extending its arms across the world in political and economic aid. Thus, he vocally opposed US entry into World War I, contra both Dewey and Lippmann. In contrast, Lippmann thought more in terms of the world becoming a more generally hospitable place, ensuing a circulation of peoples that would render their differences less noticeable. Of course, World War II placed this entire debate in a different light, giving Bourne's side of the argument the upper hand. Nevertheless, Lippmann predicted that a "State of Israel" would remain a target of Anti-Semitism simply due to its official Jewish self-identification.

"The Great Society" as Progressivism's Proving Ground

That Lippmann never stopped regarding himself as a "Progressive" throughout his long career, during which he advised every president from Wilson to Nixon, testifies to Progressivism's complexity. Moreover, he was always mindful of Progressivism's transnational nature. As a Harvard undergraduate, Lippmann significantly interacted with visiting politics lecturer Graham Wallas, who had recently cofounded the London School of Economics, a new university established on the principles of the Progressives' UK fellow travelers, the Fabian Society, a group of breakaway Liberal Party intellectuals who had recently founded the Labour Party. Indeed, Wallas dedicated his book based on those lectures, *The Great Society*, to Lippmann. It's interesting to compare Lippmann's and Dewey's attitudes toward the book's central claims, since they form part of the common context of their debate.

In the book that sparked their debate, *Public Opinion*, Lippmann regularly invokes the "Great Society," using it as a platform for characterizing mass democracy as a politically enclosed population subject to an array of fluid and overlapping special interests, the relative positions of which turn on the shifting allegiances of individuals, each of whom is limited by the "pictures in his [sic] head."[36] The allusion to Plato's Allegory of the Cave—updated for the modern age—is subtle but palpable throughout both his and Wallas's book. In this context, the policymaker (aka "philosopher-king") must operate with "selfless equanimity" in harmonizing those pictures for the greater good, armed with a yet to be determined social scientific method.[37] The main difference between Plato's world and ours is that in Plato's world it was easier to attach individuals to interests, based on the hold that heredity had on the political imagination (aka the Myth of the Metals). However, the defining feature of the modern world is that the individual is "free" from those default hereditary ties—and hence susceptible to all those special interests. However, the fundamental psychological makeup of the individual has not substantially changed in the interim. Thus, the state needs to be engaged in some sophisticated second-order social psychology.

In contrast, Dewey refers to Wallas's book only once—but tellingly, in his major response to Lippmann, *The Public and Its Problems*.[38] Dewey, in the guise of democracy's schoolmaster, observes Wallas's positive reference to Woodrow Wilson's *New Freedom*, his 1912 US presidential campaign manifesto. Wilson says that people originally dealt with each other as individuals but now they were also dealing with "impersonal organizations" (aka "big business"), which increasingly exploited them. In this context, the "New

Freedom" amounted to a rededication of the federal government to stop this by reducing the power of those impersonal organizations, thereby safeguarding the liberty of Americans. This is the "Progressive" reconceptualization of the state as "liberal interventionism." But relevant here is Dewey's objection to the foregrounding of the individual in Wilson's—and Wallas's—argument. It leads Dewey to recall how personal identity is (allegedly) primarily formed in small group contexts, and that the fixation on the individual is a distinctly modern preoccupation due to the seventeenth-century rediscovery of atomistic metaphysics, which from the late eighteenth century onward has been increasingly reinforced by capitalist ideology.

Yet Dewey's own reading of the rise of individualism is itself very modern—so much so that it renders mysterious how Plato could have been so focused on democracy's tendency to disembed people's identities from their traditional self-understandings. If Dewey's approach to individualism were correct, this should have never been a central Platonic concern. Of course, the difference between Plato's and our own times, which Lippmann deeply understood, is that Plato regarded the advent of the self-legislating individual as a threat to social order, whereas modern democratic society opens itself to exactly this risky situation in the name of political empowerment and personal growth. In any case, the strategy that Plato proposed in the *Republic* did not involve any "conservative" return to tradition. Rather, it involved a second-order rationalized reinvention of tradition. Thus, instead of people being defined by their actual parentage, Plato would identify each person with a social position that itself possesses a craft- or discipline-based lineage for which that person would be publicly recognized as qualified (again the Myth of the Metals). In this context, Lippmann's lifelong preoccupation with the production and distribution of knowledge should be understood as an attempt to recruit sociologically savvy and socially responsible journalists into a Plato-style "guardian" class that aims to maintain harmony in a new world—that of mass democracy—in which people are actively encouraged to shift social position.

Of course, the prospect of the Great Society did not die with the Lippmann/Dewey debate. The phrase acquired special resonance in the 1960s as the name of Lyndon Johnson's ambitious program of US civic renewal associated with the passage of the Civil Rights Act. It involved updating a key feature of the original Progressive agenda—its focus on developing the nation's "human capital," a phrase had that been coined by one of the leading economists of the Progressive era, Irving Fisher.[39] In the 1960s, human capital was popularly glossed on both sides of the Atlantic with the gendered term "manpower" as well as "meritocracy," which soon revealed Progressivism's vexed political legacy. Alongside this development was the rise of a new generation of renegade economists, led by Gary Becker,[40] who insisted on a strict economic reading of the state's "investment" in human capital. It was based on the long-term expectation that any specific investment strategy will be subject to diminishing marginal returns. At that point, the state should simply withdraw the policy and divert its funds to where they are likely to yield increasing returns.

Becker's argument did not make much headway with American policymakers at the height of the Cold War, given worries over the susceptibility of Black people—the target beneficiaries of Johnson's "Great Society"—to Soviet propaganda if they felt excluded from US society. However, once the Cold War ended, even self-described "social democrats" such as Bill Clinton and Tony Blair stressed balanced budgets over extending welfare benefits. In this changed political context, behavioral psychologist Richard Herrnstein and political scientist Charles Murray pushed Becker's argument to its logical conclusion by urging policymakers to take seriously humanity's biologically based differential capacities (including race and gender) as a boundary condition for human capital investment.[41] This idea had been already present in Irving Fisher's original formulation of human capital theory, which he was closely tied to eugenics. Interestingly, Herrnstein and Murray's positive proposals focused on a more explicitly tiered educational system that echoed those of former Harvard president James Bryant Conant at the end of the Eisenhower administration, just as the Cold War was heating up.[42]

It is now commonplace to speak lazily of this pushback from Johnson's Great Society as an ideological turn to the right. However, this turn had nothing to do with traditional conservatism: it presupposed just as strong sense of a scientifically informed state agency as any typical Progressive reform. Classical conservatives would never take either state power or scientific knowledge as the pretext for their policy arguments. Instead, they would appeal to "tradition," "religion," "family values" and "common sense." To be sure, in the 1980s Ronald Reagan and Margaret Thatcher co-opted substantial features of conservative rhetoric to their nationally customized versions of neoliberalism. That classical conservatives such as Roger Scruton were unable to stop this appropriation of their ideology and even became somewhat co-opted themselves is a testimony to the overall success of Progressivism in shifting the default expectations of state involvement in people's lives.[43] After all, nowadays people even need the state to render them "free," à la "liberal interventionism." The recent ascendancy of Donald Trump and Boris Johnson should be seen as taking the same dynamic to the next level.

My point in raising the fate of the Great Society is that the original Progressives would have recognized *both* sides of the controversy surrounding the application of human capital theory to public policy as their own—that is, the "social democratic" side represented by Lyndon Johnson's initiative and the "neoliberal" side represented by Gary Becker's strictures. Indeed, both sides would resonate to the term *the experimenting society*, coined by perhaps the most academically influential architect of Johnson's program, Donald Campbell.[44] The difference is that the "neoliberals" place greater stress, à la Karl Popper, on the need to recognize and learn from the negative outcomes of those experiments. Nevertheless, both sides share a vision of people as "start-ups" who would be eventually self-supporting—or "self-reliant," as Emerson would say. As I have said in the context of the eugenics backstory common to Progressivism and Fabianism, the state would be in the business of cultivating "natural born liberals."[45] The ultimate policy question, then, is how to enable people to operate in the widest sphere of freedom that will do the most good for themselves and the larger society. To recall a distinction that acquired currency in debates about the Great Society in the 1960s, the idea was to promote *equality of opportunity* rather than *equality of outcome*—the latter associated with the Soviet brand of socialism.

A common Progressive theme in the twentieth century was that the nation's "manpower" failed to be fully utilized because too many people were held back by both material disadvantage and social prejudice. However, after World War I, in light of European devastation and the rise of the Soviet Union, Progressives began to diverge significantly on strategy. The bellwether conceptual disagreement was over the scientific status of welfare.[46] The issue had been brewing since the late nineteenth century over proposals for wealth redistribution through taxation. It was prompted by John Stuart Mill's proposal that the rich suffer less from giving a fixed sum to the poor than the poor benefit from receiving it. In effect, Mill was translating a simple mathematical point into a psychological law of potentially profound policy import, especially for ideas of justice. But the legitimacy of this translation was now thrown into doubt by the proto-neoliberals, who argued that transfers of wealth are subject to significant variation in the sorts of "pain" or "pleasure" that people receive from such transactions, depending on what the parties to the transactions subjectively value. Pace Mill, there is no "objective" conception of welfare to be had—let alone one that the state could administer, say, through a "progressive" tax regime.

This point was forcefully driven home by Lionel Robbins,[47] who criticized the tendency of economists in his day, notably John Maynard Keynes, to presume that welfare is the discipline's central concept. Robbins held that "welfare" is a largely statistical illusion reinforced by a Mill-style utilitarian elision of mathematics and psychology. He had in mind the use of, say, greater personal income or greater life expectancy as proxies for increases in happiness. Had he been a Marxist, Robbins would have diagnosed the error as a willful misapprehension of capital accumulation, be it expressed in pounds or years. However, Robbins himself interestingly thought that welfare-based economics is *too* materialist, insofar as it presupposes that people can't have too much material wealth—and that the state should be in the business to make them still wealthier. But as Robbins realized, people throughout history have foregone material wealth, often in ways that have placed their own lives at serious risk. If economics is a truly universal science, welfare cannot be its focus; hence Robbins's studiously neutral definition of economics as the management of ends and means under conditions of scarcity. Although this definition has been often presented as harsh, a better sense of Robbins can be gleaned from the sort of "post-economic" conceptions of happiness championed by his last research assistant, who is nowadays understood as a justifier of "downshifting."[48]

The debate over welfare surrounding Johnson's Great Society in the late 1960s centered on whether the state could promote individual capacities without undermining everyone's freedom in the process, especially through excessive taxation or hiring quotas. This divergence in the Progressive agenda over the state's capacity to breed "natural born liberals" can be usefully understood by considering the fate of "meritocracy," a term ironically introduced in the late 1950s by UK sociologist Michael Young to characterize the post–World War relaunching of Fabianism as "upward social mobility,"[49] whereby the state would enable everyone to rise to their level of competence by providing universally free access to public education and health. I say "ironically" because this formulation invited paradoxes that sowed the seeds of discord in the Progressive ranks. Indeed, the Fabian Society, which commissioned Young's book, refused to publish it, precisely because of the ironic cast of its thesis. Moreover, forty years later, Young witnessed yet another failure to appreciate his sense of irony, this time in the form of Tony Blair's adoption of "aspirationalism," Young's term for the ideology of meritocracy, as the slogan for his "New Labour" Party. It went on to three successive UK general elections victories.

The paradoxes of Progressivism to which I allude were epitomized in the 1960s by the "Peter Principle," namely, that in practice "rising to one's level of competence" amounts to rising to the level of *incompetence*, the point at which one's achievements permit no further social mobility, which in turn breeds the traditional vices of social stasis, including a form of rentiership, whereby one's position in the hierarchy is used to block other people's advancement.[50] In the following decade, the economist Fred Hirsch generalized this insight as characterizing a "positional good," namely, one whose value is primarily tied to its scarcity.[51] As more people succeed in acquiring more merit in a certain domain, the standard of merit itself starts to erode, creating the need to multiply kinds and levels of merit, typically in the form of extra credentials, which serves to slow personal advancement. In short, the unfettered pursuit of "upward social mobility" turns out to be self-defeating and a source of personal frustration for all concerned. Over the past half century, as Progressivism increasingly divided along "neoliberal" and "social democratic" lines, each has demonized the other for fostering the sort of situation satirized by Young and codified by Peter and Hirsch. Neoliberals take Young's satire to heart as implying that a system originally designed to test and measure people's progress has been converted into an end in itself, whereas social democrats regard the satire as a mean-spirited attempt to undermine such progress altogether. At the heart of these different interpretations is the state's attitude toward those it governs.

Is Power Progressivism's Achilles Heel? A Final Take on Dewey and Lippmann

If Dewey was clearly on the losing side of history, it doesn't follow that Lippmann was clearly on the winning side. Rather, he was a "survivor," more feline than foxy.[52] He definitely understood the arrow of time in a way Dewey did not. Indeed, Lippmann's livelihood depended on hugging the arrow, perhaps like Einstein's famous thought experiment in which he imagined how someone riding a beam of light would experience time. The outcome in both cases is a constant frame of reference relative to which the world is in motion. In Lippmann's case, it allowed him to be the person most consistently involved in crafting America's self-understanding as the vanguard of global progress in the twentieth century; hence, the title of the most comprehensive work on his life, *Walter Lippmann and the American Century*.[53]

A good way to get the measure of the Lippmann/Dewey debate is to examine Frank Knight, doyen of the Chicago school of economics. Knight was a near exact contemporary of Lippmann's, openly avowed the "Progressivism" and "Pragmatism" shared by Lippmann and Dewey, and on several occasions commented on their work.[54] Generally speaking, Knight was respectfully critical of Lippmann but bemused by and sometimes dismissive of

Dewey. And while Knight delivered his judgments many decades ago when the parties were alive, they still stand. Here it is worth revisiting Knight's verdicts on Dewey's and Lippmann's understandings of that pivotal institution of Progressivism, the *state*. I shall cast the difference in terms of two positions in cognitive science: Dewey as *emergentist* and Lippmann as *dualist*.

Dewey claimed that the state derives legitimacy from being some scalable (aka "emergent") version of spontaneously generated forms of social life. Knight expressed great skepticism about this proposition, notwithstanding the Dewey-inspired experiments in deliberative democracy. He alighted on Dewey's frequent use of "transaction" as suggesting that somehow the mutual agreements reached in everyday life (aka "common law") led to the prominence of contracts in modern law. But causality is important here. The original point of contract law was to enable people to deal with potentially threatening strangers under a minimal state-based insurance policy. In this way, the state extended human freedom in a way the individuals themselves would be unlikely to do. Dewey failed to understand that what moderns take for granted as "the rule of law" is not some "evolution" from tradition but requires a specifically empowered agent to bring it into effect and maintain its efficacy. Complementing his obliviousness to the state's need to concentrate power, Dewey equally failed to see that "knowledge" is not simply a combination of techniques that people deploy in a shared environment. It also presupposes spaces for decisions, such as elections, that are not directly tied to people's material exigencies but which nevertheless result in something that transcends those exigencies.[55]

For his part, the "dualist" Lippmann clearly saw the state as manipulating the conditions under which individuals operate (aka "matter"), but it is up to those individuals to decide what to do in light of those manipulations—and then live with their consequences (aka "mind"). He thought about this issue mainly in terms of the ballot box, but obviously to us—not so much to Lippmann—it extends to consumer choice. In cognitive science terms, the state was about "matter" and the individuals about "mind." The relationship between the two is bound to be unpredictable but good governance is about harmonizing them. Lippmann was well aware of the roots of this vision in Plato, but he perhaps did not see how the vision had morphed over the centuries, via the "Occasionalism" of Ockham and Malebranche, and finally to Hobbes's turning Plato effectively on his head. For Hobbes, the question of governance begins not with the right ideas but the right resources with which to govern: how can you pretend to dictate to others if you cannot defend yourself from any potential blowback? Indeed, even if your ideas are wrong the first time, with sufficient material resources you can try again, either when the time is right or when you come up with new ideas; hence the appeal of "permanent revolution" and "experimenting society" to the Progressive imagination. Hobbes's solution was to propose the state as an artificially constructed secular deity that enjoys a monopoly of force in society—that is, the single mind in charge of all the matter.

Max Weber famously made Hobbes's anti-theology the founding principle of his version of "sociology." Knight knew this as the English translator of Weber's *General Economic History*. Weber was among the first generation of German academics to rediscover Hobbes, courtesy of Ferdinand Tönnies's translation of *Leviathan*. Hobbes gave a more concrete sense to the discourses of "power" than had been floating around in the first half of the twentieth century. It was here that Knight questioned Lippmann's political resolve.[56] As we have seen, Lippmann shifted his Progressive allegiance from Roosevelt to Wilson largely in response to Roosevelt's imperialist leanings, which Lippmann believed went against the grain of the American people. However, Knight queried whether the sort of "soft power" that Lippmann favored the state exercising would be sufficient, be it at home or abroad, to truly benefit the target populace. Knight was right insofar as Lippmann was blindsided by the Cold War arms race and, more generally, the rise of globalized liberal interventionism. And perhaps that was because Lippmann failed to fully appreciate Hobbes, the evil demon lurking behind Progressivism's Platonic dreams.

Notes

This text is a highly edited version of a longer piece that will appear as part of a forthcoming book by Steve Fuller, *Media and the Power of Knowledge* (London: Bloomsbury Press), in 2024.

1. Lippmann, *Phantom Public*.
2. Dewey, *Public and Its Problems*.
3. Plehwe, "Introduction," 13.
4. Hofstadter, *Social Darwinism in American Thought*.
5. Jackson, "At the Origins of Neo-Liberalism."
6. Rothschild, *Economic Sentiments*; Voegelin, "Liberalism and Its History."
7. Lippmann, *Cold War*.
8. Thompson, "War Best Served Cold."
9. Klein, *Shock Doctrine*; Slobodian, *Globalists*.
10. Steel, *Walter Lippmann*.
11. Kuklick, *History of Philosophy in America*, chaps. 7–9.
12. Fuller, *Post-Truth*, 88–89.
13. Steffens, "Overworked President."
14. Lippmann and Merz, "Test of the News."

15. Muhlmann, *Political History of Journalism*, 112–34, 229–42.
16. Lippmann, *Men of Destiny*, chap. 16.
17. Jones, *Soviet Concept of "Limited Sovereignty,"* 216.
18. Lippmann, *Drift and Mastery*.
19. Lippmann, *Men of Destiny*, 71.
20. Runciman, *Political Hypocrisy*, chap. 3.
21. Lippmann, *Men of Destiny*, chap. 13.
22. Lippmann, 173.
23. Dewey, *Public and Its Problems*, 195.
24. Cohen, *Science and the Founding Fathers*.
25. Lippmann, *Good Society*.
26. Keith, *Democracy as Discussion*.
27. Wallas, *Great Society*.
28. Lippmann, *Phantom Public*, chap. 7.
29. Bernays, *Propaganda*; Jansen, "Semantic Tyranny"; cf. Fuller, *Post-Truth*, chap. 2.
30. Pappas, "Dewey's Philosophical Approach to Racial Prejudice."
31. Lippmann, *Public Opinion*, 138.
32. Simon, *William James Remembered*, 253.
33. De Mey, *Cognitive Paradigm*, 93.
34. Wallace, "Against the 'Melting Pot' Metaphor."
35. Steel, *Walter Lippmann*, 188.
36. Lippmann, *Public Opinion*, 262.
37. Lippmann, 56.
38. Dewey, *Public and Its Problems*, 96.
39. Fuller, "Transhumanism's Fabian Backstory."
40. Becker, *Human Capital*.
41. Herrnstein and Murray, *Bell Curve*.
42. Conant, *American High School Today*.
43. Scruton, *Meaning of Conservatism*.
44. Campbell, *Methodology and Epistemology for Social Science*, chaps. 10–11.
45. Fuller and Lipińska, *Proactionary Imperative*, 76.
46. Proctor, *Value-Free Science?*, chap. 13.
47. Robbins, *Nature and Significance of Economic Science*.
48. Layard, *Happiness*.
49. Young, *Rise of the Meritocracy*.
50. Peter and Hull, *Peter Principle*.
51. Hirsch, *Social Limits to Growth*.
52. Fuller, *Post-Truth*, introd.
53. Steel, *Walter Lippmann*.
54. Fiorito, "Frank H. Knight."
55. Knight, *Freedom and Reform*, chaps. 2–3.
56. Knight, "Lippmann's *The Good Society*."

Bibliography

Becker, Gary S. *Human Capital*. Chicago: University of Chicago Press, 1964.
Bernays, Edward. *Propaganda*. New York: Horace Liveright, 1928.
Campbell, Donald. *Methodology and Epistemology for Social Science*. Chicago: University of Chicago Press, 1988.

Cohen, I. Bernard. *Science and the Founding Fathers*. New York: Norton, 1995.
Conant, James Bryant. *The American High School Today: A First Report to Interested Citizens*. New York: McGraw Hill, 1959.
De Mey, Marc. *The Cognitive Paradigm*. Dordrecht: Kluwer, 1982.
Dewey, John. *The Public and Its Problems*. New York: Henry Holt, 1927.
Fiorito, Luca. "Frank H. Knight, Pragmatism, and American Institutionalism." *European Journal of the History of Economic Thought* 16, no. 3 (2009): 475–87.
Fuller, Steve. *Post-Truth: Knowledge as a Power Game*. London: Anthem, 2018.
———. "Transhumanism's Fabian Backstory." In *Time, Science and the Critique of Technological Reason: Essays in Honour of Herminio Martins*, edited by Jose Esteban Castro, Bridget Fowler, and Luis Gomes, 191–207. Berlin: Springer, 2018.
Fuller, Steve, and Veronika Lipińska. *The Proactionary Imperative: A Foundation for Transhumanism*. London: Palgrave Macmillan, 2014.
Herrnstein, Richard, and Charles Murray. *The Bell Curve: Intelligence and Class Structure in American Life*. New York: Free Press, 1994.
Hirsch, Fred. *The Social Limits to Growth*. London: Routledge & Kegan Paul, 1977.
Hofstadter, Richard. *Social Darwinism in American Thought, 1860–1915*. Philadelphia: University of Pennsylvania Press, 1944.
Jackson, Ben. "At the Origins of Neo-Liberalism: The Free Economy and the Strong State, 1930–47." *Historical Journal* 53 (2009): 129–51.
Jansen, Sue Curry. "Semantic Tyranny: How Edward L. Bernays Stole Walter Lippmann's Mojo and Got Away with It and Why It Still Matters." *International Journal of Communication* 7 (2013): 1094–11.
Jones, Robert A. *The Soviet Concept of "Limited Sovereignty" from Lenin to Gorbachev*. London: Palgrave Macmillan, 1990.
Keith, William. *Democracy as Discussion: Civic Education and the American Forum Movement*. Lanham, MD: Lexington Books, 2007.
Klein, Naomi. *The Shock Doctrine: The Rise of Disaster Capitalism*. New York: Alfred Knopf, 2007.
Knight, Frank H. *Freedom and Reform: Essays in Economics and Social Philosophy*. New York: Harper, 1947.
———. "Lippmann's *The Good Society*." *Journal of Political Economy* 46 (1938): 864–72.
Kuklick, Bruce. *A History of Philosophy in America, 1720–2000*. Oxford: Oxford University Press, 2001.
Layard, Richard. *Happiness: Lessons from a New Science*. London: Penguin, 2005.
Lippmann, Walter. *The Cold War: A Study in US Foreign Policy*. New York: Harper, 1947.
———. *Drift and Mastery*. New York: Mitchell Kennerley, 1914.
———. *The Good Society*. Boston: Little, Brown, 1937.
———. *Men of Destiny*. New York: Macmillan, 1927.
———. *The Phantom Public*. New York: Macmillan, 1927.
———. *Public Opinion*. New York: Macmillan, 1922.
Lippmann, Walter, and Charles Merz. "A Test of the News." *New Republic*, August 4, 1920.
Muhlmann, Geraldine. *A Political History of Journalism*. Cambridge: Polity Press, 2008.
Pappas, Gregory. "Dewey's Philosophical Approach to Racial Prejudice." *Social Theory and Practice* 22, no. 1 (1996): 47–65.
Peter, Laurence, and Raymond Hull. *The Peter Principle*. New York: William Morrow, 1969.
Plehwe, Dieter. "Introduction." In *The Road from Mont Pèlerin: The Making of the Neoliberal Thought Collective*, edited by Philip Mirowski and Dieter Plehwe, 1–42. Cambridge, MA: Harvard University Press, 2009.

Proctor, Robert N. *Value-Free Science? Purity and Power in Knowledge*. Cambridge MA: Harvard University Press, 1991.
Robbins, Lionel. *The Nature and Significance of Economic Science*. London: Macmillan, 1932.
Rothschild, Emma. *Economic Sentiments*. Cambridge MA: Harvard University Press, 2001.
Runciman, David. *Political Hypocrisy*. Princeton, NJ: Princeton University Press, 2008.
Scruton, Roger. *The Meaning of Conservatism*. London: Palgrave Macmillan, 1980.
Simon, Linda., ed. *William James Remembered*. Lincoln: University of Nebraska Press, 1996.
Slobodian, Quinn. *Globalists: The End of Empire and the Birth of Neoliberalism*. Cambridge MA: Harvard University Press, 2018.
Steel, Ronald. *Walter Lippmann and the American Century*. Boston: Little, Brown, 1980.
Steffens, Lincoln. "The Overworked President." *McClure's*, April 1902.
Thompson, Nicholas. "A War Best Served Cold." *New York Times*, July 31, 2007.
Voegelin, Eric. "Liberalism and Its History." *Review of Politics* 35 (1974): 504–20.
Wallace, Mike. "Against the 'Melting Pot' Metaphor." *Literary Hub*, October 30, 2017. https://lithub.com/against-the-melting-pot-metaphor/.
Wallas, Graham. *The Great Society: A Psychological Analysis*. New York: Macmillan, 1914.
Young, Michael Dunlop. *The Rise of the Meritocracy*. London: Penguin, 1958.

7

PROPAEDEUTIC RHETORICAL CITIZENSHIP:
DEWEYAN IMPULSES IN DANISH
COMMUNITY-BUILDING

Lisa S. Villadsen

Contemporary readers of John Dewey's grim characterization of the eclipse of the public—distrust of politicians, widespread technocracy, PR staff masking and distorting facts, et cetera—are often struck by how it seems as apt a description of the current political landscape as what he saw almost a century ago. A similar troubling resonance holds for Dewey's comments on what characterizes community-oriented communication at the interpersonal level. Writes Dewey, "The political elements in the constitution of the human being, those having to do with citizenship, are crowded to one side. In most circles it is hard work to sustain conversation on a political theme; once initiated, it is quickly dismissed with a yawn." Arguably, overactive, aggressive political exchanges on social media constitute a significant (but no less lamentable) contemporary exception to the nonengagement described by Dewey. Yet few would disagree that dysfunction of the public sphere—be it in the shape of disintegration, fragmentation, polarization, incivility, or disengagement—is a central challenge to the health of democracies. In other words, Dewey's identification of *the* problem of the public as the need for an "improvement of the methods and conditions of debate, discussion, and persuasion" remains a pressing challenge.[1]

The current swell of populism around the world has left pundits and scholars discouraged and nonplussed over how populists in many countries succeed with projecting a particular non-inclusive national identity and collective purpose for "the people" of their countries. Lack of experience with robust democratic culture is often cited as one enabling condition explaining the rise of populism as it is linked to nationalism. This was a concern that also occupied Dewey and Lippmann, and it is tempting to see this situation as confirmation of Lippmann's point that "the democratic fallacy" consists in "failing to admit that self-centered opinions are not sufficient to produce good government." But whereas Lippmann found "the crucial interest" to be with how power is exercised because citizens "cannot . . . inspire or guide all these acts [of public officials. LSV], as the mystical democrat has always imagined," Dewey seconded the view of another contemporary, Samuel J. Tilden, that the means by which a majority comes to be so is a far more important matter than the outcome of a democratic vote.[2] In the midst of what seemed to be a time of societal disintegration Dewey thus suggested that more attention be spent on the communicative processes undergirding public and political life. While election outcomes of course are important and indicative of some aspects of the views of the voting populace, Dewey was interested in the ways people come to understand themselves as interconnected and as making up a civic collective—in other words, how they come to see themselves as *a public*. By calling for "methods and conditions of debate, discussion and persuasion," Dewey pointed to *process* as crucial to the creation of a sense of commonality conducive to democratic results. Dewey did not, however, specify what communicative practices he envisioned. This means that we cannot find examples of communicative formats that can be considered direct outcomes of his influence.

The good news is that we can find examples of activities that share and enact Deweyan ideas and ideals, and that social scientists working with deliberative democracy find that citizens are both willing and able to engage in constructive civic conversations and political deliberation, especially when provided with a framework to insure diversity and civility norms. Based on multiple studies scholars including political scientist John Dryzek call for the creation of "venues that are not simply another form of engagement for the elite. They argue that "such forms of communication may be more available to those not used to arguing in more formal terms." Their research shows that societally significant discursive interaction can involve "not just abstract argument but also storytelling and other modes of communication based on personal experience," and they concede that "rhetoric, once dismissed as the opposite of reason, can find a productive place in deliberation by engaging listeners."[3]

In this chapter I explore this claim and suggest that rhetorical thinking and practice can provide a link between Dewey's foresightful call for improved methods of debate and the facilitation of deliberative forums and public debate. Unlike Dryzek et alia, who approach public debate quantitatively and tend to study large scale events, I focus on a small-scale project to consider ways of facilitating better public engagement at the level of interpersonal emergence. A case study of two activities initiated by a community project called "Civic Desire" allows me to illustrate how thoughtful frame-setting can not only lower the threshold keeping citizens from engaging in community-oriented conversations with strangers, but also nurture their experience of being competent to do so along with making it a pleasant experience. This I call *propaedeutic rhetorical citizenship*, and I submit this concept as a contemporary supplement to Dewey's project of fostering better contact between citizens for the general purpose of strengthening the democratic society.

Dewey Among Rhetoricians

Among the several academic fields that have found inspiration from Dewey is rhetoric. Rhetoric's disciplinary history is integrally linked to the emergence of democracy, and it has a long tradition of integrating theory and practice, making it particularly well positioned to take on the Deweyan challenge to conceptualize communicative practice as community-building. Beginning in the late 1960s Dewey grew in importance as a source of inspiration for rhetoric scholars and of rhetorical didactics in America and beyond.[4] For the purposes of this chapter, Dewey's influence on the research field concerned with public sphere studies and rhetorical citizenship studies is particularly interesting.[5]

A simplified narrative of this influence starts with Lloyd F. Bitzer, whose commitment to theorizing public rhetoric's role in the creation of public knowledge drew on Dewey's work. Bitzer thus noted Dewey's expansive approach that "permits a plurality of publics, existing simultaneously in regions, sometimes overlapping in memberships, and changing or generating anew under fresh or different circumstances in the same or in different places." Dewey's view that there is "no public-in-the-abstract: publics are real, concrete entities comprised of people experiencing; and publics which alter in composition and nature according to the circumstances of their historic contexts" resonated with Bitzer's own view of rhetoric as situational and a contextually relevant resource for community-building. To Bitzer, Dewey's analysis recognized the significance of rhetorical communication in the formation of publics and as holding the potential to "enrich the public's information, sustain its experiential knowledge, and provide modes of debate and discussion needed for intelligent decision and action."[6]

Bitzer's Dewey-inspired theorizing of public life as rhetorically constituted influenced many of his students, among them Gerard Hauser. His interest in vernacular rhetoric—the interchange between "ordinary" people about shared concerns, and how their sense of a common understanding and sense of belonging with others feeds into public opinion formation—shaped his conceptualization of the reticulate public sphere. Hauser's work on vernacular rhetoric is a central source of inspiration for the discussion in this chapter because it takes Dewey's project one step further in the pursuit of theorizing discursive formats suitable for community-building and public opinion formation. Commenting on the Deweyan project, Hauser and his coauthor Chantal Benoit-Barné thus noted that "before we can have a productive civic conversation with difference, as Dewey envisioned, we first must overcome the menace of difference that provokes distrust and the antidemocratic rhetoric of intolerance, or cynicism and withdrawal from the political process. For democracy to be a functional form of governance in a society of strangers, citizens must learn how to engage difference in a way that recognizes the individual and the group as a subject."[7]

The building of such reticulate vernacular communities remains, as in Dewey's time, difficult. With the fragmentation of contemporary society into socially and politically defined subgroups who often do not share the same news sources and in some cases barely recognize the same facts, citizens have few opportunities and perhaps insufficient incentive to discuss their many differences in pursuit of common understanding and solutions. With Maria T. Hegbloom, Hauser thus identified as the greatest challenge in achieving "coordinated social action" that the individuals and groups who would be its agents are, in many respects, "strangers." In their attempt to conceptualize possibilities for public deliberation, the two authors point to three issues as central to establishing viable conditions for public deliberation: building trust in the form of mutual accountability; recognizing the necessity of rhetorical competence among ordinary citizens; and valorizing deliberative processes rather than focusing on outcome.[8]

More recently, rhetorical scholar Robert Asen has drawn inspiration from Dewey to theorize multiple publics and modes of civic engagement.[9] Robert Danisch's important work on rhetorical pragmatism stands as the most systematic revitalization of Dewey's thinking in the field.[10] Emerging at the same time, but drawing also on rhetorical scholars and on political theorists like Mouffe, Dryzek and Goodin, work by Christian Kock and myself has brought theoretical, critical, and practical issues together in the concept of rhetorical citizenship.[11]

Rhetorical scholarship thus suggests that John Dewey's ideas about what it would take to mitigate problems in the public life of democracies are alive and relevant to contemporary efforts to diversify the discursive ecology at the societal level, and also that considering such initiatives from a rhetorical perspective may help foster practice-oriented responses to Dewey's ideas. In this vein, we turn to two examples of communicative practices that I argue constitute a Deweyan perspective and which rhetorical theory can help explain. But first a few contextualizing comments.

Dewey Among Danes

It is almost impossible to exaggerate Dewey's influence on the Danish pedagogical tradition. His thoughts and ideas have influenced Danish educational thinking to such a degree that Denmark has been called his second home.[12] But also in a wider sense may Dewey's thoughts on how to build a healthy community be said to be ingrained in the Danish ethos, in part because they overlap on significant points with Danish theologian Hal Koch's notion of "conversation democracy" (*samtaledemokrati*). In a 1945 newspaper article, Koch wrote, "This is democracy. It is the conversation (the dialogue) and the mutual understanding and respect that are democracy's nature. . . . Democracy is far more extensive than a particular societal form of rule. It is a form of life that applies to all conditions where people interact."[13] Koch and Dewey were thus aligned in considering the interaction between citizens *as citizens* as crucial to the health of democracy. Koch may at times block the view to Dewey's influence on Danish society outside of the field of education, but the latter's views on what makes a democracy and how it is maintained are integrated in the Danish approach. While the project we now turn to thus may have a special resonance in the Danish society, its core principles and formats may be lifted to any democratic political setting.

Civic Desire: A Social Laboratory

Founded by Nadja Pass, an independent publicist and consultant with a master's degree in rhetoric, and anthropologist Andreas Lloyd in Copenhagen, Denmark, in 2010, "Civic Desire" (*Borgerlyst*) was an informal and nonprofit, nonpolitical, open source community.[14] Described by the founders as a "societal lab," Civic Desire experimented with bringing citizens together to foster and strengthen the appetite for community involvement independent of formal organizations or political parties under the slogan "to make it easier and more fun to use one's agency in everyday life."[15] The name, Civic Desire, plays on the more common notion of "civic duty" to suggest the possibility of voluntary and pleasurable civic engagement. During its active period, the network arranged numerous meetings and events around the country and as far away as Finland and the Faroe Islands; was featured several times at the "People's Meeting" (*Folkemødet*) (a large open air festival dedicated to political life and democracy); published three books including a "project biography" and a handbook on how to arrange conversation salons;[16] and was invited to exhibit at the Danish Architectural Center's 2015 exhibition "Cocreate Your City" (*Fællesskab din by*),[17] where it hosted a workshop for developing ideas on how to collectively improve urban spaces.[18]

Civic Desire clearly was a project aimed at creating social innovation with an eye to action and change, but my focus here will be on two particular initiatives whose function I see as something prior to actual civic action, namely the formats the "Conversation Salon" (*Samtalesalon*) and the "People's Election/Choice" (*Folkets valg*). I offer them as suggestions for Dewey's call for "improvement of the methods and conditions of debate, discussion, and persuasion."

In order to explore the relation between rhetorical frame setting and the formation of publics, I analyze the Conversation Salon as a communicative format. A Conversation Salon is a free event, open to anyone. It is held in public or semipublic spaces (city squares, parks, cafés, libraries) and typically lasts two hours. The format rests on five principles: uninterrupted time for conversing; meeting people who are not like oneself; a set framework; everyone speaks and speaks with everyone; anyone is an interesting conversation partner.[19] A Conversation Salon always has a host, and anyone can be a host. The founders of Civic Desire devised and described the framework and made it available for free on their website for anyone looking for inspiration and guidelines.[20] The host decides the theme for the salon and announces it in a shareable invitation (e.g., via Facebook). At the time of the salon, the host is responsible for facilitating various conversation "exercises" where participants are paired and offered different formats for addressing the theme in various constellations of "guests" (as participants are called). Each exercise is allotted a specified amount of time (e.g., five or ten minutes). The host keeps the time and directs the participants on what to do for each exercise. Most exercises are designed to give guests the experience of speaking with one or several other participants on one or more pre-defined questions. For example, one exercise is called the "Conversation Quadrille" and, like in the dance giving it its name, four guests circulate among one another according to a plan, allowing each guest to meet others in conversations taking their starting point in the prompts provided by the host. For the first round, the question is relatively simple and easy to talk about. With each following round, where the participants meet new conversation partners, the questions build on the previous ones and become more complex. Each conversation round lasts five to seven minutes. Since everyone has been talking about the same questions, the fact that one changes conversation partners does not stand in the way of a sense of an ongoing and increasingly reflective conversation unfolding.

Another format is the "Stance Barometer." The host presents a pointedly phrased normative statement on the theme chosen for the salon, such as "Habits are poisonous to creativity," "Age defines who you are," or "True heroes don't exist anymore." Guests are then asked to arrange themselves along an invisible spectrum with "completely agree" at one end and "completely disagree" at the other. Once in place, random participants are asked to explain why they chose the position they did. Other participants are free to change their position on the spectrum as they listen to these rationales and may find reason to review their own initial stance. They may be asked to share their reasons for this change of mind, which then may prompt yet other participants to rethink their position. Exercises like the two just described may or may not be used by the host (there are many other formats to choose between), but one format is always used: the "Conversation Menu." After several shorter "warm-up" exercises, this one takes longer, thirty minutes, and is designed to allow guests to immerse themselves in a conversation with a stranger. Guests are paired and given a "menu." These are nicely designed, good quality paper cards with six or seven printed questions all related to the theme of the salon. For a Conversation Salon on the topic of dreams, menu questions thus included: "Do you share your dreams with others? And do they believe them?"; "Why are your dreams so boring?"; "Which dream have you given up?" A menu for a salon on the topic of agency included questions such as "When did you last think 'Somebody ought to do something'?"; "When did you last feel that you made a difference?" For a salon on the topic of systems, menu questions included: "Which systems work so well you don't notice them?"; "Share an experience where two systems clashed"; "Which systems would you like to change?" As these examples illustrate, both themes and questions allow for more or less literal interpretations and invite answers and reflections that link personal experience with aspects of collective life. Some are quite open; some are deliberately presumptive in order to provoke thought and perhaps counterstatement. Guests are asked to pick and choose among the questions—as if ordering à la carte—and thus shape their conversation as they prefer. They are also encouraged to take the menu home and at a later time engage someone who did not participate in the salon.

A Conversation Salon does not involve reporting back to the host or to other participants about the content of the individual conversations, and it does not aim at reaching consensus or a common decision. The point is for participants to immerse themselves in a reflective exchange about common concerns with a stranger. The rationale behind having a host who decides the theme and introduces a series of activities is that it allows participants to focus on the designated topic (to prevent falling back on small talk topics such as vacation plans). Second, the fact that each conversation lasts only five to thirty minutes and is prescribed by the host relieves participants of certain social responsibilities and anxieties (such as how to keep the conversation with a stranger going), allowing them to focus on the moment and the content of the conversation they are having. Finally, the very structured format is meant to create a "bubble" where the conversation theme is in focus and participants' political orientation, occupation, and socioeconomic life situation bracketed. Not knowing anything about one's conversation partner other than their name (and what meets the eye) is meant to transcend the differences that can create hierarchy or distance (e.g., preconceived notions about people who live in a particular place or have a certain education or occupation) and foster conversations that sidestep the "noise" of social prejudice and facilitate a more immediate meeting of minds.[21]

My second example from Civic Desire links the vernacular conversations that are at the project's core more explicitly to civic life and politics. When the Danish prime minister called for a general election (*folketingsvalg*) in August 2011, Civic Desire launched the "People's Choice/Election" (*Folkets valg*)[22] to run parallel with the election campaign (which in Denmark typically runs for three or four weeks). Election campaigns in Denmark resemble those in other Western democracies in being characterized by massive media coverage of party leaders "dueling" with statistics and political technicalities that most people have no way of understanding or assessing. Since the ordinary voter cannot know if one statistic is more accurate than the other, or whether a particular anecdote is representative of a widespread societal problem or not, election campaigns rarely foster political reflection, let alone informed discussion, among voters. The People's Choice was intended to encourage more peer-to-peer interaction about societal issues relevant at election time, thus allowing participants a more active role than just watching a televised debate. Civic Desire sent subscribers a text message on their mobile phone every day at 11:00 a.m. The message was a question to prompt reflection and lunchtime conversations with coworkers or friends about politics, democracy, and the choices and actions citizens perform in their everyday lives and how these choices relate to the one choice voters make on election day. The questions functioned as an invitation to set one's own agenda; it could be political and eventually tie into questions of which party or candidate to vote for, but it could also remain at a more basic level of reflection about one's place and participation in society.

As with the Conversation Salons, the questions were formulated in an open-ended manner. Some were more metaphorical than others, allowing interlocutors to enter the conversation at the level they were comfortable with. Although the questions asked about people's own lives, they were still general enough to not force private divulging. Instead, by means of metaphor and generality, they offered a segue from small talk into issues of societal import where everyone could participate without having the facts about the GDP or unemployment rates. Some questions were deliberately phrased as presupposing something and thus had a slightly provocative tone such as "Why don't you get more involved?"; "How present are you really?" (about being in the moment, resisting pressure to ever increase effectiveness); "What possibilities have you ruled out?"; "What do you form an opinion on?"; "When did you get so picky?" (about holding on to old opinions and shirking conversations with people with different views); "How close do you have to be to feel responsibility?"; and "What are you willing to renounce on?" (about prioritization of public funds).[23] This campaign in a sense decentralized the concept of the Conversation Salon; if just one person at the workplace lunch table had received a question or seen it on Facebook there was the basis for a spontaneous civically oriented interaction with others.

While the People's Choice only ran once, the concept of Conversation Salons has by far been the most successful among Civic Desire's initiatives. The format has been adopted by public agencies and institutions, including municipal government, libraries, schools, and cultural institutions; private organizations and NGOs have used it for conferences and meetings. Private citizens continue to host salons, for example, on Constitution Day.

Why All the Questions?

Conversation-prompting questions are a key element to both formats described here. Pass and Lloyd explain the community-building potential baked into the questions using the metaphor of a "macroscope" to suggest how the conversations among participants are designed to start on a close, personal level, but are tailored to lead to a *meso* level concerning "the common," with perspectives to the *macro* level of "the distant." Questions are mostly phrased directly, such as "When are you open to changing your habits?" or generally, such as "Why is enthusiasm contagious?" This approach builds on an acknowledgment of a concern shared by both Dewey and Lippmann: the feeling of remoteness, perhaps even irrelevance, of larger societal issues as a major obstacle for the individual citizen's interest in participating actively in public debate and the solution of societal problems. In her work on Lippmann as Dewey's "indispensable opposition," Goodwin reminds us of how the difference between the two thinkers has been exaggerated, and she identifies their common starting point, namely that "for both men, the central problem facing democracy in the Great Society was epistemic: the inability of ordinary citizens to know the world in which they had to act." Where they differ, however, is on the nature of the knowledge required. Whereas Lippmann insisted on the desirability of expert knowledge as guiding in the solution of public issues, Dewey was more optimistic regarding the prospects of the more democratic participation. Writes Goodwin, "Knowledge for Dewey is not an individual accomplishment but a social one; through participating in any of the forms of activity made available through the organization of society, each person gains the accumulated knowledge 'embodied' in it."[24] Civic Desire as a whole is a framework for bringing strangers together to "find" social meaning and begin to engage each other with the ultimate ambition of cocreating civic initiatives. What makes Civic Desire different from other community projects is that it neither assumes familiarity (or even comfort) with civic engagement in participants, nor "pushes" participants into preset projects, but facilitates a bottom-up process allowing people to reflect on their own particular take on societal issues and in that process meet others and with them begin to formulate shared concerns. This double process of emergence (as an individual with an eye for the larger context, and as fellow community members) is propelled by particular kinds of questions by which the would-be public comes to know itself. Common to most questions is that they provide a bridge from personal grounding to matters central to civic life: how people understand their own place in society, how they define their community, what their values are, and how they would like to prioritize time, values, public funds, et cetera.

Civic Desire: Fostering Peer-to-Peer Interaction and More

The examples of communicative formats from Civic Desire may seem anecdotal and inconsequential. Indeed, the two formats I have described here are small-scale and only have tangential connections to political life. This is precisely the reason I draw attention to them. I wish to suggest that they represent a contemporary response to the Deweyan challenge of finding ways to facilitate interaction among people with the aim of increasing their sense of being interconnected and forming a public. Particular to Dewey's thinking on democracy is that it exits and extends beyond political institutions. Hence, the groundwork for political judgment begins at a prior point, in smaller, informal, local settings. Explains Dewey, "The chances of regard for distant peoples being effective as long as there is no close neighborhood experience to bring with it, insight and understanding of neighbors do not seem better. . . . Democracy must begin at home, and its home is the neighborly community."[25] We find similar views in Hauser and Benoit-Barné's description of internal and emergent public spheres as "arenas in which members enact horizontal relations of equality and develop deliberative competencies through consideration of issues that have internal and external significance for their association and the networks in which they are involved. These arenas are rhetorical constructions; they emerge from member practices by which they develop not only the voice necessary to participate in deliberative democracy but the social capital to participate in such deliberations with a trustworthy voice."[26]

Civic Desire allows people to meet and have exchanges with other citizens who differ from themselves in age, gender, education, employment, interests, values, et cetera. This sharing of experiences, values, and beliefs with people who do or do not share one's own is an effective way of creating awareness that, in spite of differences, one's life conditions overlap with others' so much so that it makes sense to think of them as communal issues. Conversation partners may not agree, but with no pressure to reach a conclusion or come up with a suggestion the format allows them to focus on learning about each other's situation or understanding each other's viewpoints (rather than waiting for a chance to try to change their minds as is common in political discussions). Salons also provide an opportunity to reflect on and formulate one's own views in a context where one's underlying values and assumptions come to the fore.

Internal Goods and the Role of Aesthetics in Civic Desire

Just one glance at its webpage suggests that aesthetics is a clear priority in the Civic Desire project.[27] The multicolored patchwork graphic and hand-drawn illustrations not only suggest that care has been put into the visual identity of the project, but also underscore the values imbuing it: being together in diversity, ingenuity, a personal touch, making an effort. In my descriptions of the Conversation Salons I have hinted at how aesthetics also plays a central role here, for example, in the well-designed and specially printed conversation "menus." My own experience as a participant in a number of Conversation Salons also includes observations of an attention to aesthetic details that feed into the salon topic. For example, at a salon on the subject of roles held around the time of the Danish holiday tradition Fastelavn (Shrovetide) (where children according to custom dress up in costumes, decorate carnival rods with colorful paper figures and ribbons, and go "trick or treating"), the host, dressed up in a colorful hat, greeted arriving guests and handed out "warm-up" questions written on colorful pieces of paper cut out in different shapes and sizes. But even at a more general level the salons reflect and inspire paying attention to the way participants engage in conversation as a mode of reflection that links the individual with the collective. The use of metaphor in salon themes, the playful phrasing of some of the questions on the menus, and the elaborate choreography of the various conversation exercises all contribute to fostering the sense that what happens at the salon is important and therefore deserves attention and care by all. This attention to manner underscores that speaking with others is valuable and that one honors that best by taking on the responsibility to speak and listen in ways that are both expressive and respectful. In his book *John Dewey and the Artful Life*, American rhetorician Scott Stroud writes about Dewey's perspective on how our everyday experience can be made more aesthetic. He argues that Dewey's thoughts on the importance of an aesthetics of communication have largely been overlooked, but that Dewey's pragmatism offers a basis for improving also seemingly mundane activities, including vernacular communication, in ways that are both morally and socially significant. Stroud quotes Dewey at length on the view that communication is both a means to an end and an end in itself as the basis for his own interpretation that "the process of communication is the end of communicating—individuals attentively responding to each other and the situation in such a way as to truly instantiate a community of interacting beings."[28] Stroud's contribution to previous work on Dewey's recognition of the connection of art and communication lies in his focus on the *manner* of engagement or, in Stroud's terms, *orientation*, of the individual, and he links this to Dewey's pragmatic project of meliorism. Stroud suggests attending to the present communicative interaction itself, cultivating habits of responding to the demands of the present communicative situation, and not focusing too much attention on the idea of a reified, separate self as three ways to improve one's communicative activities.[29] Stroud's project of developing Dewey's ideas about communication and its community-building function is one more reason to study Civic Desire as an initiative to foster community feeling and engagement. His work suggests that Civic Desire's attention to creating an aesthetically pleasing framework for citizens interested in engaging others about communal concerns can be seen as a practical instantiation of some of Dewey's more abstract ideas about the value of considering communication as also an aesthetic practice and an orientation of mindfulness as the most fruitful manner by which to approach communal argument.[30]

A related way of theorizing the potential value of initiatives such as Civic Desire is to consider its formats as the kinds of practice that bring both internal and external goods. Civic Desire has, according to the founders, on numerous occasions brought people together who decided to collaborate on a community project and in this sense achieved external goods. Here, I am more interested in the project's potential *internal* goods because I believe that understanding them will allow us to better appreciate some of the elements of communicative settings that may be useful in achieving Dewey's vision of better ways for the public to communicate. In their volume on Dewey's influence on rhetoric and democratic practice Brian Jackson and Gregory Clark refer to Alasdair McIntyre's distinction between the "extrinsic" and "internal" goods of certain practices, and they use this as a framework for addressing what they see as a key intuition with Dewey, namely that communicative practice has value in itself, as a practice, not just in ways related to skill, but also by way of attitudinal development. They thus remark, "Rhetorical practice also establishes, and emerges from, the 'goods internal' to democratic practice, such as the values, attitudes, habits, and behaviors that serve as the normative forces behind practice."[31] I develop this line of thinking in what I call the propaedeutic quality of Civic Desire.

Propaedeutic Rhetorical Citizenship

I offer Civic Desire and the two particular formats mentioned as examples of propaedeutic rhetorical citizenship and as such also as models for one way to pursue the Deweyan program of developing new ways for citizens to communicate in ways that support community-building. In what follows I lay out the theoretical basis for my claim and the arguments for the potential value to contemporary political debate culture of the Civic Desire project.

As mentioned above, the work of Gerard Hauser carries several of John Dewey's ideas into the field of rhetoric. Where Dewey wrote about communication among "ordinary people," the public as forming a cohesive unit, and the social connections tying society together, Hauser addresses similar issues in the terms *vernacular rhetoric, reticulate public spheres*, and *trust*.

Hauser's 1999 book *Vernacular Voices: The Rhetoric and Publics and Public Spheres* can be seen as a rhetoric-based response to Dewey in virtue of its focus on discursive interactions among the ordinary people that make up "the public." The project explores "the prospects for recovering awareness of our own discursive practices and their possibilities for shaping our public lives as citizens, neighbors, and cultural agents." Hauser's work contributed to an understanding of mundane rhetorical exchanges as significant to society by studying them as a way that "publics make their presences known" in what he calls the "reticulate" (network-like, interlaced) public sphere and recognizing them as "integral to civil society's continuous activity of self-regulation."[32] *Vernacular rhetoric* refers to informal and spontaneous public discourse among citizens, and Hauser's claim is that this type of interaction constitutes people in reticulate public spheres that are connected by shared concerns and interests, are constituted via common activities and never stabilized. Similar to Dewey's views on the importance of continuous communicative contact among citizens, Hauser's claim is that everyday discursive interactions are central to people's understanding of their own place in society and in the forming of their views as they meet, divert, or bend toward those of others in a collective interpretation of common concerns and societal interests. And similar to Dewey's, Hauser's definition of publics places discursive behavior at the center. He contends that "publics are emergences manifested through vernacular rhetoric" and suggests that "the rhetorical antecedents of publics influence the manner in which communicative acts occur, the relationships among public actors including those who are disempowered by institutional authority, the relationships between and among rhetors and their audiences, and the state of being shared by social actors who are co-creating meaning."[33] The conversational interactions of civil society are an arena for meeting citizens with different views and values. Such meetings are characterized by a certain measure of social risk, but by learning how to engage strangers in ways that build on mutual trust one can gain the social capital necessary to have both vernacular and institutionalized dialogue. Trust can grow from positive experiences with interactions in civil society. The rhetorical character of such encounters in turn fosters communicative competences (speaking, listening, interacting with views different from one's own and sharing reasons and motivations), and together this may result in rhetorical agency understood as a synthesis of inhabiting a trustworthy speaking position and a "voice," and possessing the communicative skills to make one's ideas matter to others.

Dewey underscores that publics are not pre-given but rather *emerge* through the discursive processes of those who participate as interlocutors in a wide range of informal expressions of their views on common issues. And if a public sphere can also be defined, as Hauser maintains, as "a discursive space in which individuals and groups associate to discuss matters of mutual interest and, where possible, to reach a common judgment about them" and as a "locus of emergence of rhetorically salient meanings,"[34] it seems that Civic Desire—albeit an intermittent, event-based community with no declared agenda—may be considered one element in a reticulate public sphere of citizens recognizing themselves and others as connected and as sharing a role in the shaping the life of the community. This is the essence of rhetorical citizenship.

As the scholarly focus of recent decades has been on how deliberation in democracies should function, less has been done in the way of helping us understand how it actually works or might work better. In Christian Kock's and my work on rhetorical citizenship we follow Dewey, Hauser, and Asen in understanding citizenship as in large part rhetorically constituted and enacted. It is in discursive exchanges that decisions are made, but also more fundamental elements such as communal norms and social knowledge emerge and are shaped in the rhetorical interactions between citizens.[35] With the concept of rhetorical citizenship we bring together two strands of thinking, namely the notion of rhetorical agency and the notion of public deliberation from the point of view of the citizen. Both pivot on the individual and their possibilities for engaging in the discursive life of the community. They are united in the critical efforts to identify ways for ordinary citizens to feel a part of public opinion and be motivated to share their views with others, be it via informal conversations, traditional formats such as letters to the editor, or as listeners. This focus on the individual's "entry qualifications," that is, skills and means for engaging public debate (be it as an anonymous listener or viewer, an interlocutor in a social or semipublic conversation, or a speaker to an audience), may seem myopic or disconnected from the fora where social change really happens. But it is where it starts.

No one is born a rhetor. Most people are hesitant about raising their voice in a crowd or among strangers. Even if people are interested in public life and follow politics, most opt out of participating actively themselves. Whether the practice of posting political comments on social media is an exception to this, or rather a confirmation that most people do not seek out direct person to person interaction on political matters and (even if they are passionately interested in an issue) prefer to comment online, is beyond the scope of this project to answer. Either way, it seems safe to claim that the general experience with online political discussion is less than positive, and this form of interaction remains unattractive to most people due to the aggressive tone that often characterizes it. As for reluctance to engage in political discussion with people outside of one's immediate circle of acquaintances the reasons for this are no doubt multiple but may have to do with social concerns such as lack of confidence in one's ability to stand one's ground and the wish to avoid confrontations and potential social conflict.

Propaedeutics means an introductory course. It is teaching and exercises designed to prepare a student to follow a course that requires certain prerequisites. Civic Desire is not a course, nor is participation in deliberative democracy, but the comparison to propaedeutics can help explain how Conversation Salons can be preparatory for taking on the role of a rhetorical citizen. They can function as a training ground for the rhetorical skills useful to someone participating in public debate. The questions participants are asked to prompt their conversations provide exemplars of the rhetorical canon of invention: discovering ways to talk about a particular topic, and the various exercises provide training in giving expression to one's thoughts, experience with presenting and explaining one's views to strangers, learning about theirs, and noticing different approaches to shared or different purposes. This experience of observing oneself as a holder of views about communal issues and as one to whom others listen is a basic rhetorical experience of having agency and as such one prone to foster a desire to enter more change-oriented community activities and to provide input to political life.

The propaedeutic function also works at a collective level. Civic Desire participants become involved in what Rosa Eberly calls "proto-publics."[36] The experience of finding oneself engaged in shared reflections on issues related to civic life can demonstrate to the individual that they can be part of something larger than themselves. In her description of the significance of rhetorical interaction in a group, Eberly makes the philological point that in ancient Greek, the medial voice of the verb *politeuein* (to be a citizen) is *politeuesthai*, which means something to the effect of "being citizens together." This particular grammatical form enables the expression that a particular action is shared, is done together. Eberly's point is that it is this "collaborative and collective nature of listening and speaking, reading and writing that remains central to the possibility of practicing participatory democracy."[37] The physical experience of "doing society" together is crucial to the fostering of a desire for future deliberative engagement.

By providing an explorative and nonbinding setting for individuals to share, test, and possibly revise their personal, social, and political thoughts and perceptions, Civic Desire's Conversation Salons and the People's Choice serve a double propaedutic purpose from the point of view of rhetorical citizenship. They both cultivate a sense in the individual of being part of something greater than just their own life, as being part of a community or society where their views are listened to with respect and interest, and they offer an opportunity to develop or practice skills useful for the role of the citizen: listening to others, presenting one's own thoughts, reflecting on ideas together with others.

The Relevance of a Case Study

Lippman and Dewey shared a concern about the scalability of democratic processes, and the question remains if this study has anything to contribute to this matter. This chapter has taken a primarily Deweyan approach in the examination of a grassroots project. It has presented a few examples of communicative formats that take place on a small scale and with no direct link to the political life of the community. The claim is not that these formats offer a blueprint for organization of more large-scale democratic engagement. The overall suggestion has been that if we follow Dewey in believing that we need better methods and conditions of debate, discussion, and persuasion we stand to benefit if we also consider even informal formats, not least as inspiration for how to facilitate better public dialogue and deliberation. As mentioned above, social scientists are confident that "careful institutional design—involving participant diversity, facilitation, and civility norms—enables well-known problematic psychological biases and dynamics to attenuate or disappear" and that "a major improvement to the deliberative system would involve enhancing moments and sites of listening and reflection and integrating these into political processes that are currently overwhelmed by a surfeit of expression."[38] I offer the principles and ideas behind Civic Desire as one answer to the question of how to begin to provide such design and to "enhancing moments and sites of listening and reflection" suitable for initiating democratic processes of civic engagement.

Rhetoric has practical purchase on issues of civic discourse. At a time of contentious and polarizing politics such as ours, it is particularly important that frustrated citizens do not turn away from public discourse. American political scientist Diana Mutz found that "crosscutting" communication is wanting, and that especially those who are most politically engaged and active have little of it. In the conclusion of the book *Hearing the Other Side* she calls for norms and instruction regarding the "civil" handling of political disagreement in dialogue, since civility, she argues, will induce more people to communicate across disagreement and allow them to find more benefit in it. Such dialogue might focus on what disagreeing individuals, from their conflicting vantage points, believe would be best for the "common good," that is, for the polity of which they are all citizens.[39] A rhetorical approach to citizenship acknowledges deep differences as givens in any polity, pointing at the same time to the necessity of reflective communication *about* such differences and *across* them. As a rhetorical praxis, the Civic Desire activities take their point of departure in formats staged to invite individuals into conversations with other people in ways that bracket the differences that might stand in the way of sharing one's thoughts. It thus represents a creative approach to the issue of fostering trust between strangers entering into dialogue with one another and thus seems one possible answer to Dewey's call for new methods of communication among "ordinary" people.

Conclusion

Civic Desire offers formats for citizens to develop themselves as citizens in dialogue with others. I have underscored the absence of expectations to participants in terms of prior knowledge, experience with public speaking, or concrete ideas about how to start a community project, and the delicate balance between the existential nature of some of the questions combined with meandering and non-extended forms of conversation. While this opens the salons to criticism of being just a different kind of social pastime, I attribute significance to these traits as enabling inclusion and involvement, not only because the setting is made as unintimidating as possible, but also because it functions as a training ground for rhetorical citizenship for participants. It invites participants to come to think of themselves as citizens and part of a greater whole and not just as private individuals surrounded by a society. This has less to do with the themes chosen than with the experience of *participating*.

Civic Desire is propaedeutic in the sense that participants may acquire and practice certain skills useful in public life. The Conversation Salons offer participants the embodied experience of having rhetorical agency in terms of both the opportunity to see oneself as occupying a legitimate speaking position and practicing speaking with strangers and narrating, explaining, and even making arguments. Such experience with rhetorical interaction can be what some people need before they venture into community projects. For others it may not lead to specific action but may strengthen their sense of belonging and commitment to the community and make them more prone to share their views in other settings, thus contributing to an ongoing strengthening of the rhetorical culture of the civic community.

This experience is also propaedeutic in a sense that Dewey seemed to have in mind when he called for new methods of dialogue and discussion. My suggestion is that rhetorical theory supplements his ideas and goes one step further in being concrete. Civic Desire activities are suitable for fostering what Eberly calls a proto-public because participants in a Conversation Salon become involved in formulating values and forming opinions in a public setting.[40] Such exchanges can foster what Hauser calls "thick moral vernaculars" and represent a richer and more democratic public opinion because such rhetorical praxis "can shift social understandings, reorder society's sense of priority and imperative, and redirect social energies into new channels of relationship and action."[41] In this sense, Civic Desire brings together the key impulses in Dewey's thinking about society: education, ethics, and community-building in miniature format.

Notes

1. Dewey, *Public and Its Problems*, 139, 208.
2. Lippmann, *Public Opinion*, 195–97.
3. Dryzek et al., "Crisis of Democracy," 1146.
4. Jackson and Clark, "Introduction," 18.

5. Asen, "Multiple Mr. Dewey"; Danisch, *Pragmatism, Democracy, and the Necessity of Rhetoric*; Danisch, *Building a Social Democracy*; Crick, *Democracy and Rhetoric*.
6. Bitzer, "Rhetoric and Public Knowledge," 78–80.
7. Hauser and Benoit-Barné, "Reflections on Rhetoric," 271.
8. Hauser and Hegbloom, "Rhetoric and Critical Theory," 481, 491–92.
9. Asen, "Discourse Theory of Citizenship"; Asen, "Neoliberalism, the Public Sphere, and a Public Good"; Crick, *Democracy and Rhetoric*; Crick, *Dewey for a New Age of Fascism*.
10. Danisch, *Pragmatism, Democracy, and the Necessity of Rhetoric*; Danisch, *Building a Social Democracy*.
11. Kock and Villadsen, "Rhetorical Citizenship as a Conceptual Frame"; Kock and Villadsen, "Citizenship Discourse."
12. Brinkmann, *John Dewey*.
13. Koch, "Ordet eller Sværdet." My translation.
14. The project ran for five years (2010–2015). The two founders have since pursued similar projects in different formats.
15. See https://borgerlyst.dk.
16. Lloyd and Pass, *Borgerlyst: Handlekraft i hverdagen*; Lloyd and Pass, *Samtalesaloner*; Lloyd and Pass, *Borgerlyst: En projektbiografi*.
17. Untranslatable pun. *Fællesskab* means "community," but read as two words it means "create together."
18. See https://dac.dk/udstillinger/faellesskab-din-by/.
19. See http://samtalesaloner.dk.
20. See http://samtalesaloner.dk.
21. While the present study is informed by the author's participation in several conversation salons and informal observation studies done in that connection, it does not aim to discuss the demographic profile of participants in particular Conversation Salons or in the activities of Civic Desire more broadly construed. Suffice it to remark that while information about the events is subject to limitations of dissemination (e.g., connections via Facebook), the turnout for Conversation Salons is surprisingly diverse in terms of age, gender, and educational and socioeconomic position.
22. An untranslatable pun: the Danish word for election also means "choice."
23. See http://borgerlyst.dk/category/folkets-valg/.
24. Goodwin, "Walter Lippmann, the Indispensable Opposition," 146.
25. Dewey, *Public and Its Problems*, 213.
26. Hauser and Benoit-Barné, "Reflections on Rhetoric," 272.
27. See https://borgerlyst.dk/category/english/.
28. Stroud, *John Dewey and the Artful Life*, 183.
29. Stroud, 186–87.
30. Stroud, "Mindful Argument."
31. Jackson and Clark, "Introduction," 2.
32. Hauser, *Vernacular Voices*, 11.
33. Hauser, 14.
34. Hauser, 61.
35. Kock and Villadsen, *Rhetorical Citizenship and Public Deliberation*; Kock and Villadsen, "Rhetorical Citizenship as a Conceptual Frame"; Kock and Villadsen, "Citizenship Discourse."
36. Eberly, "Rhetoric and the Anti-Logos Doughball."
37. Eberly, "Rhetoric and the Anti-Logos Doughball," 290, 296.
38. Dryzek et al., "Crisis of Democracy," 1146.
39. Mutz, *Hearing the Other Side*.

40. Eberly, "From *Writers, Audiences,* and *Communities* to *Publics.*"
41. Hauser, *Vernacular Voices,* 114.

Bibliography

Asen, Robert. "A Discourse Theory of Citizenship." *Quarterly Journal of Speech* 90, no. 2 (2004): 189–211.
———. "The Multiple Mr. Dewey: Multiple Publics and Permeable Borders in John Dewey's Theory of the Public Sphere." *Argumentation and Advocacy* 39 (2003): 174–88.
———. "Neoliberalism, the Public Sphere, and a Public Good." *Quarterly Journal of Speech.* 103, no. 4 (2017): 329–49.
Bitzer, Lloyd F. "Rhetoric and Public Knowledge." In *Rhetoric, Philosophy, and Literature: An Exploration,* edited by Don Burks, 67–93. West Lafayette, IN: Purdue University Press, 1979.
Brinkmann, Svend. *John Dewey: En introduktion.* Copenhagen: Hans Reitzels Forlag, 2007.
Crick, Nathan. *Democracy and Rhetoric: John Dewey on the Arts of Becoming.* Columbia: University of South Carolina Press, 2010.
———. *Dewey for a New Age of Fascism: Teaching Democratic Habits.* University Park: Penn State University Press, 2019.
Danisch, Robert. *Building a Social Democracy: The Promise of Rhetorical Pragmatism.* Lanham, MD: Lexington Books, 2015.
———. *Pragmatism, Democracy, and the Necessity of Rhetoric.* Columbia: University of South Carolina Press, 2007.
Dewey, John. *The Public and Its Problems* (1927). Athens: Ohio University Press, 1954.
Dryzek, John S., André Bächtinger, Simone Chambers, Joshua Cohen, James N. Druckman, Andrea Felicetti, James S. Fishkin, et al. "The Crisis of Democracy and the Science of Deliberation." *Science* 363, no. 6432 (March 15, 2019): 1144–46.
Eberly, Rosa. "From *Writers, Audiences,* and *Communities* to *Publics*: Writing Classrooms as Protopublic Spaces." *Rhetoric Review* 18, no. 1 (2009): 165–78.
———. "Rhetoric and the Anti-Logos Doughball: Teaching Deliberating Bodies the Practices of Participatory Democracy." *Rhetoric and Public Affairs* 5, no. 2 (Summer 2002): 287–300.
Folkets valg [The People's Election/Choice]. https://borgerlyst.dk/?s=folkets+valg. Accessed August 11, 2020.
Goodwin, Jean. "Walter Lippmann, the Indispensable Opposition." In *Trained Capacities: John Dewey, Rhetoric, and Democratic Practice,* edited by Brian Jackson and Gregory Clark, 142–58. Columbia: University of South Carolina Press, 2014.
Hauser, Gerard A. "The Moral Vernacular of Human Rights Discourse." *Philosophy and Rhetoric* 41, no. 4 (2008): 440–66.
———. *Vernacular Voices: The Rhetoric of Publics and Public Spheres.* Columbia: University of South Carolina Press, 1999.
Hauser, Gerard A., and Chantal Benoit-Barné. "Reflections on Rhetoric, Deliberative Democracy, Civil Society, and Trust." *Rhetoric and Public Affairs* 5, no. 2 (2002): 261–75.
Hauser, Gerard A., and Maria T. Hegbloom. "Rhetoric and Critical Theory: Possibilities for Rapprochement in Public Deliberation." In *The SAGE Handbook of Rhetorical*

Studies, edited by Andrea A. Lunsford, Kirt H. Wilson, and Rosa A. Eberly, 477–95. Thousand Oaks, CA: Sage, 2008.

Jackson, Brian, and Gregory Clark. "Introduction: John Dewey and the Rhetoric of Democratic Culture." In *Trained Capacities: John Dewey, Rhetoric, and Democratic Practice*, edited by Brian Jackson and Gregory Clark, 1–24. Columbia: University of South Carolina Press, 2014.

Jonsen, A. R. "Of Balloons and Bicycles; or, The Relationship Between Ethical Theory and Practical Judgment." *Hastings Center Report* 21, no. 5 (1991): 14–16.

Koch, Hal. "Ordet eller Sværdet" (1945). https://danmarkshistorien.dk/leksikon-og-kilder/vis/materiale/hal-koch-ordet-eller-svaerdet-1945/. Accessed April 27, 2023.

Kock, Christian, and Lisa S. Villadsen. "Citizenship Discourse." In *International Encyclopedia of Language and Social Interaction*, edited by Karen Tracy, Todd Sandel, and Cornelia Ilie, 115–21. Hoboken, NJ: Wiley-Blackwell, 2014.

———, eds. *Rhetorical Citizenship and Public Deliberation*. University Park: Penn State University Press, 2012.

———. "Rhetorical Citizenship as a Conceptual Frame: What We Talk About When We Talk About Rhetorical Citizenship." In *Contemporary Rhetorical Citizenship*, edited by Christian Kock and Lisa Villadsen, 9–26. Leiden: Leiden University Press, 2014.

Lippmann, Walter. *Public Opinion* (1922). New York: Free Press 1965.

Lloyd, Andreas, and Nadja Pass. *Borgerlyst. En projektbiografi*. Copenhagen: Borgerlyst, 2018.

———. *Borgerlyst: Handlekraft i hverdagen*. Copenhagen: Borgerlyst, 2013.

———. *Samtalesaloner: Små skub, der får folk til at falde i snak*. Copenhagen: Borgerlyst, 2016.

Mutz, Diana. *Hearing the Other Side. Deliberative Versus Participation Democracy*. Cambridge: Cambridge University Press, 2006.

Stroud, Scott R. *John Dewey and the Artful Life. Pragmatism, Aesthetics, and Morality*. University Park: Penn State University Press, 2011.

———. "Mindful Argument, Deweyan Pragmatism, and the Ideal of Democracy." *Controversia* 7, no. 2 (2011): 15–33.

8

A PUBLIC AND ITS SOLUTIONS: LIPPMANN AND DEWEY THROUGH THE PRISM OF NORWEGIAN SOCIAL DEMOCRACY

Kristian Bjørkdahl

In his introduction to *Experience and Nature*, in John Dewey's collected works, Sidney Hook wrote that "it might be argued with some plausibility that modern technological and cultural developments make the American condition and experience not unrepresentative of life in other Western industrialized nations."[1] Had Hook not been so careful with his wording, I would be inclined to disagree. For while his proposal might have *some* plausibility, and even though the American condition and experience are certainly not *un*representative of the West, we would be amiss to think of the United States of America and other Western industrialized nations as one and the same.

In particular, there are some significant differences between the social and political formation of the United States and that of the social democratic welfare states of Scandinavia.[2] More specifically, the Scandinavian social democracies have organized themselves in such a way that "the problem of the public," which famously plagued both Walter Lippmann and John Dewey,[3] no longer appears as such a terrible conundrum. At the danger of overextending the claim, one could even say that the Scandinavian countries have gone some way toward finding *solutions* to the problem of the public.

The Scandinavian case demonstrates that we have neither to forfeit the idea of an active democratic public forming at all (Lippmann), nor to restrict ourselves to vague speculations about how this might come to pass (Dewey). My contention here is that we, by viewing Lippmann and Dewey through the prism of Scandinavian social democracy, can loosen the grip that their alternative visions have had on many of their readers. This exercise can help us recognize that our fates are bound by neither Lippmann nor Dewey, but that there exists a fertile middle-ground where workable—though admittedly still imperfect—arrangements can grow. The Scandinavian case can have a therapeutic effect, rendering the choice between Lippmann and Dewey as a false dilemma and helping us see that the problem of the public need not be thought of as the inevitable condition of modern mass democracy, but rather as the plague of *certain* democracies among "Western industrialized nations." This does not mean, of course, that Lippmann and Dewey become irrelevant; it only means that democrats do not have to be *either* Lippmannians *or* Deweyans.

In what follows, I extend this argument with a close look at Norway's tradition for tripartism—what is also called tripartite negotiations.[4] My point of departure will be the idea that this scheme (alongside an assortment of others that work toward roughly the same end) can be read as a practical middle ground between the positions of Lippmann and Dewey—where the "practical" part is just as important as the "middle ground" part.

On Lippmann's side, the tripartite system has certain centralized features, and important decisions are taken by "insiders" in business, labor unions, and government. And while tripartism surely does not rest as heavily on expertise as Lippmann would have desired, it nevertheless manages to escape the limited perspectives that he thought hampered citizens' participation in democracy—paradoxically, by starting from the partisan interests of each party. On Dewey's side, the system is not *just* centralized but also, at the same time, local: it rests on, is fueled by, and gains its legitimacy from the participation of a myriad of decentralized associations—most notably, local sections of trade unions and individual businesses. And although the influence of these local entities on the central negotiations is not always very direct or substantial, the system has ways of balancing this deficit. Furthermore, the limits to participation are largely offset by the core political value that infuses the whole system: *compromise*. With tripartism, no one gets it all, but everyone gets something.

For all the hard, measurable results of the tripartite negotiations, however—its most important one being what the economists call "wage compression"[5]—those do not exhaust the meaning of tripartism. For in addition to the negotiations themselves, Norwegians engage in an ongoing rhetorical work of inventing tripartism as a tradition. In a great many different situations and contexts, Norwegians "culturalize" their tripartite system; they make it into an object of national pride, even to the point of projecting it as a basic trait of the Norwegian character. Although the effects of this rhetorical work are much harder to measure than are income disparities, it would not be absurd to assume that this culturalization contributes significantly to the relative success of tripartism in Norway.[6] There is reason to think that a virtuous cycle exists: Norwegians tell themselves that their intimate attachment to the tradition of tripartism has made them experts at cooperation and compromise, and hence they approach every iteration of tripartite negotiations with a desire to live up to the tradition. (After all, to approach them differently would be *un-Norwegian* of them.) This attitude increases the negotiations' chance of success, and this success in turn further strengthens Norwegians' attachment to the tradition.

I should be as careful with my wording as Hook was, since the above points are perhaps somewhat delicate. First, I am not saying that the tripartite system—or Norwegian social democracy in general—is either perfect or absolutely stable; if Norway has institutionalized certain schemes that appear to be solutions to the conundrum of democratic deliberation and decision-making, those are solutions only in a relative sense, and they are not written in stone. There are indeed signs that they have been losing their hold in recent decades and are now under threat.[7] Furthermore, I am not suggesting that Norway can stand as an example—at least not in any straightforward way—for the United States or any other country. Unlike what certain commentators claim, Norway's "solutions" are, for the most part, products of coincidence and circumstance, not carefully designed results of intention and intelligence. What others take from Norway's experience with these coincidences must remain an open question.[8]

These provisos, I should add, go against the grain of a certain tendency within Norwegian culture itself, where "the Norwegian model" is often seen almost as a function of Fate, a sort of gift given to the Chosen People of the North. There is a dark side to Norwegians' culturalization of their social and political arrangements, where history is rendered as dramaturgy and Norway is cast in the self-aggrandizing role of Annerledeslandet (literally "the Different Country").[9] Critical scholars have in this connection suggested that Norwegian political culture is steeped in a "regime of goodness," which, by way of a dehistoricizing do-gooder deontology, fails to acknowledge that Norway can be anything but good.[10] While I believe many of the arrangements of Norwegian social democracy well worth protecting and promoting, I believe this tendency to make a conceited drama of it all is both silly and counterproductive.

Defusing Lippmann/Dewey

The argument I have just sketched could be taken to say that what has often been thought of as a "debate" between Lippmann and Dewey was really nothing of the sort—and in recent scholarship on Lippmann and Dewey, this has indeed been a central contention. Sue Curry Jansen, underlining what the pair had in common, suggests that the writings of Lippmann and Dewey in the 1920s did not amount to any "debate," but that it was retrospectively reconstructed as such, in what she dubs a "phantom conflict." The main victim of the conflictual reframing from recent decades was the reputation of Walter Lippmann, whom Jansen suggests has been used and abused as a "straw man of communication research." If one, like Jansen, studies the reception history of Lippmann's and Dewey's work from the 1920s, one might find that until circa the late 1980s, hardly anyone thought of framing Lippmann and Dewey as adversaries. When such a framing did begin to gain hold, Jansen says, it had more to do with our, contemporary, concerns than with those of either Lippmann or Dewey. Michael Schudson has pursued a path that runs in neat parallel with Jansen's, placing most of the blame for the "invention of Walter Lippmann as an anti-democrat" on James Carey, whose influential writings from the 1980s created an interpretive precedent. Schudson has also been at work to resurrect Lippmann from the status of straw man, countering that Lippmann's ideas about the role of expertise in democracies are realistic and insightful. Meanwhile, other scholars, notably Lana Rakow, has mounted a counteroffensive, charging Jansen and Schudson with misrepresenting the alleged misrepresentations of Carey and others, and underlining (*with* Carey) that there really were real and non-negligible differences between the views of Lippmann and Dewey.[11]

My starting point here differs somewhat from that of these scholars. For while I believe there are indeed some obvious and important differences between Lippmann and Dewey, the positions they sketch should not be thought to stand in any *practical* opposition to each other. What I mean is that the "debate" between Lippmann and Dewey—as well as the recent debate *about* this "debate"—has been overly restricted by what Dewey at one point admits is the "intellectual and hypothetic" character of both of their efforts,[12] and that it consequently has failed to acknowledge properly that practical compromises can be struck between their respective positions.

This point, in turn, is not simply an academic one, for the Lippmann/Dewey debate appears to have formed a sort of prism through which many have understood practical political life. The Lippmann/Dewey prism has restricted our action space negatively, because it has told us that we must believe either in central decision-making or in local initiative, either in a paternalistic rule of experts who manufacture consent or in the face-to-face democracy that has its home in the "neighborly community" (368). My proposal is that, if we turn the situation on its head and use Norway's practical-political life as a prism through which to see this debate, we will discover that this is a set of false dilemmas, neither side of which offers any solid guidance for practical politics.

While it is certainly not my aim to discount the contributions of any of them, this proposal offers some resistance to Lippmann, when it comes to his lack of faith in the prospect of democratic participation, and to Dewey, when it comes to the vague object that gives him faith in the same. For Lippmann, the basic problem of the public was that society had grown so complex that no citizen could hope to gain the knowledge and oversight needed to make sensible decisions on matters of general concern. Our individual outlook on the world was so constrained that it would be pointless—maybe even irresponsible—to imagine that individual citizens could be placed in front of any significant decision-making power: "The real environment is altogether too big, too complex, and too fleeting for direct acquaintance," wrote Lippmann, and "we are not equipped to deal with so much subtlety, so much variety, so many permutations and combinations." This meant that, "although we have to act in that environment, we have to reconstruct it on a simpler model before we can manage it."[13] The situation we are in, as citizens of modern mass democracies, thus produces a need for what Lippmann variously called "fictions," "stereotypes," "pseudo-environments," and "the pictures in our heads." To put it simply, because the modern world is too complex for us to make proper sense of, we simplify, redact, and dramatize reality—we reduce it to get a handle on it.

For Lippmann, the scale and complexity of modern mass society represented a radical challenge to contemporary democracy, for if each member of the public sees nothing but what they have around them, how can a demos even come together to deliberate? Lippmann's proposal to circumvent this situation was to erect a system of experts doing "intelligence work," organized as "a net work of intelligence bureaus in politics and industry" (211), which in specific, institutionalized ways would inform central decision-making, and in this way help "break down the drama, break through the stereotypes, and offer men a picture of facts" (198). Meanwhile, the citizenry would largely be restricted to the role of spectators, who at elections would function as a test of the performance of elected officials.

Much of what Lippmann has to say about "intelligence bureaus" is quite sensible, and it has in fact also come to pass—although in somewhat different form than he envisaged. But as I will argue, the Norwegian case demonstrates that Lippmann's position is much more pessimistic about the prospects of democratic participation, of "overcoming . . . the limitation of individual experience" (213), than it needs to be. Lippmann's lack of faith is not, as is often said, a *realistic* take on democracy, it is a *cynical* one.

Dewey, for his part, did certainly not lack faith in democratic participation—indeed he staked a great deal on precisely that prospect. The trouble for him was that while we, as Lippmann also pointed out, were stuck, mentally, in "local town-meeting practices . . . we [Americans] live and act and have our being in a continental nation state" (306). Modern technology had expanded the scope of human life enormously, Dewey argued, but the "thoughts and aspirations" (323) that attached to this new situation were not successfully communicated, "and hence not common" (324). Dewey had multiple ways of phrasing this problem: The public, he suggested, was "largely inchoate and unorganized" (303), it seemed "to be lost; it is certainly bewildered" (308), it was "uncertain and obscure" (310), "amorphous and unarticulated" (317), "so confused and eclipsed that it cannot even use the organs through which it is supposed to mediate political action and polity" (311), and "so bewildered that it cannot find itself" (311–12). Finally, again echoing Lippmann, Dewey suggested that "the public . . . is not only a ghost, but a ghost which walks and talks, and obscures, confuses and misleads governmental action in a disastrous way" (313).

If Dewey's formulation of the problem can appear somewhat mystifying, his proposed solution was no less vague. The solution, he famously argued, was communication. Dewey suggested that "the essential need . . . is the improvement of the methods and conditions of debate, discussion and persuasion. That is *the* problem of the public" (365). What needed to happen was for the "ever-expanding and intricately ramifying consequences of associated activities [to be] known in the full sense of that word, so that an organized, articulate Public comes into being." This, he thought, could only happen in one way: "The highest and most difficult kind of inquiry and a subtle, delicate, vivid and responsive art of communication must take possession of the physical machinery of transmission and circulation and breathe life into it" (350).

Dewey was a democratic prophet, and to the extent *The Public and Its Problems* offered guidance, it was to a democratic faith. In this way, Dewey was strong where Lippmann had been weak. As for how Dewey's ideals might materialize—what it would mean, for example, for the "subtle, delicate, vivid and responsive art of communication [to] take possession of the physical machinery of transmission and circulation and breathe life into it"—we are left none the wiser. This, again, is where the Norwegian case is instructive, since it displays tangible, practical ways of allowing the public to find itself, take shape, step into the light, get real, solid, and organized. Whether Norway, as a case of "actually existing social democracy," would have impressed Dewey, I am not so sure. But pragmatists cannot live on faith alone; at some point, they must get out in the real world and begin experimenting.

An Enduring Compromise Between Labor and Capital

Historians, sociologists, political scientists, and others have made various proposals about how the Scandinavian social democracies are distinct vis-à-vis other liberal democracies.[14] Given my concern in this chapter, one angle of particular interest is the tradition that identifies Norway as a country marked by a characteristically pluralist form of corporatism.[15] A key contribution to understanding this aspect of Norway's political organization is the work of Stein Rokkan, who, with his work from the 1960s, especially, offered a reading of Norwegian political life that emphasized its crosscutting "cleavages."[16] The term referred to the various layers of interest that had been added to Norway's political life over time, and which had made its political culture a thick mesh of intersecting agendas. His basic idea was that, since citizens were typically attached to several of the central axes of conflict in Norwegian politics, conflict as such was contained.[17] The crosscutting cleavages were thus—paradoxically, it might seem to some—a cause of solidarity; the different agendas that intersected in Norway's political culture were in fact what made Norway into *one* public. Some have referred to this feature of the Norwegian (or more generously, the Scandinavian) way of doing politics as "the conflict partnership."[18]

According to Rokkan, key to this situation were the corporatist mechanisms that ensured that Norwegians with different perspectives would be brought together on a regular basis, around "the bargaining table where the government authorities meet directly with the trade union leaders, the representatives of the farmers, the smallholders, and the fishermen, and the delegates of the Employers' Association."[19] Scholars from the outside have made similar observations of Norwegian political life. In 1976, the American political scientist Robert Kvavik noted that, in contrast with the United States, interest groups in Norway did not engage in a "competitive struggle for access" to decision-makers (i.e., lobbying), but were rather "coopted by the government into the administration's advisory, managerial, or policy-making commissions."[20] Later, political scientists Hege Skjeie and Birte Siim would suggest that the two most central aims of Scandinavian corporatism were "that governments are able to bring large organizations into binding collaboration, and that professional expertise is well represented," adding that "the aim of corporatism is simply to build consensus on major policy moves through unanimous proposals."[21] More recently, Nik Brandal and Dag Einar Thorsen have written that, in the Scandinavian way of doing politics, "inclusion (and co-option) into the political process has been extended to an array of stakeholders within civil society," in such a way that "vested interests are included in drawn-out political discussions, tying stakeholders to an eventual outcome." Over time, they suggest, this has primed "the participants towards cross-political, cultural and social compromise favouring evolution and cooperation."[22]

One can recognize this way of doing politics in various corporatist mechanisms within the Norwegian political system, but they are perhaps nowhere as apparent as in the tripartite negotiations, which is also called simply tripartism.[23] In essence, tripartism is a scheme that brings workers, employers, and government together around an imperative to come to an agreement on the issues raised. The mechanism operates mainly to regulate matters of work—wages, employment regulations, working conditions, and so on—but equivalent mechanisms are also used in other areas, though often in somewhat less institutionalized ways.

The history of this mechanism makes it clear that it came about under quite contingent, even coincidental, circumstances, so when I dub it a "solution," this should not be taken too literally. It is rather more like an inheritance, something that the forebears of contemporary Norwegians created, under a certain duress—"fought for within a chain of situations of choice," as the historian Finn Olstad puts it[24]—and which their descendants developed, fine-tuned, and adapted to changing circumstances, and which they would come to cherish in the process.

According to leading Norwegian historians, the system stems from the first tariff agreement, in the iron sector, from 1907, and then, most directly, from the "Main Agreement" of 1935, which, according to Olstad, amounted to "a historical compromise between capital and labor," and which came to be known as the "constitution of working life" in Norway. With these agreements, he writes, "the labor movement's liberation project was transformed into a negotiation game, where one did not challenge the principles of capitalism." The battle between capital and labor, which had raged for several decades, had ended in "a draw," as workers and capitalists realized that "none of them was strong enough to trump the other." This became "the basic premise of enduring stability and an understanding between the parties that eliminated the possibility of any general showdown."[25]

A central precondition for the negotiation game was the labor movement's willingness to forfeit its previous aim of class struggle for a more inclusive political agenda. While class conflicts were still raging in the early 1930s, an increasing number of centrally placed labor politicians now began directing their rhetoric toward creating a "broad popular culture." One, Halvdan Koht, argued to fellow party members in the Labor Party, in 1930, that "all class culture will, sooner or later, come to its demise. Only a general people's culture can hope to live and to be a [force of] progress without end."[26] More than one historian of Norwegian history has described this as the "growth of a new class into the nation," pointing out that, in Norway, from the 1930s onward, "the nation gained territory as an overarching identity in the political-democratic [sphere], at the same time as class identity was mobilized to create adherence to the national project."[27] This relative shift from class identity to national identity was in turn made possible by the creation of a new repository of trust between the parties. The negotiations leading up the general agreement were instrumental in "creating mutual confidence and trust," argues Olstad, and "the agreement would have been worthless without this trust."[28] Another historian, Francis Sejersted, has argued, similarly, that the Main Agreement established a "solidarity game" between capital and labor: "In order to have a well-functioning capitalism—something that both parties were interested in—it is assumed that the two parties, capitalist and labor, must play their respective roles in the game. If one of the parties, for instance the capitalists, does not do so, then the system does not function, and the opposing party's opposition has to take the form of a critique of the system; in other words, it has to become more revolutionary."[29] But although the system could be described as a "game" once it had been established, Sejersted emphasizes that "the path to these agreements was long and convoluted," and that the ensuing trust, cooperation, and will to compromise was the result of "periods of revolutionary atmospheres and periods of intense conflict," where the parties nevertheless shared a goal, namely "the development of a modern industrial state."[30]

The Art of "Together-Talking"

While elements of this story echo in the history of other Western countries (including the New Deal era in the United States), a peculiar aspect of Norway and Scandinavia is that "the conflict partnership," and the trust on which it rests, was never really abandoned. In fact, it has only grown deeper over time. One key to this development has been the fact that conservatives, even the far-right populists, are largely committed to the "Norwegian model" and to what is seen as its foremost result, the universal welfare state.[31] The core of this model, the tripartite system, has become ever more entrenched over the years, and is now a feature of Norwegian politics to which most everyone—from the far left to the far right—attaches a certain pride.

One way to understand this system is as a mechanism that overcomes at least some of the problems identified by Lippmann and Dewey. When seen from a particular perspective, tripartism is precisely what Dewey called for: it is, quite literally, a formation of a public, and it arguably places "the methods and conditions of debate, discussion and persuasion" at the very center. Interestingly, tripartism might be seen to engage Dewey's definition of the public, as a coming together of those affected by an issue. The system does include a variety of face-to-face interactions between people who know each other, but at the same time it goes far beyond Dewey's idea of the "neighborly community"; in some ways, the tripartite negotiations look more like the informed, central decision-making system that Lippmann envisioned. As such, it transcends the limited perspective of single individuals or groups of individuals—indeed, this is the whole point of the mechanism.

The tripartite system has in many ways been a great success, and arguably one key to this success is that it brings people and perspectives together under the imperative to transcend the particular positions of each. While it might perhaps appear to rest on a harmonious notion of the public, that is not so; tripartism does not assume that a public can only form once everybody is the same. In fact, one might argue that the "oneness" implied in this term, *the* public, is somewhat foreign to tripartism, since what it does is to organize an *agonistic* space—a format in which each party is called on to promote its agenda, though with the other central stakeholders as face-to-face interlocutors.[32]

A skeptic might argue that the actual negotiations themselves are not very "public," that they take place largely behind closed doors. This, however, is to miss the point; it is to assume that a public can only "find itself" if it uses a form of communication that we have come to associate with the idea of "the public"—notably mass media. But this assumption is quite unhelpful. It prioritizes theory over practice; it blinds us to the fact that we often can accomplish in practice what theory, on the basis of abstract criteria, has deemed impossible. Lippmann and Dewey agreed that the public was, as the latter wrote, "confused and eclipsed," but if the conflict partnership that comes alive in the tripartite system shows that this need not be so, that tells us more about the limits of their imaginations than it does about this system.

To get into what tripartism does and how it does it, I will stipulate that the tripartite system works as a networked, representative mechanism for scaling up decision-making, in which mutual solidarity and compromise along vertical as well as horizontal axes is a central imperative.

First, contra Lippmann's proposals, the action in this system is not located solely at the central level, but rather distributed across various points along a vertical axis—from local to national to central—along which each of the parties in the system is organized, as well as in the rhetorical traffic between those points. The small number of people who take part in the central negotiations collect most of their legitimacy from the networked processes whereby interests and concerns are scaled up from, say, local sections of a trade union on to its national division and then onward to the big union alliances (the "main organizations," which take part in the negotiations). At the end of a round of negotiations, decisions travel back down again, to the local level, where they regulate the relation between employers and workers (not least in the form of tariff agreements, but also in other, less formal ways).

Even in cases where there is not much traffic to speak of, there is nevertheless an imperative toward coherence between the levels. This is in some measure because the central negotiators perform in a representative function; they negotiate on behalf of a large, and often quite diverse, mass of members. At the local level, union sections and businesses often complain about the results of the central negotiations, but they are aware, most of the time, that there are limits to what can be gained in negotiations as complex as these.

Do the various local organizations, say the local sections of a union, make any decisions in this system? Are they, to speak in Lippmann's terms, self-determining? To some extent, yes, because bargaining also takes place at the local level. More generally, though, it is clear that decisions are taken mainly at the central level—and in this way, the system might be said to align with Lippmann's impulse against naive notions about local democracy. That said, the system simply would not work if the central union alliances did not rest on, listen to, and hold themselves accountable to those local organizations. Likewise with the employer side: if businesses felt that the entities who act on their behalf did *not* in fact act on their behalf, those entities could not retain their function for very long.

The tripartite system not only co-opts organized interests into the administration, as Kvavik suggested, it also connects local participation to national and central sites of decision-making. While local groups do not make the decisions, the system can nevertheless be seen, by way of representation, to be a mechanism for scaling up decision-making. But this scaling up comes to life only through a notion of citizenship that political scientist Helga Hernes has identified with "an activist, participatory and egalitarian ideal."[33] Because it, at its most basic level, is built on the type of face-to-face interaction that Dewey envisioned, tripartism is one way to do precisely what Lippmann doubted could be done—namely, to involve the average citizen in a real way in central political decisions. Granted, the involvement is probably slighter than what Dewey would have wished to see, but the tripartite system has the obvious benefit, contra Dewey's contributions, of offering a set of *tangible* political mechanisms: tripartism actually exists and demonstrably works.

The point of tripartite negotiations is not simply to allow representatives for various—opposing—parties to meet and fight it out. It is also, at the same time, an opportunity for each party to convey to the others how it *knows* the world, to present and display the interpretive frame it relies on to make sense of its surroundings. In this way, these negotiations go some way toward counteracting Lippmann's emphasis on the limited perspective allowed by our particular situations. Tripartism counteracts "stereotypes" in the sense that it invites, or even forces, the stitching together—into a more reliable whole—of various stereotypes that emanate from different social positions. The mechanism at work here *relies* fundamentally on the participation of small groups, but does not *stop* at them: rather, the system transcends stereotypes only to the extent it successfully scales up from particular, partial, perspectives to a composite perspective—or, more simply put, to a compromise.

While I would argue the tripartite system works well, that is not to say the movements within this system are necessarily smooth. In fact, they are basically agonistic. But this only shows how the scheme as a whole works toward solidarity also along the horizontal axis, meaning between workers, employers, and the state. While local groups will always try to persuade their national organizations of the importance of a certain priority, and while those national organizations will in turn do what they can to put a stamp on the position of their "main organization," the system as a whole rests on an ideal of compromise.

Truth is arrived at, in this system, not so much in a marketplace of ideas as within a communicative circuitry of concern. The tripartite system is a way to make sure that people who rely mutually on each other—as labor and capital do—see the world from the other's perspective, and to place each of them in front of an imperative to reach an agreement with the other. It asks each party to keep alive—in fact, to reenact—the historical compromise between labor and capital in each new round of negotiations.

Understood as a practical form of political-organizational communication, tripartism's most distinctive feature is its propensity toward what we might call "together-talking." While this term is not distinguished by its stylistic elegance, it nevertheless captures (in a literal translation of the Norwegian *samsnakke*) quite closely what goes on within the tripartite system, along the vertical as well as the horizontal axes. Not only does tripartism on a practical level consist of a set of talks (i.e., negotiations), but the system can more broadly be seen to rest on the ideal of conversation. As I would have us understand it, tripartism rests on the ideal of bringing people together, to talk things through, so that everyone can emerge, at the end of the talks, in a state of being together-talked. Indeed, there is a tremendously strong expectation that the parties should emerge from the talk in precisely this state—it is, one might say, the whole point of the mechanism.

To emerge together-talked means that a temporary agreement has been made, that one leaves the negotiations without disturbing resentments or grievances, and that one will keep the peace for another year. In between negotiations, one may of course voice what one believes was not achieved in previous negotiations, what still needs to change, and so on, but these moves will be largely contained by the knowledge that one will have to come back to the negotiating table fairly soon—and regularly, in the foreseeable future. A deep commitment to the value of compromise is a prerequisite for together-talking to work, and this creates a constant push to move beyond one's own narrow perspective and agenda, since compromises can only be had if each party is willing to move beyond its starting point.

Culturalizing Tripartism

So far, I have suggested that the corporatist element in Norway's political administration has offered this country a set of communicative mechanisms that go some way toward rendering the Lippmann/Dewey debate a false dilemma. To put it simply, there are practical ways to get around "the problem of the public," as both Lippmann and Dewey described it. I want, however, to take this reading somewhat further. For in addition to the immediate workings and effects of tripartite system itself, tripartism is routinely "culturalized" by Norwegians, that is, made into an object of national pride and veneration. As such, it is used rhetorically—in a variety of contexts that go far beyond the parties to the negotiations—to create, enhance, and reproduce Norwegian national identity. As historian Francis Sejersted notes, the agreements at the core of the tripartite system "are viewed as national treasures, cornerstones upon which the Social Democratic order was built."[34] The culturalization of tripartism tells Norwegians that they should take pride in their ability to talk things through and reach an agreement, and this sentiment is fed back into the tripartite system itself—setting it up for success, as it were, since now, anyone who does not value compromise is seen as un-Norwegian.

The rhetorical uses of the tripartite system, which makes a topos of values like cooperation and compromise, might seem like mere embellishments—like forms of self-congratulatory boasting. They are that, too, but my contention here is that they are also a substantial part of the longevity, solidity, and success of tripartism in Norway. Simply put, I believe the actual workings of the tripartite system combine with cultural images of how it works, and that the result is a further boost to the system and its underlying values.

To illustrate this point, I will in the remainder briefly present examples of this type of culturalization, taken from each of the parties represented in the system—capital, labor, and government—to show how they present tripartism in their communications. I offer them in this context more as illustrations than as objects of detailed critique. In this case, a simple juxtaposition is itself quite effective, though, since it demonstrates how broadly the tripartite vocabulary and the values they express is spread across Norwegian society.

We might look first at a statement from the Norwegian government, offered by Anniken Hauglie of the Conservative Party, Minister of Labour and Social Affairs, in 2017, at the 106th session of the International Labour Conference. The title of Hauglie's talk flagged some of the key elements of how tripartism is culturalized: "Part of the Same Future: Experiences from the Norwegian Social Dialogue." Emphasizing collective bargaining in particular, the minister noted that "there is a broad consensus on the guidelines for wage formation," and noted that the continuous efforts of the authorities to facilitate the arrangement "generate a broad consensus on the basis for the yearly bargaining session between the social partners." Social dialogue was used in Norway in a wide variety of contexts, she noted, again underlining the authorities' efforts to safeguard and develop this tradition: "For the Government, it is a conscious policy to invite to cooperation and to hear the views of all organized parties in the working life." As for the purposes of this practice, she suggested that tripartite schemes yielded a "good working climate," that it operationalized the "right to consultation and negotiation," that it—interestingly—"establishes more shared perceptions of reality between workers and company management and lays a foundation for extended cooperation," which in turn would yield "a more inclusive workplace." Further, she acknowledged the presence of conflict and disagreement within this system but concluded that "such disagreement does not threaten the fundamental willingness to cooperate that characterizes the Norwegian labour market."[35]

As with any speech of this kind, Hauglie's talk worked not so much by the transmission of arguments as by the iteration of key words—in this case, "social dialogue," "cooperation," "partners," and the like. Words like these were repeated throughout her speech, less to build a formal case than to leave a certain impression on the audience—their effect being more likely pathetic than logical—of the relations between various actors in the Norwegian labor market and the atmosphere in which they routinely meet. *We, Norwegians, talk things through*, Hauglie seemed to say, *and we really make that work*.

The most telling part of her talk, however, was given as concluding remarks, when she suggested quite emphatically that what she had just presented was not her individual "take" on the tripartite system, but rather a widespread, indeed *shared*, legacy—which was maintained by everyone and anyone. It was the basic tone and value of Norwegian society, what gave life to the whole: "The politicians and the social partners share a commitment to compromise and seek consensus to solve problems and upcoming challenges. It takes time but it builds trust and legitimacy in the society. Tripartism works as a living way to address difficult questions and provide fair and legitimate answers, which, if perfect to nobody, are acceptable for all."[36]

Moving from government to capital, one hardly notices any shift in vocabulary. If one considers articles from the webpages of NHO—the main organization for employers (i.e., business owners)—the first thing one notices is just how eager Norwegian capitalists are to express their support of the tripartite system. One can also not fail to notice the rhetorical work being done to present tripartism as Norwegian (despite the fact that similar arrangements exist in both Sweden and Denmark).[37] The heading of one such article is "The Norwegian Model," adding a subtitle that leaves no doubts about the merits of the model: "The Tripartite Cooperation Creates Jobs and Increases Profitability." The article summary further consolidates the Norwegianness as well as the success of this model: "The result of the Norwegian Model of work is high participation in work life, solid welfare arrangements, and a well-developed tripartite cooperation scheme." The text further emphasizes that the key to the success of the Norwegian Model is how participation fuses with central institutional factors: "A report on management in Norway shows that trust, short distances, and participation has ensured high productivity and capacity for change. Norwegian leaders are a result of Norwegian culture, but also of the institutions, agreements, and laws that make up the Norwegian Model." What is peculiar, I would argue, is how tightly these texts connect these features to Norwegian national identity, how Norwegianness becomes the main frame around how tripartism is represented. The NHO text drives the point home when it explicitly states, "The Norwegian tripartite cooperation is unique in the global context."

Entirely similar rhetorical moves are found if one moves to the trade unions. One particularly striking example of the culturalization of tripartism comes from Finansforbundet, a national union for employees in "banking, insurance, technology, real estate, accounting, auditing, and debt collection."[38] On its website, the union presents its take on tripartite negotiations under the heading "The Art of Being Norwegian," and refers, throughout, to tripartite negotiations as the "Norwegian Model." This model, the union adds—using almost verbatim the same hyperbole as the employer organization—is "unique in the world." Incidentally, hyperbole also occurs throughout, as when the page states, "We can think of the cooperation between employers, workers, and the state almost as a little work of art."

This particular notion is one the union has pursued quite consistently, we soon discover, as the site goes on to describe how the union gave a group of artists the task of rendering the tripartite system as artworks. Users of the union's webpage can then choose to play a series of videos—very professional ones to boot—where each artist describes their work, and where we trace the artistic process and product in response to the task given to them by the union: "Interpret the relation between employers, workers, and the state in the big collective bargaining agreements." One, a graphic artist, admits that this was a particularly challenging assignment, and at first responds, simply, "I think I'll just have to start grinding a rock, and see how it goes." As the video progresses, however, her artistic instincts seem to kick in: "I didn't want to simply illustrate three parties sitting around a table. I got to thinking that this is really about mutual cooperation. So it occurred to me that we can see the tripartite negotiations as the body's most central organ: it is like the heart and lungs, that pump blood and oxygen into the system, to the entire body, and make sure that everything is distributed equally." And indeed, while the finished artwork does not represent an actual organ, it gives an abstract form—consisting of three blobs connected by what might recall an umbilical cord—that can easily leave the viewer with the impression of something organic, something of the body. The Norwegian *body politic*, perhaps?

Beyond the Historical Coincidence That Is Norway

The institutional arrangement known as tripartism has come to carry a peculiar cultural significance for Norwegians. As the above examples illustrate, tripartism is understood as the democratic "way of life" in Norway, and in this way it arguably manifests Dewey's ambition, however imperfectly. It does so, however, by *means* that we would perhaps sooner identify with Lippmann—that is, by scaling up decision-making to a highly centralized level, and by creating institutional pressures that ensure that individual limitations are transcended. Importantly, tripartism does this work without any need for fancy philosophical notions like "ideal speech situation" or a "veil of ignorance"; to the contrary, the system has its origins in conflict, and is, still today, a means of encapsulating what some have called the "conflict partnership." Finally, the ongoing rhetorical work in which this mechanism is culturalized makes sure that the partnership aspect is maintained: we, Norwegians, are the people who talk our way through conflicts; we are the compromising kind.

If I am right in suggesting that the tripartite arrangement (along with certain other corporatist schemes) goes some way toward defusing the problem of the public, what does this mean for anyone outside Norway? My first inclination in response to this question, I fear, is *you tell me*. Self-determination is important—or actually, self-determination is what democracy means—and I am not going to make the case for a particular variety of democracy by telling anyone else what to do.

There are certain implications of what I have said, though, that do not translate so directly into advice about what anyone should do. First, when I have read the tripartite system as a mechanism that allows us to defuse significantly the problem of the public, one obvious implication of this is that we should give up any "literalist" reading of Lippmann and Dewey, which is to say that we should not approach the issue as though it were a choice of two clearly predefined alternatives: either the "elitist" Lippmann who validates the manufacture of ordinary citizens' consent because their understanding is inevitably limited and thus insufficient, or the "blue-eyed" Dewey who resists this conclusion and thinks that we by updating and fine-tuning our communication arts can arrive at a place, the "Great Community," where the public will have found itself. This, the practical example of tripartism shows, is a false dilemma. It shows that there exists, in actually existing social democracy, mechanisms that allow us to pick elements from each of these options and achieve a working arrangement that combines democratic participation with effective decision-making. The result surely falls far short of the respective utopias of Lippmann and Dewey, but the tripartite tradition has a response even for this, namely that *utopias are good, but practical compromises even better*. Indeed, the tripartite tradition is a testament to what one can achieve if one—in a figurative as well as a literal sense—settles.

Another implication of what I have said is that the stories we tell about our democracy, in particular times and places, matter to the actual workings of that democracy. The story we can tell about Norwegian social democracy by way of the tripartite system is one that allows us to dispel Lippmann's pessimism about the chances of citizens' effective participation in democracy, on the one hand, while making concrete and realistic some of Dewey's vague—or, as he himself wrote, "intellectual or hypothetical"—pronouncements about what needed to happen. As Lippmann and Dewey both knew, such stories are tremendously effective, but they should be tended with care. As I have tried to show, the story that Norwegians tell themselves about tripartism contributes significantly to the success of this system. At the same time, Norwegians are constantly tempted to essentialize and dramatize—to imagine, say, that this system is a basic expression of "the Norwegian character," or that the history of compromise is coextensive with the history of the Norwegian people.

The relevance of the Norwegian case outside the historical coincidence that is Norway should become clear if we acknowledge that this temptation is not just morally unacceptable, but also historically faulty. It fails to acknowledge that the events that culminated in the tripartite system were both conflictual and bitter. In editing out the struggles and the animosity that were in fact the central precondition of those agreements, while highlighting the trust and stability that ensued, it fails to explain how the latter are traits of the Norwegian character while the former allegedly are not. It fails, in short, to acknowledge that historical contingency and coincidence played a big part in the realization of the tripartite arrangement. If we, contrariwise, do acknowledge the contingency and coincidence of this case, a prospect opens up where we might apply its lessons with intentionality and intelligence. What anyone outside of Norway is inclined to do with such a prospect, I cannot guess. But I do not mean to direct these cautions just—or even primarily—to anyone outside Norway, but equally to those within this country, who are constantly at risk of tossing away the accomplishments left to them by history.

Given the case I have presented here, what kind of story about democracy should we be telling? I think it suggests that we should talk about democracy as a basically conflictual, and often quite messy, but nevertheless collective work in progress that calls for creative use of whatever action space is available to us in any given situation. It advises us to be agnostic about pessimism and optimism, and instead turn our attention toward the practical effort to *make* democracy—as much of it as we can possibly manage to make. It suggests, with one of our protagonists, that democracy is the creative task we have before us. If this is what motivates our efforts as democratic citizens, we will recognize (like Lippmann) the need for large-scale institutional structures, but we also see (with Dewey) that such structures will remain hard and cold and morally problematic until they are brought to life by the active participation of citizens.

Notes

1. Hook, "Introduction," viii.
2. For an extended elaboration of this point, see Esping-Andersen, *Three Worlds of Welfare Capitalism*.
3. The key texts, of course, are Lippmann, *Public Opinion*; Lippmann, *Phantom Public*; and Dewey, *Public and Its Problems*.
4. In English, it is sometimes referred to as "collective bargaining," but I believe this is misleading in more ways than one. First, there is no commonly used equivalent in the Scandinavian languages for this term; in Norway, which I will focus on, it is generally referred to as "the tripartite cooperation." Second, as I hope to show, the negotiations themselves, as well as how they are rendered in culture, extend beyond "bargaining." It is not just about "getting a good deal," but about coming to the negotiations in mutual respect, trying to arrive at a result that each party can accept.
5. Barth, Moene, and Willumsen, "Scandinavian Model."
6. Brandal and Thorsen in "Between Individualism and Communitarianism" make a related point.
7. Two recent books trace the incursion of neoliberalism on Norway's social democracy: Hammer, *Sosialdemokrati versus nyliberalisme*; and Innset, *Markedsvendingen*. Taking a somewhat broader view, Brandal and Thorsen in "Between Individualism and Communitarianism" note three challenges to the Nordic "way of doing politics": globalization, technocratization, and mediatization. Another challenge, more to the point of the example I am using here, is the fact that the number of workers who are organized has been going down in later years.
8. Though, clearly, there is no shortage of either historical or contemporary examples of those who want to elevate Scandinavia, or any one of the Scandinavian countries, to the status of "model." See, for example, Marklund "Nordic Model on the Global Market of Ideas"; and Byrkjeflot et al., *Making and Circulation of Nordic Models*.
9. This moniker became widespread when Norway, for the second time, declined to join the EU, in 1994, in contrast even to its Scandinavian neighbors. It arguably resurrected older, national-romantic notions of Norway as a particularly egalitarian and independent nation.
10. Tvedt, *Verdensbilder og selvbilder*; Tvedt, *Utviklingshjelp, utenrikspolitikk og makt*; Witoszek, *Origins of the "Regime of Goodness"*; see also Bjørkdahl, "Nobel Savage."
11. Jansen, "Phantom Conflict"; Jansen, "Walter Lippmann"; Schudson, "'Lippmann-Dewey Debate'"; Schudson, "Trouble with Experts"; Schudson, "Walter Lippmann's Ghost"; Rakow, "Family Feud"; Rakow, *John Dewey*.

12. Dewey, *Public and Its Problems*, 333. Further citations of this work in this section are given in the text.
13. Lippmann, *Public Opinion*, 8. Further citations of this work in this section are given in the text.
14. Perhaps the most famous is Esping-Andersen, *Three Worlds of Welfare Capitalism*. See also Bendixsen, Bringslid, and Vike, *Egalitarianism in Scandinavia*.
15. A standard work on Norwegian corporatism is Nordby, *Korporatisme på norsk*.
16. Rokkan, "Norway."
17. I believe there is a case to be made that the empirical tendencies documented and analyzed by Rokkan can be seen as an instance of antagonisms being redirected into agonism; cf. the writings of Chantal Mouffe, for example, *Agonistics*. I cannot, however, make that case here.
18. See Dølvik et al., *Den nordiske modellen mot 2030*, 17.
19. Rokkan, "Norway," 106. See also Rommetvedt, "Scandinavian Corporatism in Decline."
20. Kvavik, *Interest Groups in Norwegian Politics*, 15.
21. Skjeie and Siim, "Scandinavian Feminist Debates on Citizenship," 348.
22. Brandal and Thorsen, "Between Individualism and Communitarianism," 162–63.
23. See, for example, Brandal, Bratberg, and Thorsen, *Sosialdemokratiet*.
24. Olstad, *Frihetens århundre*, 99.
25. Olstad, 95, 55, 93.
26. Cited in Slagstad, *De nasjonale strateger*, 235.
27. Slagstad, 236. See also Johansen, *Komme til orde*.
28. Olstad, *Frihetens århundre*, 95.
29. Sejersted, *Age of Social Democracy*, 158.
30. Sejersted, *Sosialdemokratiets tidsalder*, 163.
31. See, for example, Brandal and Thorsen, "Between Individualism and Communitarianism"; and Brandal, Bratberg, and Thorsen, *Sosialdemokratiet*.
32. Again, I would see a potential for developing the Norwegian case with the vocabulary offered by Chantal Mouffe; cf. note 18, above.
33. Helga Hernes cited in Skjeie and Siim, "Scandinavian Feminist Debates on Citizenship," 347.
34. Sejersted, *Age of Social Democracy*, 159.
35. Hauglie, "Part of the Same Future."
36. Hauglie.
37. See, for example, https://www.nho.no/tema/arbeidsliv/artikler/partssamarbeidet-skaper-jobber-og-bidrar-til-lonnsomhet/ and https://arbinn.nho.no/arbeidsliv/lonn-og-tariff/tariff/artikler/den-norske-modellen/.
38. See https://www.finansforbundet.no/om-oss/. The Finance Sector Union is in turn a member of the main organization called YS, or the Confederation of Vocational Unions.

Bibliography

Barth, Erling, Karl O. Moene, and Fredrik Willumsen. "The Scandinavian Model: An Interpretation." *Journal of Public Economics* 117 (2014): 60–72.
Bendixsen, Synnøve, Mary Bente Bringslid, and Halvard Vike, eds. *Egalitarianism in Scandinavia: Historical and Contemporary Perspectives*. London: Palgrave Macmillan, 2018.

Bjørkdahl, Kristian. "The *Nobel* Savage: Norwegian Do-Goodery as Tragedy." In *Do-Gooders at the End of Aid: Scandinavian Humanitarianism in the Twenty-First Century*, edited by Antoine de Bengy Puyvallée and Kristian Bjørkdahl, 60–79. Cambridge: Cambridge University Press, 2021.

Brandal, Nikolai, Øivind Bratberg, and Dag Einar Thorsen. *Sosialdemokratiet: Fortid–nåtid–framtid*. Oslo: Universitetsforlaget, 2011.

Brandal, Nikolai, and Dag Einar Thorsen. "Between Individualism and Communitarianism: The Nordic Way of Doing Politics." In *Sustainable Modernity: The Nordic Model and Beyond*, edited by Nina Witoszek and Atle Midttun, 160–86. London: Routledge, 2018.

Byrkjeflot, Haldor, Lars Mjøset, Mads Mordhorst, and Klaus Petersen, eds, *The Making and Circulation of Nordic Models, Ideas and Images*. London: Routledge.

Dewey, John. *The Public and Its Problems* (1927). In *John Dewey: The Later Works, 1925–1953*, edited by Jo Ann Boydston, 2:235–372. Carbondale: Southern Illinois University Press, 1984.

Dølvik, Jon Erik, Tone Fløtten, Jon M. Hippe, and Bård Jordfald. *Den nordiske modellen mot 2030: Et nytt kapittel?* Oslo: FAFO, 2014.

Esping-Andersen, Gøsta. *The Three Worlds of Welfare Capitalism*. Princeton, NJ: Princeton University Press, 1990.

Hammer, Svein. *Sosialdemokrati versus nyliberalisme: Norsk styringskunst og samfunnsforming, 1814–2020*. Oslo: Solum Bokvennen, 2020.

Hauglie, Anniken. "Part of the Same Future: Experiences from the Norwegian Social Dialogue." Address presented to the 106th session of the International Labour Conference, Geneva, June 7, 2017. https://www.regjeringen.no/en/aktuelt/tripartism-part-of-the-same-future—experiences-from-the-norwegian-social-dialogue/id2555610/.

Hook, Sidney. "Introduction." In *John Dewey: The Later Works, 1925–1953*, edited by Jo Ann Boydston, 1:vii–xxiii. Carbondale: Southern Illinois University Press, 1981.

Innset, Ola. *Markedsvendingen: Nyliberalismens historie i Norge*. Bergen: Fagbokforlaget, 2020.

Jansen, Sue Curry. "Phantom Conflict: Lippmann, Dewey, and the Fate of the Public in Modern Society." *Communication and Critical/Cultural Studies* 6, no. 3 (2009): 221–45.

———. "Walter Lippmann, Straw Man of Communication Research." In *The History of Media and Communication Research: Contested Memories*, edited by David W. Park and Jefferson Pooley, 71–111. New York: Peter Lang, 2008.

Johansen, Anders. *Komme til orde: Politisk kommunikasjon, 1814–1913*. Oslo: Universitetsforlaget, 2020.

Kvavik, Robert M. *Interest Groups in Norwegian Politics*. Oslo: Universitetsforlaget, 1976.

Lippmann, Walter. *The Phantom Public* (1925). Abingdon: Routledge, 2017.

———. *Public Opinion* (1922). Abingdon: Routledge, 2017.

Marklund, Carl. "The Nordic Model on the Global Market of Ideas: The Welfare State as Scandinavia's Best Brand." *Geopolitics* 22, no. 3 (2017): 623–39.

Mouffe, Chantal. *Agonistics: Thinking the World Politically*. London: Verso, 2013.

Nordby, Trond. *Korporatisme på norsk, 1920–1990*. Oslo: Universitetsforlaget, 1994.

Olstad, Finn. *Frihetens århundre: Norsk historie gjennom de siste hundre år*. Oslo: Pax, 2010.

Rakow, Lana F. "Family Feud: Who's Still Fighting About Dewey and Lippmann?" *Javnost—the Public* 25, no. 1 (2018): 75–82.

———. *John Dewey: A Critical Introduction to Media and Communication Theory*. New York: Peter Lang, 2019.

Rokkan, Stein. "Norway: Numerical Democracy and Corporate Pluralism." In *Political Opposition in Western Democracies*, edited by Robert A. Dahl, 70–115. New Haven, CT: Yale University Press, 1966.
Rommetvedt, Hilmar. "Scandinavian Corporatism in Decline." In *The Nordic Models in Political Science: Challenged, but Still Viable?*, edited by Oddbjørn Knutsen, 171–92. Bergen: Fagbokforlaget, 2017.
Schudson, Michael. "The 'Lippmann-Dewey Debate' and the Invention of Walter Lippmann as an Anti-Democrat 1986–1996." *International Journal of Communication* 2 (2008): 1031–42.
———. "The Trouble with Experts—and Why Democracies Need Them." *Theory and Society* 35, no. 5 (2006): 491–506.
———. "Walter Lippmann's Ghost: An Interview with Michael Schudson." *Mass Communication and Society* 19, no. 3 (2016): 221–29.
Sejersted, Francis. *The Age of Social Democracy: Norway and Sweden in the Twentieth Century*. Princeton, NJ: Princeton University Press, 2011.
———. *Sosialdemokratiets tidsalder: Norge og Sverige i det 20. århundre*. Oslo: Pax, 2005.
Skjeie, Hege, and Birte Siim. "Scandinavian Feminist Debates on Citizenship." *International Political Science Review* 21, no. 4 (2000): 345–60.
Slagstad, Rune. *De nasjonale strateger*. Oslo: Pax, 1998.
Tvedt, Terje. *Utviklingshjelp, utenrikspolitikk og makt: Den norske modellen*. Oslo: Gyldendal, 2003.
———. *Verdensbilder og selvbilder: En humanitær stormakts intellektuelle historie*. Oslo: Universitetsforlaget, 2002.
Witoszek, Nina. *The Origins of the "Regime of Goodness": Remapping the Cultural History of Norway*. Oslo: Universitetsforlaget, 2011.

9

DEMOCRACY NOW: RECOVERING THE POLITICAL PRAGMATISM OF WALTER LIPPMANN AND JOHN DEWEY

Scott Welsh

It is difficult to write about what Walter Lippmann and John Dewey have to do with us today when we have so little sense for what tomorrow might bring. The beginning of the third decade of the twenty-first century has been nothing if not unpredictable. Hence, it is not clear that a chapter initially drafted before the COVID-19 pandemic, the Russian invasion of Ukraine, and stubbornly high inflation is worth revising. Add to all this a US president attempting to undermine a democratic election by lying about the results and perhaps we cannot all help but wish that we could just start over. Do-overs and mulligans are the order of the day, it seems.

At the same time, Lippmann and Dewey were no strangers to crisis. Lippmann was especially uncertain that his *Public Opinion*, published in 1922, was prepared to do much more than describe the problems the public faced, just as Dewey would still be doing, five years later. "In the present state of political science there is," Lippmann concluded, "a tendency for one situation to change into another, before the first is clearly understood, and so to make much political criticism hindsight and little else."[1] Perhaps, though, we might be permitted to take some inspiration from their hindsight, looking back, as they did, on a crisis that was unlike anything that had come before it.

The standard account of Lippmann and Dewey suggests that Lippmann takes the realistic route and Dewey the idealistic. And while the paths to a more democratic future that they mark out are certainly different, it is not clear that either is ultimately more realistic than the other, for both end in the same place: both project democratic futures in which citizens, with great effort, and quite consciously, come to understand more fully the wider world in which they live, the plight of others within it, and act in concert to pursue the good of each and all in a fully inclusive way. The method by which Dewey imagines we can arrive at something approaching an ideal democratic future is "on the winged words of conversation" in which the artfully reported results of scientific investigation become the subject of daily, face-to-face conversation.[2] Lippmann imagines that we can get there through expert inquiry, more effective reporting of the results of inquiry, and citizens educated to properly gauge the value of their opinions (251–57).

In *The Public and Its Problems*, Dewey argued that the "idea" of democracy is indistinguishable from "the idea of community life itself" (148). Genuine community occurs, Dewey explains, "wherever there is conjoint activity whose consequences are appreciated as good by all singular persons who take part in it, and where the realization of the good is such as to effect an energetic desire and effort to sustain it in being just because it is a good shared by all." According to Dewey, "the clear consciousness of a communal life, in all its implications, constitutes the idea of democracy" (149). Scholars who seek justice, inclusion, and equality do nothing if not promote consciousness of the wide range of activities that produce life in society and all their radiating, unpredictable consequences. This idea lies at the heart of democracy for Dewey because democracy, as an idea, "denotes effective regard for whatever is distinctive and unique in each, irrespective of physical and psychological qualities" (151). In other words, if a society does not consciously tend to the consequences that affect each and every individual in distinct and unique ways, that society is not truly governed by *all* the people. This language is certainly resonant with the reformist democratic spirit that has emerged from the Black Lives Matter movement, especially as it intersects with a recognition that the poor and people of color experienced the most devastating consequences of COVID-19 at much higher rates, at least initially, compared to white people.[3]

That Lippmann performs a similar attitude throughout *Public Opinion* is not often acknowledged.[4] Even for Lippmann, the democratic idea is similarly bigger than elections and majority rule. "No electoral device," he argues, "no manipulation of areas, no change in the system of property, goes to the root of the matter." And "no reform, however sensational, is truly radical, which does not consciously provide a way of overcoming the subjectivism of human opinion based on the limitation of individual experience." As much as alterations to "systems of government, of voting, and representation" may invite people to broaden their perspective, it is only through education,

Lippmann argues, that "the enormous censoring, stereotyping, and dramatizing apparatus can be liquidated" (249, 255, 257). Of course, Lippmann did not believe that such enlargement of perspective would bubble up spontaneously from the hearts and minds of citizens in conversation, but would instead require a "Socrates," or educators and mediators, who could help people "separate" words, emotions, and images that become uncritically "entangled." Nevertheless, according to Lippmann, sorting out fictions from expertly identified facts, for the benefit of elected officials and voters alike, would form the basis of a democracy that is genuinely, and consciously, in the interest of all and not only some (254–56). While Lippmann and Dewey were certainly not revolutionaries, they did look forward to a day in the future when a more robust democratic spirit will have fully revolutionized actually existing democratic practice.

Yet for all their idealistic projection into the future, Lippmann and Dewey emerged out of the "war to end all wars" with a clear-eyed sense for what the practice of democratic politics, in their time, fundamentally entailed. And what they both saw, as they looked around them, was a practice of democratic politics that looks very much like what we see today. They saw politicians competing for the votes of variously engaged and resigned, foolish and wise, angry and peaceful citizens just trying to get through the day. When Lippmann and Dewey identified the practices that represented the most basic exercise of democracy, which is to say the existing practices that they believed would need to be leveraged to produce any approximation of a more ideally democratic future, they looked, equally, to the give-and-take, rough-and-tumble, of day-to-day political contest.

Speaking pragmatically about democracy as they saw it enacted around them, Lippmann and Dewey described democracy as a relationship between rulers and the ruled in which the rulers were accountable to a voting public. This accountability was mediated by what they called "publicity agents" competing for the attention, support, and votes of those who they thought they might be able to turn out to vote. "This is not the most inspiring of the different meanings of democracy," Dewey recognized, "but it contains about all that is relevant to *political* democracy," he made very clear (132, 82). Dewey's distinction between what he called *political* democracy versus the *idea* of democracy (or "the idea of community life itself") is perhaps especially relevant to the frustrated democratic idealism of the present, among both citizens and theorists. This distinction might allow us to appreciate better that the competition for votes—and the ongoing existence of that competition—constitutes the very avenue through which "community life itself" can be improved. The need to win elections is precisely what leads to political efforts better focused and political coalitions better conceived—which is to say the constitution of governing majorities. In other words, the democratic pragmatism that unites Lippmann and Dewey is their shared insistence that improvement pretty much only occurs through the tireless efforts of individuals (what we might call "activists") working with and through symbols to secure electoral and legislative victories. Consequently, inasmuch as Dewey and Lippmann imagined that ideal democracy, in the future, could perhaps resemble something like a mode of scientifically inflected, consciously inclusive, mutually respectful deliberation in pursuit of the common good, they were no less cognizant of what political democracy now demands.

The trouble Lippmann and Dewey share is that they often demeaned the practice of democratic politics in the moment as they envisioned an allegedly more genuine democracy in the future. They did this by isolating what they each regarded as the most essential democratic characteristics or qualities in the present (science and deliberation) and imagined that those good or promising elements might eventually displace the bad or unfortunately necessary elements (the manipulation of symbols in order to win electoral majorities). The problem with this way of imagining progress from present to future is that all the things that must be done now, in the realm of actually existing political democracy, end up being marked as somehow compromised, tawdry, or democratically second-rate—and precisely at the moments when we need those things most. The aim of this essay, in contrast, is to feature directly what Lippmann and Dewey nevertheless did identify as the practices essential to actually existing democratic politics even as they imagined a future in which those practices would no longer be necessary. In other words, this chapter attempts to reclaim the pragmatism in Lippmann's and Dewey's accounts of democracy. This is important because building a bridge to something approaching more effective and equitable forms of political association will require that we not become discouraged. While we must undoubtedly continue to draw inspiration from a revolutionary democratic spirit, the less inspiring work of day-to-day politics will still need to be done, and for it to be done we are going to need a language with which to value it.

The Early Twentieth-Century Scene of Democracy

Although we tend to emphasize Dewey's hopefulness more than his discouragement, Dewey was no less attentive to the realities of political democracy than was Lippmann. Much of *The Public and Its Problems* is a direct affirmation of *Public Opinion*'s description of democratic practice at the time, or what Dewey famously described as the "most effective indictment of democracy as conceived ever penned."[5] We need to be clear, however, about what, in fact, Lippmann was indicting. Lippmann was not so much indicting the practices he described but was, instead, indicting theories of democracy that suggested that democratic practice could work any other way given the current state of scientific inquiry, reporting, and education. Yet, not unlike Dewey, Lippmann also hoped that with improvements to inquiry, reporting, and education, "it will become more possible" to "reduce the discrepancies between the conceived environment and the effective environment," and for government then to operate "more and more by consent" and "less and less by coercion." But in the absence of improved inquiry, reporting, and education, where "masses of people must cooperate in an uncertain and eruptive environment," Lippmann maintained that "it is usually necessary to secure unity and flexibility *without real consent*" (249, 153; emphasis added). Hence, in the absence of a persistent and reliable alignment of the public's *conception* of reality with *reality itself*, the ongoing existence of democratic politics is premised on leaders' uses of symbols that elicit demonstrations of support that are not indicative of fully informed consent—or what many scholars writing in this volume would recognize as a familiar account of rhetoric.

Neither Lippmann nor Dewey describes a state of affairs or a democratic scene that is unfamiliar to contemporary political observers. Their relentless empiricism can still be bracing, however, especially when the subject turns to citizens' ability to meet the challenges that representative democracy thrusts on them. Walter Lippmann reviewed research that suggested that even the best informed citizens spent little more than thirty minutes per day with a newspaper given the numerous other work and domestic responsibilities that occupy most everyone (37–40, 228). Dewey agreed that citizens largely do not pay attention to political details outside of the final few months of an election cycle, and even those who do bother to pay attention in those waning months constitute no more than half of the electorate (132–37). The half that is paying attention, Lippmann makes clear, and Dewey affirms, are invariably motivated by "complexes of all sorts" as well as "economic interest, personal animosity, racial prejudice, [and] class feeling," which "distort our reading, our thinking, our talking and our behavior in a great variety of ways." And good intentions often do not allow us to avoid casting votes on such grounds, which include what we would describe today as unacknowledged and unearned "privilege." Even worse, Lippmann argues, are the "mass of absolutely illiterate, of feeble-minded, grossly neurotic, undernourished and frustrated individuals" that politicians must attempt to win over "who are mentally children or barbarians, people whose lives are a morass of entanglements, people whose vitality is exhausted, shut-in people, and people whose experience has comprehended no factor in the problem under discussion." "The stream of public opinion," Lippmann notes, "is stopped by them in little eddies of misunderstanding, where it is discoursed with prejudice and far-fetched analogy" (48).

Dewey was no more sanguine about the then-current public's ability to carry out the function of citizenship. Dewey's response to Lippmann's charge that the public was a "phantom" was to say that individuals do not exist in isolation but are socialized as they grow up in association with others, which provides for a share in common symbols that makes meaningful communication, and publics, possible. Nevertheless, "socialization," Dewey clarifies, "is as marked by the formation of frivolous, dissipated, fanatical, narrow-minded and criminal persons as in that of competent inquirers, learned scholars, creative artists and good neighbors." This would explain why "popular opinion is little troubled by questions of logical consistency," in Dewey's estimation, and all-too-readily accepts a nonsensical "amalgam" of contradictory ideas. For "what is logic between friends?" he wryly concludes (70, 91).

Moreover, with industrialization and new modes of transportation and communication, the society that citizens must form logical opinions about, Dewey argues, is no longer merely one's hometown or region, but has expanded, in the United States, to a "continental nation state" and all of its attending and complex interactions with other nations (110–11, 114, 127). This Great Society "has so enormously expanded, multiplied, intensified and complicated the scope of indirect consequences, formed such immense and consolidated unions in action, on an impersonal rather than a community basis, that the resultant public cannot identify and distinguish itself" (126). And it is not only citizens who have trouble sorting through all the details. "Even the specialist," Dewey notes, "finds it difficult to trace the chain" of "cause and effect" well after an event is over, let alone looking to the future, as citizens must (135). "Conjoint actions which have indirect, serious consequences are multitudinous beyond comparison, and each one of them crosses the others and generates its own group of persons specially affected with little to hold these different publics together in an integrated whole" (137).

There is no daylight between Lippmann and Dewey on this subject. And no amount of willpower or good intentions can possibly solve the problem of too many issues and too little time to make sense of them all. Even limiting the scope of concern to just oneself provides no greater opportunity for success. For "no one can take into account" Dewey argues, "all the consequences of the acts he performs. It is a matter of necessity for him, as a rule, to limit his attention and foresight to matters which, as we say, are distinctly his own business" (52). Or, as Lippmann states, "the real environment is altogether too big, too complex, and too fleeting for direct acquaintance. We are not equipped to deal with so much subtlety, so much variety, so many permutations and combinations." Instead, to function within such an environment, "we have to reconstruct it on a simpler model," through the medium of what Lippmann calls stereotypes, fictions, and symbols. These combine to produce what Lippmann refers to as "pseudo-environments" or "pictures in our heads" that serve the purpose of providing us with operative visions of reality that are not reality itself, but are radically simplified, truncated versions that merge with the dramatic forms and genres we use to give meaning to everything that is important to us (10–11).

Dewey acknowledges that it is tempting to imagine a way to strip human thought of such fictions "and stick to the facts verifiably ascertained." But even if publics could focus long enough to make sense of even a narrow band of facts, such facts "do not exist outside human desire and judgment" for "ideas belong to human beings who have bodies." As desiring beings, humans "are naturally short-sighted, and the short-sightedness is increased and perverted by the influence of appetite and passion" (6, 8, 56). These appetites and passions, as Lippmann indicates, combine with cultural socialization to teach us to stereotype and dramatize the world around so that we each become characters in our own unique world-making dramas (110). Or, as Dewey puts it, in the absence of a controlled laboratory environment, in what he calls "the field of social discussion," the "human imagination" is more often than not permitted to "run wild in its theories of interpretation" even when "we suppose the brute facts to remain the same." That human beings must actively make sense of events around them, with the aid of imagination, explains "how and why," according to Dewey, "publics and political institutions differ widely from epoch to epoch and from place to place" even though the facts themselves may overlap considerably (3, 65).

That people must use their imaginations to construct a whole world out of the fragments they encounter accounts for why even apparent agreement, among citizens, is rarely as it seems. For even as people are socialized in shared and overlapping ways, "the conflicting streams of social influence," Dewey argues, nevertheless "come to a single and conclusive issue only in personal consciousness and deed." This means that even when citizens appear to be acting in concert, on the surface, and even share a wide range of influences, there is still a high degree of diversity at the level of *personal* meaning and intent as no two people identically rank or sort those influences in the context of their own attempts to make sense of the world. Consequently, a public "acts" only in the metaphorical sense, since votes and allegiances are only conducted "through the medium of individuals." This means, according to Dewey, that "the public" is "a collective name for a multitude of persons each voting as an anonymous unit" with each person voting to "express" a will that, while on the surface in support of a common candidate or shared resolution, remains nevertheless unique to each individual's particular nexus of socialization, imagination, and desire (75). In other words, Dewey does not imagine *real consent* to be any more achievable than does Lippmann.

As previously noted, Lippmann describes human interpretation as dramatization. What is especially interesting, and little remarked on, is that he does not merely describe political speech as a mode of dramatic projection or storytelling but sees individual audience members as dramatists or storytellers. An "identical story" he explains, "is not the same story to all who hear it." Rather, each audience member "will enter it at a slightly different point, since no two experiences are exactly alike; he will reenact it in his own way, and transfuse it with his own feelings." Consider, for example, just the simple act of discussing "the meaning" of a television show, movie, or speech with a group; Lippmann's insight becomes apparent so quickly that it barely registers as insight. Nevertheless, the net effect may not often be appreciated: "It is as if a play," Lippmann argues, "were rewritten each time it is performed with all the changes of emphasis and meaning that the actors *and audience* inspired" (emphasis added). But it is not only that different audience members have different interpretations. Instead, "in almost every story that catches our attention we become a character and act out the role with pantomime of our own." For Lippmann, the script is not just performed by audience members, it is effectively "edited and revised by all who played with it as they heard it, used it for their daydreams, and passed it on" (110). Hence, to "assume that all who voted your ticket voted as you did" is a "disingenuous thing to do." Instead, "all these voters were inextricably entangled with their own desire." Moreover, as time passes, the stories we tell ourselves evolve and change to such an extent that the reasons we gave on election day for voting a particular way may no longer be the reasons we are giving come inauguration day (126–27).

In their descriptions of the scene of democracy, Lippmann as well as Dewey describe citizens overwhelmed by the vastness of the range of facts and concerns that compete for their limited attention. Moreover, they are equally explicit in their rejection of any sense that citizens are able to comprehend, regularly or reliably, the complexity of even single issues with any degree of depth or complexity, unless the issue happens to match their particular vocational specialty. Consequently, citizens must, out of necessity, simplify and dramatize the world around them to such a degree that their senses of the world often come to bear only a passing relationship to reality and often even less to each other's. Add to this the normal human tendencies toward selfishness, tribal allegiances, racial animus, class resentment, insufficient education, and a press that is consistently no better able to render the world in other than reductive, stereotyped, dramatized, and sensational terms, and it does seem, as Dewey initially concludes, "close to denial of the possibility of realizing the idea of a democratic public" (185).

The Idea of Democracy

Of course, the scene of actually existing political democracy was, for Dewey, something different than "the idea of a democratic public" (185) in the same way that actually existing democracy was different, for Lippmann, than an imagined democratic future "liquidated" of "censoring, stereotyping, and dramatizing" (255). The "idea" of democracy is fundamentally an "ideal," according to Dewey: "the tendency and movement of some thing which exists carried to its final limit, viewed as completed, perfected." Yet, "since things do not attain such fulfillment" he adds, "but are in actuality distracted or interfered with, democracy in this sense is not a fact and never will be" (148). In this sense, Dewey is actually far less idealistic than Lippmann. In contrast, Lippmann says in the concluding section of *Public Opinion* that government intelligence agencies, in cooperation with university researchers and the press, had shown him that "there is a way out, a long one to be sure, but a way" out of the problem of people being unable to perceive and understand a single, common, true version of events. With the additional help of expert mediators, political actors would be able to cleanly distinguish facts from stereotypes which, he claims, "disintegrates partisanship" (249, 254).

One cannot help but imagine that Dewey had Lippmann's conclusions in mind as he began *The Public and Its Problems*, starting, as he did, by saying, "If one wishes to realize the distance which may lie between 'facts' and the meaning of facts, let one go to the field of social discussion." At the same time, Dewey imagines a future quite in line with Lippmann's in this respect. While "the power of physical facts to coerce belief does not reside in bare phenomena," it can emerge, he argues, "from method, from the technique of research and calculation" (3). The problem, for Dewey, is that this "kind of knowledge and insight" does "not yet exist" within public discourse writ large, and therefore this "prime condition of a democratically organized public" will "be one of the last to be fulfilled." For the *idea* or *ideal* of democracy to be approximated, even if not fully realized, the results of scientific inquiry must be broadly "disseminated." Such dissemination, however, is not simply "scattering at large" but "must take root and have a chance of growth" (166–67). The problem is that "the mass public is not interested in learning and assimilating the results of accurate investigation." The solution, according to Dewey, is "art," for "artists have always been the real purveyors of the news." Properly disseminated, the results of scientific inquiry, Dewey insists, "would have such an enormous and widespread human bearing that its bare existence would be an irresistible invitation to a presentation of it which would have a direct popular appeal" (183–84).

Perhaps anticipating readers raising an eyebrow or two, Dewey notes how it might be "easy to exaggerate the amount of intelligence and ability" that might be "demanded" even for publics to render meaningful judgments on artistic presentations of the results of scientific inquiry. But he does little to address our concerns. Instead, he raises the bar still higher. He writes, "Until secrecy, prejudice, bias, misrepresentation, and propaganda as well as sheer ignorance are replaced by inquiry and publicity, we have no way of telling how apt for judgment of social policies the existing intelligence of the masses may be." In other words, by the final chapter of *The Public and Its Problems*, *not* sardonically titled "The Problem of Method," Dewey is calling for the same liquidation of stereotyping, dramatizing, and censoring from public discourse, to be replaced by the results of scientific research, that Lippmann projected on the future (209). The main difference between Lippmann and Dewey is that while Lippmann largely imagines citizens variously engaging and disengaging from public deliberation depending on their specific expertise, leaving citizens to participate indirectly through voting and supporting research and advocacy organizations, Dewey looks ahead to citizens directly engaging the results of inquiry (251). "Systematic and continuous inquiry into all the conditions which affect association," Dewey argues, "is a precondition of the creation of a true public." Once again, however, mere dissemination of the results of inquiry is not enough. Rather, "their final actuality is accomplished in face-to-face relationships by means of direct give and take." "That and only that," he concludes, "gives reality to public opinion" that is authentically democratic (218).

Dewey, of course, is probably right. If legislative and electoral choices are ever to be free of systematic bias, injustice, and exclusion and reflect the fully conscious assent of all of those affected by a decision, then "free social inquiry" will probably need to be, indeed, "wedded to the art of full and moving communication." "The highest and most difficult kind of inquiry and a subtle, delicate, vivid and responsive art of communication" would, indeed, likely need to "take possession of the physical machinery of transmission and circulation and breathe life into it." Short of a form of human neurobiological evolution now only possible in science fiction, some sort of improved mass communication coupled with extensive face-to-face communication would probably be required for each and all to learn an "effective regard for whatever is distinctive and unique in each, irrespective of physical or psychological qualities" (184) and demonstrate "a clear consciousness of a communal life, in all its implications" (149). Maybe artificial intelligence companies are collecting all the necessary data right now. Or, as Dewey mused, perhaps one day in the future, "a state which will organize to manufacture and disseminate new ideas and new ways of thinking may come into existence" (59). Lippmann certainly wished for the same, writing, "My conclusion is that public opinions must be organized for the press if they are to be sound, not by the press as is the case today" (19). Not to put too fine a point on it but, at the very least, their guesses are probably as good as anyone else's. And, to be fair, it would be another twenty-two years before George Orwell would publish *Nineteen Eighty-Four*.

Political Democracy

Looking back a century later, it is striking how often Lippmann and Dewey referred to the future. For all the problems they chronicled, public and otherwise, they shared a vision for the future in which it surely seems like science and communication should have already helped us more fully realize the idea of democracy in the present. It's hard not to look back in longing. For all the scientific, technological, and even social problems that have been more and more effectively addressed over the past hundred years, the practice of democracy has remained as challenging as ever. People are still largely disengaged and are still unable to comprehend the complexity of even a few pressing issues, let alone the many that vie for our attention at any given moment. Racialized, tribal politics ebbs and flows rather than having been long ago eliminated. Public discourse is no less characterized by ignorance, wild flights of imagination, dramatization, and stereotypes. Public opinion seems equally impervious to the results of inquiry, even with the exponential increase in the availability of artful renderings of such results across a constantly expanding number of modes of digital media. How many more artful renderings are required before the devastating reality of climate change will be acknowledged across the political spectrum? How many more expert panels need to be convened? Living in their future, it is hard to share their optimism for ours.

At the same time, as Lippmann said following World War I, "Great as was the horror, it was not universal. There were corrupt and there were incorruptible. There was muddle and there were miracles." Concerning unmet ideals, he wrote, "You can despair of what has never been. You can despair of ever having three heads." But, "if amidst all the evils of this decade, you have not seen men and women, known moments that you would like to multiply, the Lord himself cannot help you" (262). The challenge is to know where to look, and often the greatest challenge, as Orwell said, is "to see what is in front of one's nose."[6] Hence, it may be that Lippmann and Dewey were most prescient when they did not look to the future. Rather, Lippmann and Dewey were, perhaps first and foremost, keen observers of actually existing political democracy. And what the politically concerned had to do, then, to improve life in community is perhaps very much what we still have to do today.

This distinction between community and democracy is crucial, even though, in the realm of ideals, Dewey reduces the latter to the former. In practice, we engage in democratic politics, not fundamentally to instantiate "community" in some abstract sense, but to improve our lives as members of groups who experience particular consequences, what Dewey calls "publics." In other words, speaking pragmatically, Dewey argues that what citizens do in democracy is perceive consequences of behaviors, whether imagined or real, and then attempt to elect officials who will pass legislation that addresses those consequences (35).

It is important to note, however, for all of Dewey's intimations about the collective agency of "publics" or a public somehow "recognizing itself," that *he*, no less than Lippmann, repeatedly and insistently clarifies that it is individuals who do the work of producing the symbols that attract the votes that elect particular candidates who pass laws. He repeatedly states that there is no "meeting of wills" or "mind or reason" manifest by publics. Speaking even more pragmatically, he says, there is never a "mysterious collective agency" "making decisions." Instead, "some few persons who know what they are about are taking advantage of massed force to conduct the mob their way, boss a political machine, and manage affairs of corporate business" (20). Dewey's language may not be congenial to contemporary ears, but he has no illusions about how change takes place. Whenever "the public or state is involved in making social arrangements like passing laws, enforcing a contract, conferring a franchise, it still acts through concrete persons" (18). The actions of a state, he argues, are never a "direct result of organic contacts," "brooding indwelling spirit," or any other "superstition." Instead, individual political actors draw attention to particular consequences, through the medium of carefully chosen symbols that resonate with a large number of fellow citizens; politically calculating representatives are elected; bills are passed; and state agencies are created to "care for and regulate these consequences" (37–39).

Dewey, like Lippmann, often discusses such uses of symbols in derogatory terms. He says that "we seem to be approaching a state of government by hired promoters of opinion called publicity agents" who, "at election time, appeal to some time-worn slogans" in order to convince people to adopt shallow "convictions on an important subject." The method of these "exploiters of sentiment and opinion," Dewey argues, is to "take advantage" of "emotional habituations and intellectual habitudes of the part of the mass of men." They have "an extraordinary facility in enlisting upon their side the inertia, prejudices and emotional partisanship of the masses" to "manipulate social relations for their own advantage" and must be "reckoned with" (132, 169).

At the same time, Dewey is nevertheless emphatic in his insistence that "all deliberate choices and plans are finally the work of single human beings" (21). Or, as Lippmann puts it, "no common idea emerges by itself." Rather, "the art of inducing all sorts of people who think differently to vote alike is practiced in every political campaign" and is accomplished by politicians and publicity agents practiced in the art (146, 127). Inducing cooperation through symbols is possible, according to Lippmann, because symbols are inherently vague and their meanings are uniquely supplied by individual audience members, allowing them to project their own needs, desires, and stories onto the symbols employed by speakers. Leaders can use speech as a "handle" to "move a crowd" because the "idiosyncrasies of real ideas are blotted out" by symbols, preventing precise distinctions and difference of opinion from emerging into view. The symbol, Lippmann argues, "obscures personal intention, neutralizes discrimination, and obfuscates individual purpose." It is "the instrument by which in the short run the mass escapes from its own inertia, the inertia of indecision, or the inertia of headlong movement" (150, 153). A symbol has the "power to syphon emotion out of distinct ideas," becoming equally a "mechanism of solidarity" as well as "exploitation." Nevertheless, it is only through the strategic use of symbols, and diversely appropriate-able stories, that diverse and diversely informed members of the public, within actually existing political democracy, can come to support a "common end" (151, 131, 110).

Perhaps surprisingly, especially after he dismisses the machinations of publicity agents and politicians as "exploiters of sentiment and opinion," Dewey concedes that "if individuals had no stated conditions under which they come to agreement with one another, any agreement would terminate in a twilight zone of vagueness or would have to cover such an enormous ground of detail as to be unwieldy and unworkable" (54). The making of laws, instead, is an exercise in rhetorical leadership and what Dewey repeatedly calls "canalization," in which energies are directed toward concrete ends through use of symbols. For "only when there exist signs and symbols of activities and of their outcome can the flux be viewed as from without, be arrested for consideration and esteem and be regulated." In this way diverse "wants and impulses are then attached to common meanings" by "means of shared signs." "Thus," he says, "there is generated what, *metaphorically*, may be termed a general will and social consciousness: desire and choice on the part of individuals in behalf of activities that, by means of symbols, are communicable and shared by all concerned" (emphasis added). Hence, "force" is "not eliminated" by this sort of sharing "but is transformed in use and direction by ideas and sentiments made possible by means of symbols" (152–53).

In other words, Dewey is not so naïve as to suppose that this sharing is *literally* a "meeting of wills," as noted previously, or actually a "general will." Instead, he is explaining, much like Lippmann, that what we call a "general will," or what Lippmann calls "public opinion," is actually a product of symbol usage that transforms conflicting "desire and choice on the part of individuals" into something that can be held in common due to the ability of symbols to select for what is perceived as common while at the same time obscuring difference. This makes clear the broader significance of Dewey's earlier discussion of the fundamental relationship between facts, desire, and interpretation. "Political facts" he says, "are not outside human desire and judgment." Rather, "change men's estimate of the value of existing political agencies and forms, and the latter change more or less" (6).

The further challenge is that diverse political actors are constantly competing to change our "estimate of the value" of things. "Bodies of men," Dewey does not need to remind us, "are constantly engaged in attacking and trying to change political habits, while other bodies of men are actively supporting and justifying them." As Dewey is well-known for having argued, the problem of the public is as much too many publics as too few. The number and variety of consequences that warrant our consideration have the effect of inciting the production of more and more varied publics than citizens are capable of thoughtfully addressing. Each resulting interest group must therefore compete for attention with all the rest, as not everything is able to be addressed at once. Moreover, even when a group coalesces around the symbol-induced perception of a particular set of consequences and manages to attract, imaginatively and dramatically, the attention of enough citizens to spur legislative action, representatives of existing publics will then work to "obstruct the organization of a new public" out of fear that their earlier concerns may no longer be addressed. As a result, "Retrogression is as periodic as advance" (30–31).

Democracy Now

Neither Lippmann nor Dewey, of course, fully approved of the actually existing practice of democracy as they described it. Like contemporary interpreters of each, public sphere theorists, and deliberative democrats, among others, Dewey hoped that conflict might be significantly curtailed (72) and Lippmann imagined a form of communication that might dissolve partisanship with the help of expert mediation (254).[7] Both looked forward to an overwhelming expansion of the role of the results of scientific inquiry, as well as the administrative state, in public discussion and decision-making. Such an expansion, they hoped would eventually cultivate a public far less susceptible to the persuasive designs of publicity agents, electoral strategists, and political machines. Ultimately, a more thoroughly informed public, they hoped, would learn to discount their fictions and stereotypes and see the world more like it actually is instead of how interested parties preferred that they imagine it to be. This would lead to what Dewey called *genuine* community or what Lippmann referred to as the constructive use of reason. Both envision a state of affairs in which the unique needs of all would be understood, respected, and addressed.

The problem is that, in the meantime, achieving all the incremental improvements to the communities in which we live (and that we so desperately and immediately need) requires people engaging in all the activities that occupy the attention of publicity agents and electoral strategists. These political professionals and politicians must (as Lippmann and Dewey make clear when operating in a fully pragmatic mode) engage a diverse public composed of variously uninformed, prejudiced, and busy people who have only a passing interest in most issues relevant to an electoral campaign. These are citizens who, as Lippmann and Dewey make clear, understand the world fundamentally with the aid of conflicting uses of imagination. In the absence of a clear understanding of systematic, scientific inquiry concerning an issue, we have no choice but to assemble pictures in our heads from the material of our past education, experience, fleeting news reports, and appeals from interested parties.

Professionals and politicians assembling electoral majorities out of citizens as we are, and not as we wish to be, is democracy as it is practiced. And this practice is one of inventing dramatic stories and combinations of symbols drawn from cultural materials at hand. It is building electoral coalitions, yielding on one's principles, and meeting audiences where they are. To make the communities we live in more just and more inclusive, now, we need to accept that elections need to be won and legislative victories need to be secured. Speaking empirically, democracy is, first and foremost, a tactical practice, in a moment, of generating a vote from a majority that appears to be rooted in concretely shared plans and intentions. Democracy as immediately practiced, Lippmann and Dewey carefully documented, is not only frustrating and compromising, but deeply pragmatic about means and ends.

Future engagement with Lippmann and Dewey might do well to consider, even more thoroughly, what they thought democracy was, above and beyond what they wished it could become. As it is, democracy is the name of the form of government in which foolish, shortsighted, distracted, sometimes angry, sometimes hopeful, underinformed, misinformed, well-informed, racist, sexist, inclusive, kind, and confused citizens get to have a say in who governs them and what those governments do. They get to have a say by voting for politicians and parties who dramatize facts and events in ways that make them into stories that citizens might care about, even just momentarily. As much as public discourse and citizen engagement might conceivably be improved, politicians and communication professionals, for better and worse, do the daily work of stitching together narratives and locating symbols that groups of citizens might mutually applaud, often for divergent reasons, but mutually applaud nevertheless. In other words, Lippmann and Dewey offer grounds for reappraising what might be called unapologetically *rhetorical* politics, as it is actually practiced, above and beyond how we wish it might be.[8]

As immediate crises fade into the past, and resolve inevitably weakens, what might seem at one moment like a new collective identification with the common good will inevitably return to being a point of contention. Outrage will need to evolve into legislative victories and collective relief will need to be politically overcome (lest we forget). And, at every turn, elections will need to be won and governing majorities constituted through appealing to diversely informed, diversely motivated, and diversely affected publics. Most important, citizens must continue to believe that democratic politics—as it exists and not as we wish it to be—is worth the trust we place in it. This is why we must recover the deeper pragmatism equally present in Lippmann and Dewey—the pragmatism that is attuned to the political management of consequences moment by moment, and not just envisioning how they might be better managed in the future. For when a society becomes broadly impatient with democracy in its immediate, political manifestations, we are left only with ideal democracy, which as Dewey plainly stated, "is not a fact and never will be" (148). In other words, as tempting as it will likely always be to draw Lippmann and Dewey into debate through an emphasis on their idealized prescriptions, we should repeatedly return, rather, as I have here, to their detailed agreement on what actually existing democracy entails, both then and now—as well as for the foreseeable future.[9]

Notes

1. Lippmann, *Public Opinion*, 260. Further citations of this work in this chapter are given in the text.
2. Dewey, *Public and Its Problems*, 218. Further citations of this work in this chapter are given in the text.
3. Leonhardt, "Covid and Race."
4. See Schudson, "'Lippmann-Dewey Debate,'" for more on the tendency to draw Lippmann and Dewey into debate while minimizing their similarities.
5. As quoted in Westbrook, *John Dewey and American Democracy*, 294.
6. Angus and Orwell, *George Orwell*, 125.
7. Schudson, "'Lippmann-Dewey Debate.'" For more on the ideals animating public sphere theory and deliberative democracy, see Welsh's *Rhetorical Surface of Democracy* and "Deliberative Democracy and the Rhetorical Production."
8. See Welsh, *Rhetorical Surface of Democracy*.
9. Schudson, "'Lippmann-Dewey Debate.'"

Bibliography

Angus, Ian, and Sonia Orwell, eds. *George Orwell: In Front of Your Nose, 1946–1950*. Boston: Nonpareil Books, 2000.
Dewey, John. *Public and Its Problems* (1927). Athens, OH: Swallow Press, 1991.
Leonhardt, David. "Covid and Race." *New York Times*, June 9, 2022. https://www.nytimes.com/2022/06/09/briefing/covid-race-deaths-america.html.

Lippmann, Walter. *Public Opinion* (1922). New York: Free Press, 1997.
Schudson, Michael. "The 'Lippmann-Dewey Debate' and the Invention of Walter Lippmann as an Anti-Democrat, 1986–1996." *International Journal of Communication* 2 (2008): 1031–42.
Welsh, Scott. "Deliberative Democracy and the Rhetorical Production of Political Culture." *Rhetoric and Public Affairs* 5 (2002): 679–707.
———. *The Rhetorical Surface of Democracy: How Deliberative Ideals Undermine Democratic Politics*. Lanham, MD: Lexington Books, 2012.
Westbrook, Robert B. *John Dewey and American Democracy*. Ithaca, NY: Cornell University Press, 1991.

10

DEMOCRATIC DELIBERATION, IDENTITY, AND INFORMATION

Patricia Roberts-Miller

When I was in graduate school, it was conventional to present the debate between Lippmann and Dewey as an argument between a technocrat and democrat. Jean Goodwin summarizes the way the debate was turned into a false, but elegant, binary: Lippmann was "pessimistic, where Dewey was optimistic; concerned to remove decision-making from a feeble public to a technocratic elite, where Dewey would solve the problem of democracy with more democracy; invested in value-free scientific rationality, where Dewey embraced reasoning joined with aesthetic, emotional, and ethical responsiveness."[1] Thus, having been told that's what the debate was, that's how I read it, as did many others. Dell Champlin and Janet Knoedler, for instance, summarize Lippmann's point as follows: "Rather than striving for an impossible ideal of participatory democracy in complex societies, successful democracies would instead have to rely on trained experts in government and journalism *to make decisions* and *to disseminate those decisions to the citizenry*."[2]

If one reads the debate this way—elitism versus populism—then it would seem that Lippmann lost. Given the twentieth century's history of disastrous decisions made by various experts, their endorsement of tragic policies, and their willingness to be involved in appalling practices, Lippmann's faith in experts seemed to have been thoroughly discredited (a point discussed in more detail below). Now, however, at a point in time when fake news, bots, bizarre conspiracy theories, and blazing factionalism are acknowledged to have major impacts on voting, political action, and political deliberation, it may seem that Lippmann won, and Dewey's faith in popular reason was misplaced. After all, empirical research on voting preferences, decision-making, and cognitive biases shows that many voters make decisions on precisely the bases Lippmann criticizes.³ Most voters are not interested in doing the difficult cognitive work that is ideal for policy deliberation, don't take the time to do a lot of research, tend to rely on cognitive shortcuts (such as in-group favoritism), and are prone to rely on charismatic leadership (or identification). In light of that research, it might seem that Dewey's optimism about voters' capabilities is unfounded, and he has fallen for what political scientists call "the folk theory of democracy" (that the political action in a democracy begins with the people.) And it may therefore seem that Lippmann's solution—shifting political power to the elite—is more reasonable than it looked for some time. Perhaps Lippmann won after all.

Or perhaps Lippmann never made that argument, and it was never a debate that Lippmann or Dewey could win or lose. As others have argued, the two parts to my (mis)reading were common—that Lippmann and Dewey's writings can be usefully framed as a "debate," and that it was a neat binary of technocrat versus democrat, elitist versus populist, fatalist versus optimist. What I want to do in this chapter is three-part: first, discuss how it is a misreading, in that scholars now argue it was a much less binary and more nuanced exploration and development of ideas than the nice binary suggests; second, look at the argument normally attributed to Lippmann in light of recent research on expert and nonexpert deliberative practices; third, consider what that sometimes very pessimistic research suggests for a more hopeful democratic practice.

The Debate That Wasn't

As Michael Schudson points out, "It was never, in fact, a debate, and it is not clear that Lippmann ever considered himself to be in dialogue or discussion with Dewey."⁴ Lippmann wrote several books, over a long period, two of which are always included in the canon of the debate that wasn't (*Public Opinion* [1922] and *The Phantom Public* [1925]), and one that sometimes is (*Liberty and the News* [1920]). Dewey's book reviews of Lippmann's books and *The Public and Its Problems* (1925, in which he mentions Lippmann specifically) are always included, and various other articles and books of his are sometimes discussed. It wasn't a debate, then, in the sense that, while Lippmann changed his position repeatedly (Goodwin says, "At one time or another he experimented with a democracy that institutionalized virtually every possible arrangement of the available roles"),⁵ he didn't appear to do so in response to Dewey specifically, let alone refute any of Dewey's arguments.

In addition, their positions were not as stable nor as divergent as the term *debate* suggests, nor as much as scholarship assumes. Dewey and Lippmann changed their own arguments, agreed on many points, and disagreed on many, but their disagreements have "been distorted into a clash between elitism and populism."[6] Schudson similarly posits that Lippmann's argument specifically was distorted, in that he never argued that citizens were incompetent, nor that policy decisions should be left to experts.[7] Lippmann had two parts to his argument—the negative case and the affirmative case. His negative case, what Goodwin calls his "critique of contemporary democratic practice,"[8] concerned "the folk theory of democracy," the notion that "democracy begins with the voters. Ordinary people have preferences about what their government should do. They choose leaders who will do those things, or they enact their preferences directly in referendums. In either case, what the majority wants becomes government policy. . . . Democracy makes the people the rulers, and legitimacy derives from their consent."[9] In this view, policies are always the consequence of the policy preferences of most voters. Voters begin with a stable understanding of their needs or interests, with "fixed preferences."[10] We vote to get policies that will serve those needs or interests either indirectly (voting people in or out of office on the basis of whether those politicians served those preferences) or directly (through referenda). Lippmann's argument is that people don't really know what our needs or interests are because we don't understand the issues well enough, and we don't have the time to do so. Robert Westbrook points out that Lippmann's explanation was that "the environment of most modern political perceptions was expansive and only indirectly accessible to citizens."[11]

Dewey not only agrees with this critique but shares Lippmann's narrative as to how this situation came about. There was a simpler time when ordinary voters did have the capacity to make good political decisions—when they lived in rural townships and were able to make decisions isolated from larger issues and factors.[12] The major problem, Lippmann argued, was that, when it comes to issues outside their immediate experience, they rely on stereotypes. Dewey shared that concern, and for both, the issue had come about because of the increased complexity of the decisions facing voters, and the inability of the media to provide the relevant information: "The common problem to which Dewey and Lippmann responded was not only the increasing difficulty for citizens of an increasingly mobile and fragmented society to comprehend complex . . . global affairs; they also responded to the failures of twentieth century corporate liberal notions of democracy which relied on eighteenth century notions of the public sphere."[13] That is, both Dewey and Lippmann believed the democratic deliberation was hindered by political issues being more complicated than they used to be, and both shared the assumption that a "free" press would provide citizens with all the information we need.

Lippmann's affirmative case—what should we do about this (what Goodwin calls his "proposed communicative solution")[14]—varied from one text to another and, in general, was where he disagreed with Dewey. While he was never the technocrat bogeyman he is often accused of being, he was certainly *more* trusting of experts than Dewey was: "Although stereotypes are inescapable, it is the scientist—the same character who will shortly become Lippmann's expert—who knows that fictions are fictional."[15] Scientists can recognize fictions as such because they are more familiar with the truth—it is their job. And, interestingly enough, there is a way Dewey shares that same perception—that familiarity makes a person better able to make good decisions. Both Dewey and Lippmann privileged direct experience and direct knowledge; Dewey seemed to think that voters might find ways to get that direct experience, but Lippmann did not. Schudson says, "Lippmann argued that ordinary citizens do not perceive the world directly but only through the set of forms and stereotypes provided by the press. People could still comprehend their immediate environment, but they saw the wider world that impinged on their lives through a media-constructed 'pseudo-environment.'"[16] That is, both Lippmann and Dewey seem to suggest that the problem is the mediation of information, that direct knowledge is preferable. They disagree as to how we get that kind of unmediated knowledge, or who has it. As long as people were making decisions about that direct environment, such as in small agrarian towns, their capacities were adequate. The increased complexity of the world, however, meant that they were asked to make decisions about world wars, national policies, and scientific questions that their otherwise adequate means of reasoning couldn't manage.

Setting aside the question of whether their politically nostalgic narrative is right (that people could reason well in small towns or about things within their direct experience), it is worth noting that the fairly negative assessment of voters' capacities to understand complicated situations is supported by empirical research. Much scholarship shows that large numbers of voters rely only on partisan information and vote in purely partisan ways.[17] Achen and Bartels show that voters will vote out incumbents for such incoherent reasons as bad weather or shark attacks. They also show that partisanship is not reduced by more information—that partisanship, information, and misinformation have a complicated relationship.[18] (Stroud discusses similar research). John Hibbing and Elizabeth Theiss-Morse show that many

Americans don't even agree with the premise of democracy: "People's perception seems to be that the common good is not debatable but rather will be apparent if selfishness can be stripped away." That is, many people believe that we don't really disagree. And many people have unrealistic assumptions about what the government should do: "They somehow believe it should provide them with everything they want." Further, it isn't that people can't be informed about politics, but that they don't want to be: "The people's desire to become informed on (at best) all but a few issues makes it difficult for them to comprehend any legitimate justification for intense disagreement on other issues."[19] That there is no legitimate justification for disagreement means there is no reason to listen to anyone who disagrees—and that's a problem in a democracy. The problem isn't simply that people reason badly, with far too many issues framed as a zero-sum between in- and out-group(s), but that they don't see any particular reason to reason very much at all, let alone differently. And they're perfectly happy relying exclusively on in-group sources of information, on the false assumption that media that agrees with them is not biased.[20]

Does that suggest Lippmann was headed in a better direction—that experts shouldn't make the decisions, but that they should have a larger role?

When Doctors Disagree

As mentioned above, both Lippmann and Dewey seem to have assumed they were looking at *new* problems in democracy because the world was more complicated in their era than it had been previously, and a "free" media might engage in manufacturing consent rather than usefully informing the citizenry. Yet that's a very problematic assumption.

It is not actually clear that citizens in the early twentieth century were having *more* trouble comprehending complex global affairs, nor that an unleashed media that could create war fever was new, nor even that people did better when they weren't debating major world issues but only things within their immediate experience. The antebellum debate over slavery was often framed as an issue with global implications (as it was), about the international slave trade, cotton mills in Britain, competition with Indian cotton, the need to create new markets for slaves and, therefore, the need to expand slavery (the cause of war with Mexico).[21] Henry David Thoreau spent a night in jail in a small town in New England (the kind of place Lippmann and Dewey seem to favor as sites of good deliberation) because of slavery and the implications for international relations. Thoreau acknowledged the global implications of his political decisions, but, even if they didn't acknowledge it, people debating in a town hall in a small New England town were affected by global issues.

Many of those (perhaps unwittingly) global issues were fueled by partisan commitment and a fear-mongering media. Neither Lippmann nor Dewey mentioned anything about the slavery debate, the toxic role of the fear-mongering anti-abolitionist media in the antebellum era, the role of media and propaganda in the demagogic anti-Reconstructionist media, genocidal rhetoric about First Peoples that was still going on while they were writing, the role of media in an important debate during their time about lynching, the Red Scare happening around them, or the xenophobic rhetoric of their moment that would result in the 1924 Immigration Act. All those instances of manufactured consent would have been examples to support the claims they were making about the flaws of ordinary citizens' voting practices but would have complicated their claim that the problem was new. While there are reasons to be concerned about the ability of the government to use media to manufacture consent regarding the Great War, it's striking that they both share blind spots regarding other instances of manufactured consensus and propaganda, ones that affected them less directly.

My point is that citizens in Lippmann and Dewey's era were not faced with problems that were bigger, more complicated, more mediated, or less clear than what people had faced in earlier eras. The people in those earlier eras just didn't necessarily know how complicated, global, and risky the decisions were. They could *feel* that they were masters of the decision simply because they didn't know what factors were influencing them—how a volcanic eruption far away might influence their apple crops, what political events in other countries would do for their ability to hire farm workers, what industrialization elsewhere might mean for their local economy.

We are still in that world, where many people think that their direct experience tells them all they need to know in order to make a good political decision. Many voters believe you can look a man in the eye and know that he's a good man, that the right course of action is obvious to "real Americans,"[22] that experts are eggheads who have no contact with the real world.[23] Jan-Werner Müller is eloquent, and a little scary, on how the populist demagogue creates what feels like an authentic connection to a group of voters.[24] Kenneth Burke called that move "identification" in his 1939 analysis of Hitler's rhetoric. Jeffrey Berry and Sarah Sobieraj argue that "the outrage industry" is so profitable and politically consequential because outrage hosts create a "safe space" in which they come across as authentic, trustworthy, and knowledgeable while they present political issues in ways that seem clear and obvious. Viewers feel that they have seen the evidence for themselves.

In fact, I would suggest that it's precisely that false privileging of direct knowledge that is at the base of how and why people reason badly. A surprisingly common argument among Young Earth creationists is that evolution must be wrong because it's so hard to imagine how old the earth is according to the Big Bang theory; a common argument against evolution is that children do not inherit tattoos; Flat Earthers have videos about what the world looks like from a plane; white supremacist arguments invite people to rely on their perception that members of other races are bad; anti-vaxxers point out that you can google the ingredients in vaccines and see that they are in dangerous in some quantities. Those are poor arguments that are effective because they appeal to what Paul Saurette and Shane Gunster have called "epistemological populism." This epistemology privileges the beliefs of "'the common people,' which they possess by virtue of their proximity to everyday life," the notion that "opinions based upon first-hand experience are much more reliable as a form of knowledge than those generated by theories and academic studies," and the faith that a rhetorical "appeal to 'common sense'" is "a discussion-ending trump card."[25] Lippmann and Dewey were right about many things, but they were very wrong about epistemology, and unintentionally endorsed one that fuels partisanship, toxic populism, and demagoguery.

And I would suggest that there are two dominant ways of thinking about democratic deliberation that are damaging to democracy. The first is the one on which many people have commented: that there is a tendency to think that there is a kind of person (WASP, male, property owner) who is capable of good deliberation, and that we should give them power, while purifying our political sphere of the others. Michael Mann argues that genocide comes about when a nation decides that ethos is the same as ethnos, and that killings of political, class, or religious groups similarly happen when "the nation" is identified as one group, and every other group is, therefore, a threat.[26] Müller similarly describes how populists (I would add the modifier "toxic" to his argument) declare one group to be the real group. Democracy requires pluralism. Rhetors advocating antidemocratic policies and ideologies frame themselves as (and probably sincerely believe themselves to be) democratic insofar as their direct experience of the world tells them that they are the only people who really count: populists claim "to speak in the name of the people as a whole—and . . . morally delegitimize all those who in turn contest that claim."[27] They want a democracy of the people who matter.

Müller is both clear and persuasive that this way of thinking about democracy—that there is a real group of real people—is profoundly antidemocratic and incipiently authoritarian.

The second way of thinking about deliberation is what might be called "folk pragmatism," the notion that we only need to worry about outcomes, that as long as we're getting what we want politically, we shouldn't look into how the sausage is made. This notion can be made even stronger, in what has been called "outcomes-based ethics"—that is, assessing the effectiveness *and* ethics of a process, policy, or individual purely on the basis of whether the desired outcome was achieved.[28] Folk pragmatism says if it ain't broke, don't fix it; don't look a gift horse in the mouth—that is, it says don't worry about the process. Outcomes-based ethics says the proof is in the pudding—a good outcome is proof that that the process was good. Müller argues that populism always involves "mass clientelism," which he defines as "trading material benefits or bureaucratic favors for political support by citizens who become the populists' 'clients.'"[29] Steve Levitsky and Daniel Ziblatt point out the ways the authoritarians kill democracy partially through irresponsible practices that inflate the economy.[30] These authors are all pointing to ways that the proof is not in the pudding—it might just be a soufflé about to fall.

Scholars often note the role that unreasonable optimism plays in the debate, as when Schudson says, "Lippmann is as starry-eyed about sophisticated experts as John Dewey [is] about small-town democrats." I would suggest that they are both nostalgic about small town democracy—they were relying on stereotypes. Schudson summarizes their concern: "What is almost erased from historical memory is why Lippmann and others were so drawn to the topic of expertise. Their vision was not one of expert judgment, as superior to the personal experience of ordinary citizens, but of disinterested and expert judgment as superior to decisions that would be made by malleable citizens prey to the propaganda of urban bosses and machines and their business partners."[31] Certainly in the 1920s there were urban bosses and machines that were corrupt and got people to vote on far from reasonable bases. This was the height of Tammany Hall, a world of recent (non-WASP) immigrants mobilized to vote as their bosses dictated. But political corruption was hardly specific to urban areas, let alone non-WASP groups. The post-Reconstruction strategies for intimidating potential African American voters were corruption Lippmann and Dewey don't seem to have been concerned about, although it happened in rural areas.

This isn't to say that they were bad people for failing to think about how racist much contemporary discourse about democracy was, but just that, although they were experts thinking and writing about democratic deliberation, they, too, relied on stereotypes and fictions. I mentioned above that it's now a consensus that there was a scholarly consensus for quite some time that was grounded in a misreading of Lippmann and Dewey. Experts of communication got it wrong, probably because, as Schudson argues, that misreading was friendly to other issues and agenda the scholars had. And this was their area of expertise. In other words, how Lippmann and Dewey argued, and how scholars argued about their argument, shows that experts are not necessarily immune from the problems Lippmann and Dewey saw in nonexperts.

While Lippmann and Dewey were writing, and Lippmann was being starry-eyed about expert opinion, an especially troubling instance of the problem of expert blindness—of scientists not knowing that fictions are fictional—was expert testimony in service of the racist and damaging 1924 Immigration Act. Dr. Harry Laughlin testified that the more recent group of immigrants, from Central and Eastern Europe, were genetically prone to feeblemindedness, criminality, and mental illness on the grounds that comparison of the ethnic makeup of public mental hospitals showed those ethnicities were disproportionately represented (relative to the 1910 immigration statistics). Laughlin didn't control for income, and recent immigrants are more likely to be poor. Thus, what his data actually showed was that state mental hospitals have a lot of poor people—nothing about genetics. Laughlin's bias—his stereotype, in Lippmann's terms—was that Italians, Jews, Poles, and so on were genetically inferior, and he interpreted his data through those fictional stereotypes.[32]

Laughlin wasn't partisan, and there is no reason to think he was personally corrupt. He was an expert about and sincere supporter of "negative" eugenics—sterilizing people whom experts like him had determined were genetically inferior. As an expert, he helped states draft forced sterilization laws, exactly the kind of advisory expert Lippmann advocated. And eugenics was well accepted by many experts—it was disputed, but often on moral or pragmatic grounds. When the case about Carrie Buck—whether she should be forcibly sterilized—went before the US Supreme Court (as *Buck v. Bell*), Harry Laughlin provided the expert opinion that she was second of three generations of genetic feeblemindedness. He was, by the way, completely wrong; Carrie Buck wasn't feebleminded, nor were the other two generations.[33] Eugenics was eventually more or less discredited, not by scientific debate, but by its association with Nazis.[34]

Since eugenics provided a scientific defense of segregation and white supremacy, it wasn't entirely abandoned—just the term was avoided. Experts formed racialist science societies, funded research, founded journals, and continued to provide expert advice for lawsuits, legislation, and pundits. It's clear enough that they were politically motivated (they believed the scientific claims because they were committed to the ideology of white supremacy) but accusing their opponents of being biased by politics was a constant refrain.[35] There were similar creations of ideologically committed organizations providing expert advice when other scientific consensuses shifted: about the health consequences of smoking, the status of homosexuality as a mental illness, climate change, evolution. The problem with Lippmann's argument is his faith that "expertise" is some kind of neutrally determined, easily identified status is false; when a scientific consensus shifts such that important (or, in the case of tobacco or global warming, profitable) ideologies have their legitimacy threatened, experts can always be found.

Experts are not necessarily objective; they don't have unmediated access to information; they aren't even necessarily more logical in their reasoning. Studies have shown they also aren't very good at predictions, and many don't learn from their previous mistakes because they won't admit they made them.[36] Milton Lodge and Charles Taber have a sobering summary of the research on rationality and voters, research that included professors as subjects. They reject as "outmoded" the notion that "citizens *cause* their issue stances, candidate preferences, and vote decisions through careful, intentional reasoning." Instead, they conclude, "Looking across the experimental evidence, what we find is biased processing at every stage of the evaluative process, with the strength of associative priming effects far exceeding our expectations, and truth be told far beyond our comfort zone. Even when we ask participants to stop and think, to be even handed in their appraisal of evidence and arguments, we find precious little evidence that they can overcome their prior attitudes, or override the effects of incidental primes."[37] This is not a question of lay versus expert participants. Nor is it a question of inadequate information; it's a tendency that humans have to reason badly, especially about issues that trigger hot cognition.

The Possibilities of Persuasion

The research on how people reason may sound hopeless, and, in fact, Lodge and Taber are openly fatalistic about the ability of people—anyone—to reason well. But there is an intriguing aside in Lodge and Taber's passage: "truth be told far beyond our comfort zone." Lodge and Taber didn't much like the conclusions their research led them to. Yet they were persuaded by the data to say that people don't make decisions on the basis of a logical assessment of data. Or, as I heard a neuroscientist say, "Studies are clear that people aren't persuaded by studies." If that's the case, why did he mention the studies? Why did he change his mind? Why did Lodge and Taber? Certainly the studies about persuasion show that people, even experts, strongly rely on confirmation bias and in-group favoritism when presented with information. We try to make new information fit old beliefs, and, if we can't, we are strongly motivated to reject the information as biased.

But we *do* change our minds. Books like *Leaving the Fold* (about people who left fundagelical Christianity) or *How I Changed My Mind About Evolution* (narratives of people who abandoned creationism for evolution) show people who made major ideological shifts, sometimes at considerable personal cost, and partly or largely on the basis of new data and logical reasoning.[38] People leave cults, join cults, get persuaded by elaborate (and data-heavy) conspiracy theories, change political parties, come to believe that their reading of the Lippmann/Dewey debate was wrong, and so on.

The work on deliberative publics (such as Robert Asen's *Democracy, Deliberation and Education*) and inclusive peacemaking (such as the "Hands Across the Hills" project) show that people can change their minds about policies or prejudices, but that the process is complicated, influenced by various cognitive biases and frames (such as scarcity), affective affinities (such as trust), and that it can be very slow. There has been considerable research on deliberation within mini-publics, with some of the conclusions very hopeful.[39] But there are criticisms of such publics, and even the premise of them that agreement should be the telos of deliberation.[40]

We keep trying to solve the wrong problem, as both Lippmann and Dewey framed it: for both, the question is who has the best judgment when it comes to political decisions? And while they appear to disagree (or even keep changing their minds) about the answer, where they agree is that it should be the group with unmediated knowledge, people who are not subject to thinking by stereotype. For Dewey, conversation brings the issues into the realms in which people reason well; for Lippmann, it's various solutions, but it's still about giving decision-making power to the people whose identity, experience, or knowledge base makes them better judges of truth. Robert Westbrook summarizes one part of Lippmann's criticisms of "most men's" capacities for effective political reasoning: "They had to rely on others for information, and their sources of contact with the world were often inadequate."[41] And for both Dewey and Lippmann, mediation introduces misperception. They simply and only sometimes disagree as to who is most likely to have the most unmediated exposure.

There's nothing really wrong with Lippmann and Dewey sharing the notion that beliefs are on a range of direct to mediated, with that range also being a range of reliability—that was the dominant epistemology of their time. More recent research, however, shows that model to be wrong. And, to be blunt, so do many other things—Harry Laughlin, deeply immersed in data about immigration, was just wrong; for years, it was common knowledge that women have one more rib than men (we don't), even in communities where they must have seen skeletons. Were we to line up common knowledge and expert knowledge, there would not be a clear win on either side. Because, again, that's asking the wrong question.

Philip Tetlock's *Expert Political Opinion* is often cited as having shown that, as Tetlock would later say, "the average expert was roughly as accurate as a dart-throwing chimpanzee."[42] But what he concluded after a twenty-year research project about experts' ability to predict was much more complicated than that: it wasn't about lay versus expert, but rather about the model of knowing. Certain kinds of people were especially bad at making accurate predictions, as well as even remembering what prediction they had actually made. He called these people hedgehogs—they tended to have one theory, to think in either/or terms, to see themselves as having excellent judgment. Others, whom he called foxes, were more ideologically versatile, made nuanced predictions (often involving likelihood rather than either/or states), remembered their past predictions more accurately, and were more likely to remember and admit mistaken predictions. In short, while it's true that, on average, experts weren't better than random chance, how well experts did was strongly influenced by how they thought about their own relationship to knowledge, and their comfort with uncertainty. Tetlock and Dan Gardner's 2015 work *Superforecasting* describes how they put together a team of nonexperts who were very good at making predictions. What is shared by the experts and the superforecasters wasn't expertise, but how they thought about their own thinking.

Tetlock and Gardner summarize the processes and approaches that lead to superforecasting (that is, the most effective processes for and qualities of assessing evidence). Their "Ten Commandments for Aspiring Superforecasters" are primarily about thinking about, but not overthinking, one's own thinking—continually assessing how likely it is that one is right, what information would change the prediction (or the assessment of likelihood). The ideal superforecaster would believe that reality is complex and undetermined, that their "beliefs are hypotheses to be tested, not treasures to be protected." They are "intellectually curious, . . . introspective and self-critical, . . . comfortable with numbers," they "judge using many grades of maybe," they revise their beliefs ("when facts change, they change their minds"), they are "not wedded to any idea or agenda," and they are conscious of cognitive biases while holding a growth mindset (they believe you can get better at things).[43] If we think about deliberation this way, then it isn't about who makes decisions, or what information they have, but what model, as a culture, we have about thinking. My argument is that we should shift away from the question Lippmann and Dewey both worried over (what sort of individual voter—expert or nonexpert—has the right kind of knowledge for making good decisions) to promoting, as a culture, different models of thinking, something much closer to what Tetlock and Gardner describe.

Granted, the superforecasting experiment involved predictions and assessments that would eventually be confirmed or falsified, such as whether North Korea would develop a nuclear weapon by a certain date, and voting often involves decisions without moments of closure, such as whether Barry Goldwater would have taken a better course of action regarding Vietnam than did LBJ. There is inherently a lot of uncertainty about voting, which may be why we are so drawn to substituting factionalism for deliberation. Here, too, the issue isn't who should be making decisions, but how we should think about processes of deliberation. We are drawn to factionalism and its brother demagoguery in order to avoid uncertainty. Perhaps we should instead become more comfortable with uncertainty.

Factionalism and demagoguery—the dark side of democracy—reduce questions of policy options to questions of identity.[44] My argument is that, perhaps paradoxically, trying to determine *who* has the right information, whose knowledge is less mediated, who should be trusted with power, makes that reduction of policy questions to questions of identity seem attractive.

Good deliberation is a process, not an identity. It involves the ability to step back and think about one's processes of deliberating. That isn't a skill anyone is born having, that isn't a skill one necessarily gains by becoming an expert, that isn't a skill that results from access to more (or better) information. It is a skill we should and could be teaching. Thus, the solution isn't to try to find ways to distribute political power to the people with better judgment, but to try to create a culture, media world, and educational system that value, enable, and nurture effective and ethical processes of thinking about thinking.[45]

Müller says, "Put simply, democracy is a system where you know you can lose, but you also know that you will not always lose."[46] It is not, and never should be, a system in which all policies benefit the only kind of person defined as the "authentic" citizen. If we think of democracy that way, then what we need is not to find the people who have the kind of direct knowledge that makes them reliable sources of information and judgment. What we need is for citizens to gain a different understanding about what democracy is, value pluralism, understand cognitive biases, and think about thinking. And that brings us back to Dewey and his notion of conversation, a conversation that is unending, never closed, always contingent, often uncomfortable, and realistically hopeful. So perhaps Dewey won the argument after all.

Notes

1. Goodwin, "Walter Lippman, the Indispensable Opposition," 142.
2. Champlin and Knoedler, "Media, the News, and Democracy," 137–38.
3. See especially the summary of research in Lodge and Taber, *Rationalizing Voter*; and Stroud, *Niche News*.
4. Schudson, "'Lippmann-Dewey Debate,'" 1031.
5. Goodwin, "Walter Lippman, the Indispensable Opposition," 148.
6. Crick, "Search for a Purveyor of News," 492.
7. Schudson, "'Lippmann-Dewey Debate,'" 1033.
8. Goodwin, "Walter Lippman, the Indispensable Opposition," 143.
9. Achen and Bartels, *Democracy for Realists*, 1.
10. Binder and Lee, "Making Deals in Congress," 242.
11. Westbrook, 295.
12. See especially Lippmann, *Public Opinion*, 203–5.
13. Crick, "Search for a Purveyor of News," 488.
14. Goodwin, "Walter Lippman, the Indispensable Opposition," 143.
15. Tell, "Reinventing Walter Lippmann," 121.
16. Schudson, "Trouble with Experts," 492.
17. See especially Abramowitz, *Great Alignment*; Levendusky, *How Partisan Media Polarize America*; Mason, *Uncivil Agreement*; and Ellis and Stimson, *Ideology in America*.
18. See Achen and Bartels, *Democracy for Realists*, 118–38, 278–84.
19. Hibbing and Theiss-Morse, *Stealth Democracy*, 9, 119, 133.
20. See especially Benkler et al.
21. Roberts-Miller, *Fanatical Schemes*.
22. See Lodge and Taber, *Rationalizing Voter*; and Müller, *What Is Populism?*
23. Cramer, *Politics of Resentment*; Lecklider, *Inventing the Egghead*.
24. See especially Müller, *What Is Populism?*, 33–36.
25. Saurette and Gunster, 5.
26. Mann, *Dark Side of Democracy*.
27. Müller, *What Is Populism?*, 68.
28. Roberts-Miller, "Demagoguery," 241.

29. Müller, *What Is Populism?*, 4 (see also 46–48).
30. Levitsky and Ziblatt, *How Democracies Die*.
31. Schudson, "'Lippmann-Dewey Debate,'" 1034, 1040.
32. It's interesting that Lippmann remarks on the ways that people essentialize the "backwardness" of groups it is useful to keep backward, even noting the way that an expert can be brought in, without this observation cooling his enthusiasm for direct knowledge; see Lippmann, *Public Opinion*, 115–18.
33. See especially Lombardo, *Three Generations*.
34. For a more thorough discussion of Laughlin specifically and eugenics generally, see especially Lombardo, *Three Generations*; and Kevles, *In the Name of Eugenics*.
35. See Jackson, *Science for Segregation*.
36. See especially Tetlock, *Expert Political Judgment*.
37. Lodge and Taber, *Rationalizing Voter*, 43, 227.
38. Vance, *Leaving the Fold*; Applegate and Stump, *How I Changed My Mind About Evolution*.
39. See for example the contributions by Simone Chambers (52–71) or Michael MacKenzie and Mark Warren (95–124) in Parkinson and Mansbridge, *Deliberative Systems*.
40. See especially Rosenblum.
41. Westbrook, 295.
42. Tetlock and Gardner, *Superforecasting*, 4.
43. Tetlock and Gardner, 191–92.
44. Roberts-Miller, *Rhetoric and Demagoguery*.
45. This solution may seem ambitious; however, were it easy to solve the problem of democratic deliberation and cognitive biases, it would have been resolved long ago.
46. Müller, *What Is Populism?*, 79.

Bibliography

Abramowitz, Alan I. *The Great Alignment: Race, Party Transformation, and the Rise of Donald Trump*. New Haven, CT: Yale University Press, 2018.

Achen, Christopher H., and Larry M. Bartels. *Democracy for Realists: Why Elections Do Not Produce Responsive Government*. Princeton, NJ: Princeton University Press, 2016.

Applegate, Kathryn, and J. B. Stump. *How I Changed My Mind About Evolution: Evangelicals Reflect on Faith and Science*. Downers Grove, IL: InterVarsity Press, 2016.

Asen, Robert. *Democracy, Deliberation, and Education*. University Park: Penn State University Press, 2015.

Benkler, Yochai, Robert Faris, and Hal Roberts. *Network Propaganda: Manipulation, Disinformation, and Radicalization in American Politics*. New York: Oxford Academic, 2018.

Berry, Jeffrey, and Sarah Sobieraj. *The Outrage Industry: Political Opinion Media and the New Incivility*. New York: Oxford University Press. 2014.

Binder, Sarah A., and Frances E. Lee. "Making Deals in Congress." In *Solutions to Political Polarization in America*, edited by Nathaniel Persily, 240–61. New York: Cambridge University Press, 2015.

Burke, Kenneth. "The Rhetoric of Hitler's Battle" (1941). In *The Philosophy of Literary Form: Studies in Symbolic Action*, 191–220. Berkeley: University of California Press, 1974.

Champlin, Dell P., and Janet T. Knoedler. "The Media, the News, and Democracy: Revisiting the Dewey-Lippman Debate." *Journal of Economic Issues* 40, no. 1 (2006): 135–52.

Cramer, Katherine J. *The Politics of Resentment: Rural Consciousness in Wisconsin and the Rise of Scott Walker*. Chicago: University of Chicago Press, 2016.

Crick, Nathan. "The Search for a Purveyor of News: The Dewey/Lippmann Debate in an Internet Age." *Critical Studies in Media Communication* 26, no. 5 (2009): 480–97.

Ellis, Christopher, and James A. Stimson. *Ideology in America*. New York: Cambridge University Press, 2012.

Goodwin, Jean. "Walter Lippman, the Indispensable Opposition." In *Trained Capacities: John Dewey, Rhetoric, and Democratic Practice*, edited by Gregory Clark and Brian Jackson, 142–58. Columbia: University of South Carolina Press, 2014.

Hands Across the Hills of the Leverette Alliance. "Hands Across the Hills." Last modified July 6, 2019. https://www.handsacrossthehills.org/.

Hibbing, John R., and Elizabeth Theiss-Morse. *Stealth Democracy: Americans' Beliefs About How Government Should Work*. New York: Cambridge University Press, 2002.

Jackson, John P. *Science for Segregation: Race, Law, and the Case Against Brown v. Board of Education*. New York: New York University Press, 2005.

Kevles, Daniel J. *In the Name of Eugenics: Genetics and the Uses of Human Heredity*. Berkeley: University of California Press, 1986.

Lecklider, Aaron. *Inventing the Egghead: The Battle over Brainpower in American Culture*. Philadelphia: University of Pennsylvania Press, 2013.

Levendusky, Matthew. *How Partisan Media Polarize America*. Chicago: University of Chicago Press, 2013.

Levitsky, Steven, and Daniel Ziblatt, *How Democracies Die*. New York: Crown, 2018.

Lippmann, Walter. *Public Opinion*. New York: Harcourt, Brace, 1922.

Lodge, Milton, and Charles S. Taber. *The Rationalizing Voter*. New York: Cambridge University Press, 2013.

Lombardo, Paul A. *Three Generations, No Imbeciles: Eugenics, the Supreme Court, and Buck v. Bell*. Baltimore: Johns Hopkins University Press, 2008.

Mann, Michael. *The Dark Side of Democracy: Explaining Ethnic Cleansing*. New York: Cambridge University Press, 2005.

Mason, Lilliana. *Uncivil Agreement: How Politics Became Our Identity*. Chicago: University of Chicago Press, 2018.

Müller, Jan-Werner. *What Is Populism?* Philadelphia: University of Pennsylvania Press, 2016.

Parkinson, John, and Jane Mansbridge, eds. *Deliberative Systems: Deliberative Democracy at the Large Scale*. Cambridge: Cambridge University Press, 2012.

Roberts-Miller, Patricia. "Demagoguery, Charismatic Leadership, and the Force of Habit." *Rhetoric Society Quarterly* 49, no. 3 (2019): 233–47.

———. *Fanatical Schemes: Antebellum Rhetoric and the Tragedy of Consensus*. Tuscaloosa: University of Alabama Press, 2009.

———. *Rhetoric and Demagoguery*. Carbondale: Southern Illinois University Press, 2019.

Schudson, Michael. "The 'Lippmann-Dewey Debate' and the Invention of Walter Lippmann as an Anti-Democrat, 1985–1996." *International Journal of Communication* 2 (2008): 1031–42.

———. "The Trouble with Experts—and Why Democracies Need Them." *Theory and Society* 35, no. 5 (2006): 491–506.

Stroud, Natalie Jomini. *Niche News: The Politics of News Choice.* New York: Oxford University Press, 2011.

Tell, Dave. "Reinventing Walter Lippmann: Communication and Cultural Studies." *Review of Communication* 13, no. 2 (2013): 108–26.

Tetlock, Philip E. *Expert Political Judgment: How Good Is It? How Can We Know?* Rev. ed. Princeton, NJ: Princeton University Press, 2005.

Tetlock, Philip E., and Dan Gardner. *Superforecasting: The Art and Science of Prediction.* New York: Crown, 2015.

Vance, Laura. *Leaving the Fold: Testimonies of Former Fundamentalists.* Berkeley: University of California Press, 2000.

Westbrook, Robert. *John Dewey and American Democracy.* Ithaca, NY: Cornell University Press, 1991.

II

RHETORICAL SOCIOLOGY AND THE MANAGEMENT OF PUBLIC DISCOURSE

Robert Danisch and William Keith

How do we understand the macro context of rhetoric? If we want to move on from philosophical arguments about whether rhetoric is good or bad, we need a way of thinking in the broadest sense about how rhetoric operates in a society. We propose rhetorical sociology as a way of examining the role of communication in making, maintaining, and changing social organizations and structures. At the same time, it is also a way of showing how social organizations and structures can condition the forms of communicative agency available to us as members of society. The idea that our agency is implicated in the structures that we inhabit, and that communication is perhaps our central way of negotiating the tensions that arise from our social situatedness, would not have been a surprising argument to either John Dewey or Walter Lippmann. Late nineteenth-century philosophical pragmatism and Chicago sociology foregrounded a concern with the way symbols mediate, construct, and maintain the social order. Through the lens of rhetorical sociology, we argue that Dewey and Lippmann were less in debate with each other in the 1920s than they were addressing a common set of problems, ones that remain with us today. The problem was that American society in the 1920s had reached a level of size and complexity that seemed to burst the bounds of the systems that had seemed to function well in the nineteenth century. This shift meant that the forms of agency social structures made possible were also changing radically. The social order itself seemed very much in flux to both Dewey and Lippmann, and both were aware of the important role that communication played in maintaining and fostering a social order. Therefore, we believe both Dewey and Lippmann offered a rhetorical sociology, or a systemic account of the theoretical and normative ways in which social structures, institutions, and forms of individual agency are both guided by and constituted by communicative practices.[1] Their insights are valuable ways for us to assess our own deformed and defective rhetorical sociology. In the midst of waves of populism, rising sea levels, and neofascist political leaders, we face similar concerns in new variation. As protests over police violence against people of color spread all over the world and conspiracy theorists spread misinformation and disinformation on the internet, our own social order seems very much in flux, just as it did at the beginning of the previous century. Therefore, Dewey and Lippmann may help us understand ourselves, and might offer a constructive path forward.

Neither Dewey nor Lippmann lacked faith in the public or in public deliberation. Lippmann worried that then-current institutions presumed an epistemically glorified version of the public (individually and collectively), one that fell too far short of the reality of individual and collective decision-making. This seems just as clear today with the ubiquitous concern with "fake news." Dewey was concerned that the United States was failing to activate its deliberative possibilities, which he viewed as flowing from particular kinds of civic relationships. The rising levels of divisiveness in our own public discourse has amplified this concern with civic relationships. Their rhetorical sociology contains, however, more than people, ideas, and arguments. Both recognize that the communication needed in a society of such scale, diversity, and specialization required appropriate institutions to nurture healthy and functional public spheres. Hence, they are, in two senses, republicans just as much as they are democrats. They accept that the United States is a representative republic (defined by a set of mediating political institutions between the people and the state), and they are civic republicans, albeit believing more in orders of expertise than moral virtue. This stance is not dissimilar from Aristotle's institutionalism, which holds that good governance and legal outcomes result from the combination of citizen skills and correctly organized and maintained institutions. We ought to be asking whether our own systems are up to the task of nurturing healthy and functional public discourse.

Our work in this chapter will be, first, to thicken our description of the problem. We will use some language connected to our current predicament, while recalling that their era, with the rise of tabloid and yellow journalism as well as the communication professions of public relations and advertising, was not completely different from our own. Second, we will try to outline, based on Dewey and Lippmann's work, the kinds of institutional solutions required, a model for which can be found in Roger Pielke's work on "honest brokers."[2] Our aim is to use the connections between Dewey and Lippmann to argue for a sociology of rhetoric that might describe and prescribe a better system for effective decision-making in our own moment. On the one hand, for Dewey this involves institutional mechanisms capable of forming, building, and maintaining social relationships between diverse sets of strangers (what we might call "weak ties"). On the other hand, for Lippmann this involves institutional mechanisms for ensuring that the information circulating in public discourse is reliable and accurate so that we can trust the decisions we reach. These are not mutually exclusive commitments, but instead different approaches to foregrounding essential components of the management of public discourse. Our argument is that if we think through the lens of rhetorical sociology, we're likely to see Dewey and Lippmann as complementary figures attempting to improve the conditions for public decision-making and helpful resources for us now as we confront a similar set of threats to democratic life.

Obviously, "rhetorical sociology" was not part of Dewey or Lippmann's vocabulary. We are creatively reading it into their work to clarify our current predicament, and so that it might better ground some suggestions for intervening in our moment. Neither Dewey nor Lippmann gives us a specific set of communication practices that we might use to navigate our world. Instead, they describe a defective communication system (which is defective in ways similar to what we are experiencing now) and prescribe some ways for making sure our system is guided by accurate information and constructive relationships between diverse citizens. We think our own moment, marked as it is by fake news, conspiracy theories, agonistic divisions between competing identity groups, and the absence of trust between strangers, is badly in need of a communication system guided by accurate information and constructive relationships. The question Dewey and Lippmann pose, seen through the lens of rhetorical sociology, is the following: how might we construct a communication system that relies on, fosters, and circulates accurate information and that allows strangers and diverse citizens to collaborate and constructively engage one another to solve collective problems?

The Problem of Managing Public Discourse

We aim, with rhetorical sociology, to shift our focus from rhetoric's traditional concern with specific practices and interactions (embodied, for example, in public speech or debate) and toward a structural account of what makes an interaction possible in the first place, following the path set out by the Chicago school of sociology. Instead of asking about what figures of speech a public speaker used in crafting an argument or what impact those figures of speech had on an audience, we want to ask what visible and invisible systems were in place that made a particular speech possible. Some historical context can help show how, and with what kind of language or set of terms, Dewey and Lippmann may have thought through their own state of public discourse in more systemic terms, and how we might recover some of that intellectual history for use in our own moment. By using the term *rhetorical sociology*, we are practicing (methodologically) intellectual history for the purposes of theorizing the role of rhetoric in democratic life.

One of the major contributions of Chicago sociology was "symbolic interactionism," which is a way of viewing all action as mediated by symbols. The term was coined by Herbert Blumer, a student of George Herbert Mead, who described the three basic assumptions of "symbolic interactionism" as follows: "Humans act toward things on the basis of the meanings they ascribe to those things. . . . The meaning of such things is derived from, or arises out of, the social interaction one has with others and the society. . . . [And] these meanings are handled in, and modified through, an interpretive process used by the person in dealing with the things he/she encounters."[3] This means that sociologists who conduct research as symbolic interactionists are concerned with how people create meaning during social interactions, how people present and construct a self, and how people collectively coproduce definitions of particular situations. These social interactions are public discourse at work, and Dewey was acutely aware of this in his pragmatism. Dewey's pragmatism gives us an account of action guided by a conception of collective deliberation as problem-solving (and not an account of a solitary actor rationally pursuing her ends), what we might call, building on symbolic interactionism, a philosophy of interaction. Dewey sought to critique the ideas of self-reflection and epistemological realism derived from Descartes and to rethink the relationship between cognition and reality in more concretely social, or interactive, terms (building on symbolic interactionism). For example, Dewey, in his 1896 article "The Reflex Arc Concept in Psychology," critiqued the attempt to establish causal relations between stimuli and an organism's reactions. He claimed that we cannot conceive of action as composed of phases with a discreet external stimulus, an internal processing of a stimulus, and an external reaction. Instead, he claimed that it is the action that determines which stimuli are relevant within the context defined by the action. With such an account of cognition in place, Dewey was able to argue that the Cartesian ego was not an adequate descriptor of thinking, and that it ought to be replaced by the idea of a community constituted by collective problem solving. In other words, Dewey's pragmatism was committed to the proposition that notions of a self depended on the communities to which the self belonged, or that psychological questions about agency and mind were also always already sociological questions about contexts and structures. These considerations lay at the core of how we manage public discourse. One problem, therefore, was to develop an explanation of how social interaction was linked to self-reflection. This is what George Herbert Mead contributed to pragmatism and psychology.[4] Mead became a central figure in pragmatism, psychology, and sociology through his account of human gestural and linguistic communication and the role of symbols in social interactions. Mead never went so far as to establish a rhetorical theory or an account of persuasion in his theory of communication, but he did, by virtue of his emphasis on symbols, interpretation, and community, bring psychology and sociology very close to some of the most enduring concerns of the rhetorical tradition, and he shed light on what Dewey would describe as some of the central problems in managing public discourse and building relationships that can give rise to effective communities.[5]

Embedded in Dewey's philosophy of interaction was a normative conception of a social order based on the ideals of democratic self-rule and unrestricted communication within a community of inquirers. This is what Dewey described in *The Public and Its Problems* by defending a theory that takes the process of collective action as a starting point. Communication plays an essential role in this process, and everyone affected is motivated to participate in such communication. In the light of this, the work of people like Jane Addams and Robert Park in Chicago makes sense both as kinds of sociology and forms of political participation that issued from a pragmatist philosophy *and* as a pragmatist psychology oriented toward social interaction. Addams, for example, believed that the mission of Hull House was to help Chicago immigrants interpret one another's interests and thus serve as a space for interpersonal interaction of the kind that Mead, Dewey, and symbolic interactionism championed. In so doing, she invented sociological methods and practices for use within the context of Chicago political culture. Dewey's work aligned with sociology, then, not just through the symbolic interactionism of Mead and Blumer, but also through the reform projects carried out at places like Hull House. In such cases, the Chicago School was concerned with empirically tracking the results of professionalization, urbanization, and immigration and suggesting modes of action to improve the conditions of life in Chicago based on the collection of quantitative data. This meant that social research was essential to reform projects and to the "Progressive Era" in general and relied on the same kind of quantitative and data-driven research that Lippmann championed in *Public Opinion*.

In numerous research projects that focused on the city of Chicago, Robert Park, who also influenced Dewey, developed a theory of human ecology that understood cities as kinds of natural environments. For Park, and others of the Chicago School, the city was a laboratory for studying social interaction.[6] He argued that biological metaphors and ecological models were appropriate framing devices for understanding social interactions. The social structures within human ecologies could be viewed as complex webs of dynamic processes. Chicago School sociologists also focused on groups as part of a human ecology. Studies of groups ranged from whole urban regions to occupational teams and to extended families. These groups showed a high degree of both immersion and isolation, either internally encouraged or externally enforced. Both the barriers to entering a social group and the impetus for the group to maintain a degree of cohesion were fascinating parts of the human ecology of Chicago. Park and other members of the Chicago School began to try to map the ways in which cooperation and competition governed social interactions and what they eventually called "communities of practice" in order to understand how and why these groups functioned as they did.

In 1936, almost ten years after *The Public and Its Problems*, Park published an essay in the *American Journal of Sociology* called "Human Ecology." That essay provides a fascinating perspective on what we'd call rhetorical structures. It is Park's attempt to apply theoretical insights about the interrelations of plants and animals to human associations: "In plant and animal communities structure is biologically determined, and so far as any division of labor exists at all it has a psychological and instinctive basis. . . . In a society of human beings, however, this communal structure is reinforced by custom and assumes an institutional character." This is an early attempt at a systems theory approach to sociology. Competition, which is prevalent in biological ecologies, is limited by custom and consensus produced in and through institutional structures. Human society, as distinguished from plant and animal society, "is organized on two levels, the biotic and the cultural. There is a symbiotic society based on competition and a cultural society based on communication and consensus." The economic, political, and moral order that arises on a cultural level incorporates individuals into "a control organization" through practices of communication and consensus. The function of society is "to organize, integrate, and direct the energies resident in the individuals of which it is composed. One might, perhaps, say that the function of society was everywhere to restrict competition and by so doing bring about a more effective co-operation of the organic units of which society is composed."[7] In other words, animal ecology is based on competition, but human ecology is based on a social order made possible by cooperation. Lippmann argues in *Public Opinion* that the way in which society chooses to organize and integrate information about the world is critical to the health of a democracy—this would not seem like a radical argument to a Chicago sociologist. Park claims that the "human community" consists of a population and a culture, and that a culture is made up of a body of customs, beliefs, technologies, artifacts, and institutions that help form the social order. Lippmann's major preoccupation in *Public Opinion* is with the cultural beliefs about the world that circulate through the ecology and the institutions (such as democratic governance) that help preserve the social order of an ecology. Problems with public discourse arise when the institutions that help form the social order are not appropriately fit to the complexity of the historical moment.

When Lippmann describes the challenge of matching the "pictures in our heads" and the "world outside," he is describing precisely the problem that Park and other sociologists tried to tackle—not as a problem of representation, but as one of interaction. They were aware of the complexities of such a project given what they knew from symbolic interactionism and the necessity of structural or institutional mechanisms for "mapping" accurately the world as they knew it. Communication was an omnipresent but under-theorized and relatively ambiguous concept within Park's sociology, Dewey's philosophy, and Lippmann's intellectual work. But the conclusion that we think we ought to draw from Chicago sociology is that democratic societies need specific kinds of social structures able to foster cooperation among diverse populations. We've chosen to call these social structures "rhetorical structures" because we want to highlight their importance in promoting forms of communicative agency. Those structures are aimed at managing public discourse, and Dewey and Lippmann each emphasize different components of those structures. For Dewey, managing public discourse is a matter of fostering relationships between strangers (thus making forms of symbolic interactionism a lived reality for democratic citizens). For Lippmann, managing public discourse is a matter of building institutions or organizations fit for the complexity of the moment's human ecology so that citizens had the necessary resources for decision-making. Lippmann's interest was less in the kinds of relationships built in public and more in the kinds of evidence that mediate those relationships. Both were critical concerns for Chicago sociology and American pragmatism.

Ecology is an apt metaphor to use within the context of the Dewey/Lippmann debates for two reasons. First, the biological concept of ecology was developed in Chicago during Dewey's time there and was linked to human societies through pragmatist sociology. In other words, we have historical reason to employ this metaphor. Second, the concept of ecology highlights interactions between organisms and their environment, as well as the diversity and open-endedness that characterize such interactions. Both Dewey and Lippmann were privileging in their work interaction and the socially encumbered and relational characteristics of human life. The dynamically interacting parts of an ecology include both forms of human association and the institutions and structures in which those forms are practiced. Pragmatism is itself a philosophy of interaction through and through, by which we mean it is concerned with interactions between agents and between agents and their environments. Dewey may see great potential in activating and leveraging the power of social relationships for effective decision-making, while Lippmann may see the danger that those relationships will be governed by fake pictures in our heads that aren't objectively related to our world, but both try to offer ways of improving our ecology through communication practices and communication structures.

What this ought to tell us about the practice of communication is that it is not just a matter of one person transmitting a message to another. Any two participants in a communicative act (or interaction) are embedded within a larger social structure that conditions the ways that interaction can and does take place. The Dewey/Lippmann debate opens a set of serious questions about how the structures that we inhabit condition the possibilities for our agency and what the best structures for our democracy ought to look like. Both Dewey and Lippmann turn our attention to the ways our communication practices are embedded within these larger structures and institutions while leaving aside the practical suggestions about how we ought to engage in communication. This is not necessarily a limitation of their work. Instead, it speaks to the complexity of the American democratic experiment. Massive immigration and huge numbers of citizens all within a vast geographical space posed structural challenges different in kind from those faced by any other democracy in the history of the world. At the same time, advances in communications technologies, public relations, mass media, and capitalism also transformed the human ecology within which citizens found themselves.

Lippmann (while writing editorials and books), Dewey (in *The Public and Its Problems* and elsewhere), and Park (throughout his analyses of Chicago) were all preoccupied by how both immigration and industrialism affected social organization. For each, immigration highlighted the challenges of pluralism and diversity in generating both community life and an objective consensus about the world. At the same time, industrial capitalism pointed to how economic relations might undermine or affect social relations in dangerous and damaging ways. (In *The Good Society* [1936], Lippman argues for a well-regulated market economy, since centrally managed economies appeared to him to go hand in hand with authoritarian/antidemocratic politics—he liked the policies of the New Deal, just not a slippery slope to authoritarianism.) Thus, Lippmann's commitment to "organized intelligence" and Dewey's "Great Community" were meant as theoretical and practical descriptions, as well as prescriptions for how the ecology of American democracy might be improved. Each saw the importance and vitality of social structures because political democracy was a limited mechanism for promoting freedom, equality, and the self-development of individual citizens. The forms of cooperation characteristic of community life in general were, for Dewey and Lippmann, essential for understanding democracy as a way of life. Therefore, both were concerned with the building of deliberative ecologies. We use the word *deliberative* to refer to the process of long and careful consideration and discussion of public issues.[8] Deliberation is a face-to-face, uncertain, open-ended process that requires broad participation and reliable or accurate information. It employs reason, dialogue, and care, all with the end of broad consensus in mind. But individual agents within a democracy cannot practice deliberation without specific structures within which face-to-face, open-ended conversations based on sound evidence can take place. A deliberative ecology holds the potential to bring Dewey's Great Community into being and requires institutional structures like those Lippmann proposes.

Both Dewey and Lippmann suggest that we can test and evaluate our own democratic society by assessing the "health" of the human ecology within which we interact with other citizens. A healthy "deliberative ecology promotes forms of deliberation" supported by rhetorical structures that make possible a kind of communicative agency that privileges cooperation. Such an ecology would be essential for improving American democracy (this is the common theme between Dewey and Lippmann). If, however, our ecology does not promote deliberation and does not possess the kinds of structures that make cooperation possible, then one of our intellectual burdens is to figure out how to nurture structures that might do that kind of work.

Throughout the course of the twentieth century, Communication Studies and Cultural Studies have offered relentless critiques of the ways that industrial capitalism has affected, damaged, or eroded the quality of human interactions within our human ecology. The promise of the work that both Dewey and Lippmann did in the 1920s lies in their suggestions about how we might be able to imagine and nurture structures that would make possible our forms of communicative agency capable of counteracting the impact of industrial capitalism. The Dewey/Lippmann debate ought to leave us with the hope that we could invent, foster, and maintain such structures, and if we did that, we might be able to build a democracy capable of generating good decisions, coping with conditions of unremitting pluralism, and counteracting the alienating forces of industrial capitalism. Such structures would form integral parts of a deliberative ecology in which democracy would be practiced.

Lippmann and Dewey come at this problem from different angles, which can produce the impression that they are on opposite sides. In *Public Opinion* and *The Phantom Public*, Lippmann had argued that average citizens of a democracy were defective as ideal deliberative citizens because they were too busy, too ignorant, and too reliant on stereotypical representations of a world that they could never really know. Lippmann endorsed a democracy that integrated experts that had the time and methods to collect data and render better judgments and decisions in the light of their superior knowledge—just like Chicago sociologists did when they intervened in city affairs. Dewey described democracy as both a system of government and a social ideal. Against Lippmann, he asserts that the capacity of the expert few to discern the public interest tends to be distorted by the institutional position of those experts. Democratic participation is then a safeguard against government by elites, while the necessary expertise can exist in the general public, given the right circumstances (of education and the construction of democratic institutions). In addition—and this is Dewey's innovative and radical contribution to political theory—democracy is not simply and solely a form of government or a set of political institutions. Instead, democracy is a social idea, a way of life, and a set of social relationships embodied in the social structures within which we interact with other citizens. According to Dewey, "the strongest point to be made in behalf of even such rudimentary political forms as democracy has attained, popular voting, majority rule and so on, is that to some extent they involve a consultation and discussion which concerns social needs and troubles."[9] The emphasis here is clearly on the importance of discussion, consultation, persuasion, and debate in democratic decision-making. These processes articulate, develop, and deepen the public understanding of the problems under discussion, and help to inform the administrative experts of social needs, but only if they rely on and use accurate evidence. Democracy as public discussion is the best way of dealing with conflicts of interests and the general conditions of pluralism in a society: "The method of democracy—inasfar as it is that of organized intelligence—is to bring these conflicts out into the open where their special claims can be discussed and judged in the light of more inclusive interests than are represented by either of them separately."[10] This method relies on both the kinds of social relationships Dewey argued for and the kinds of institutions for preserving the social order and organizing intelligence that Lippmann argued for.

Like most works of political theory, *The Public and Its Problems* tries to explain the origins and functions of the state, and Dewey devotes the first half of the book to that task. As had become typical of pragmatism more broadly, Dewey argued that forms of associated living drove the development of the state as a set of institutions that could respond to the consequences of those forms of association. Interaction and association between people came first and the state came after as a consequence of association. From such a perspective, Dewey defined the "public" as "all of those who are affected by the indirect consequences of transactions to such an extent that it is deemed necessary to have those consequences systematically cared for."[11]

Organizing all those affected is an ongoing, plural, and uncertain process. Part of that process leads to the formation of the state, but part also leads to the formation of a community and, as Lippmann argued, the formation of non-state institutions. When the public was organized into a state, it could act through representatives and officers of the state (including Lippmann's experts), but it also needed to organize itself into a community to hold officials accountable and to widen and deepen the discussion of public problems and solutions, and in so doing also rely on Lippmann's suggested organizations. For Dewey, the institutional machinery of the state was not sacred. Democratic governments had helped to create the Great Society, marked by vast, impersonal webs of interdependent relationships. But "the same forces which have brought about the forms of democratic government, general suffrage, executives and legislators chosen by majority vote, have also brought about conditions which halt the social and human ideals that demand the utilization of government as the genuine instrumentality of an inclusive and fraternally associated public. The new 'age of human relationships' has no political agencies worthy of it." Dewey claims, therefore, that the "Great Society" needed to become the "Great Community," which required "the perfecting of the means and ways of communication of meanings so that genuinely shared interest in the consequences of interdependent activities may inform desire and effort and thereby direct action."[12] Robert Westbrook claims that this is a "problem of inquiry and communication."[13] It is also the problem that Lippmann describes in the opening pages of *Public Opinion*.

In the concluding passages of *The Public and Its Problems*, Dewey suggested that the development of the Great Community also meant the revitalization of the local community: "In its deepest and richest sense a community must always remain a matter of face-to-face intercourse." Place matters for community because interpersonal associations and attachments are "bred in tranquil stability; they are nourished in constant relationships."[14] Only in face-to-face associations could citizens of a community participate in dialogue about pressing problems, and such dialogues were critical to the organization of the public. This is perhaps the point at which he most diverges from Lippmann on the surface because these forms of symbolic interaction are almost sacred for Dewey, while Lippmann highlights the necessity and potential of our interactions with institutional structures.

The famous proclamation from *The Public and Its Problems* is a normative endorsement of communicative agency that aligns with Lippmann's claims in *Public Opinion*: "The essential need ... is the improvement of the methods and conditions of debate, discussion, and persuasion. That is *the* problem of the public. We have asserted that this improvement depends essentially on freeing and perfecting the process of inquiry."[15] Lippmann wanted such improvements as well and sought out the institutional mechanisms to make them possible, while Dewey sought out the kinds of relationships that made them possible. Thus, both *The Public and Its Problems* and *Public Opinion* are attempts to outline the practical and intellectual conditions for community-based inquiry as a method of channeling communicative practices for the benefit of democratic society. Lippmann lacked faith in ordinary citizens, but Dewey's belief in participation rested on a "faith in the capacity of human beings for intelligent judgment and action if proper conditions are furnished."[16] The stipulation of "proper conditions" is what matters most and why we introduced the idea of human ecology here. We take both *The Public and Its Problems* and *Public Opinion* as deeply concerned with what those "proper conditions" look like.

At the core of Dewey's commitment to inquiry as a vital matter for the organization of community life lie two complementary but distinct practices: inquiry that requires deliberation and discussion, and inquiry based on the methods of scientific thinking. These two prescriptions would improve

American democratic culture, and the latter is clearly deeply aligned with the way Lippmann argued public discourse ought to be managed. Given Dewey's commitments, communication is both a matter of relationality and social solidarity, on the one hand, and practices of empirical investigation governed by a kind of fallible, revisable ethos or collective discussion and argumentation, on the other. In other words, we ought to read Dewey as simply extending two commitments, one to organized intelligence articulated by Lippmann through an awareness of symbolic interactionism and the other to the importance of relationships. Lippmann points out how deeply fallible human thought processes are, and how prone to simplistic stereotyping we can be. These limitations may appear cynical next to Dewey's more hopeful and rosy descriptions of the Great Community, but they don't emerge from a radically different worldview. Lippmann is equally worried about how burdened citizens can become given the overwhelming amount of information we are exposed to in the modern world. He was rightly concerned with propaganda and the more nefarious side of public relations, or the ways in which meaning can be distorted or manipulated so that an ordinary citizen is ill equipped to make good judgments. Our own moment is replete with the circulation of faulty information and ever-cascading degrees of complexity related to the problems we face. These forms of cynicism do not imply a radical break with Dewey's optimism of the great potential of community-based inquiry. Instead Lippmann's cynicism raises enduring questions about the management of our human ecology, questions that complement, in important ways, Dewey's optimism about building a cooperative ecology that could make good decisions.

Improving Public Decision-Making Through Rhetorical Structures

Lippmann was not (simply) an elitist, thinking that ordinary people weren't intellectually capable of understanding technical issues and making complex decisions, as many have asserted. Rather, his critique is more systemic and nuanced. Lippmann thought that the stereotype of the ideal citizen, what he calls the "omnicompetent citizen," doesn't cohere with the way their roles are structured in a democracy like the United States:

> These various remedies, eugenic, educational, ethical, populist and socialist, all assume that either the voters are inherently competent to direct the course of affairs or that they are making progress toward

such an ideal. I think it is a false ideal. I do not mean an undesirable ideal. I mean an unattainable ideal, bad only in the sense that it is bad for a fat man to try to be a ballet dancer. An ideal should express the true possibilities of its subject. When it does not it perverts the true possibilities. The ideal of the omnicompetent, sovereign citizen is, in my opinion, such a false ideal. It is unattainable. The pursuit of it is misleading. The failure to achieve it has produced the current disenchantment.[17]

He tried to illuminate a number of ways the mismatch between the normative conception of citizenship, the one to which we pay homage and direct our educational efforts, and the realities of citizenship. Lippmann focuses his critique in two main directions, on the opportunities for citizens and the motivations/interests of citizens in participating. He never seemed to tire of pointing out that US democracy of the early twentieth century isn't like small town councils of early, rural America, which oversaw relatively simple government systems, with a simple democratic vote or delegation to a mayor. As cities grew larger and more complex, mayors and their staffs turned out often enough to be corrupt or incompetent that the Progressive Era saw the rise of the city-manager system, where the manager is accountable to a city council. This need for differentiation of function and specialization of knowledge is where Lippmann puts pressure; since no one person can know or do enough to rationally make government decisions, this implies that no citizen could be in such a position either; yet, he thought, we put people in this position when we ask them to vote on policies or politicians where making a "good" choice requires knowledge and experience they don't have.

Lippmann's solution was a bit hazy, but it was something like reconfiguring the system so that the participation of citizens (e.g., voting) would be made meaningful. Voting would be meaningful when citizens were presented with choices they could understand, which also would make a significant difference. Yet this would require realigning the interests and motivations implicit in the system. Essentially the later chapters of *Public Opinion* argue for a complex relationship between the government and media that present to people choices that have been vetted by experts and stated in a form that voters can contemplate. A version of this has evolved in the US state of Oregon, which introduced vote-by-mail in 2000. Oregon allows for "ballot measures," which are essentially laws placed on the ballot through citizen signatures; if approved by a majority of voters they become law, bypassing the legislature. (Vote-by-mail itself was the product of a 1998 ballot measure.) Since forty or fifty measures on a single ballot are not unusual, the state produces a "Voter's Pamphlet" giving arguments for and against each proposal. Anyone may submit arguments, but for ballot measures the state provides explanatory and fiscal impact statements. In 2009 the state then launched the Citizens Initiative Review, which is a committee of randomly selected citizens tasked with weighing all the arguments and data for and against a ballot measure.[18] John Gastil's research team has shown that voters find the relative impartiality of the state's statement extremely important to their voting decisions, and this is just as Lippmann might have wanted; the ordinary voter doesn't need to become an expert on the state budget to evaluate the worthiness of a ballot measure.[19]

Lippmann, however, downplays or ignores the role of legislatures, focusing instead on the lack of omnicompetent citizens relative to direct democracy. Legislatures have the time, money, and resources to collect knowledge and the expertise to make decisions on our behalf, and the best of them do this. While it's true that concerns about corruption (then as now) fueled calls for direct democracy in the Progressive Era, these reforms were piecemeal. Whether direct democracy is possible at scale or not, the US democracy was quite deliberately designed not to be direct, and there are few examples of direct democracy left at any level. In addition, as the Citizens Initiative Review example shows, a great deal of space exists between the ideal citizen and actual voters. Lippmann asserts that the system quashes voter motivation making the task of being an ideal citizen seem impossibly difficult. But he takes for granted a specific picture of average voters and their motivations that appears unfair from our vantage point.

As Sue Curry Jansen and others have pointed out, *The Public and Its Problems* has a rather complex relationship to Lippmann's text, less a refutation than a rejoinder.[20] Dewey doesn't reject Lippmann's diagnosis but accepts parts of it while restating and redescribing it. We don't, he thought, have the relationship right between political mechanisms and problem solving in other contexts. Here is where the problem of the public enters, since while it would be good for the "public" to lard the political system and bureaucracy with experts, no public has emerged to fill this function.[21] But this is also where Dewey takes some argumentative steps that will get him in trouble with generations of readers. He has to theorize what a more general public (or publics) would look like, and he stakes out very different, though not incompatible, territory from Lippmann. Lippmann focuses on individual voters, understood in the psychology of the time, when propaganda was thought to be able to "socially engineer" outcomes by manipulating minds.[22]

Dewey wants to begin in a different place, with the quality of communication between people in society. To manage this, he has to do some setup work about modern media (which strikes us as fairly prescient and quite relevant to the contemporary scene) and dispense with the metaphysics of social theory. He was interested in the nature of high-functioning democratic communication and thought he had identified the soil in which it grew: just like Thomas Jefferson, he pegged the (New England) small town, before factories and industrial farming, as the source "of genuine community life."[23]

The term *genuine* strikes most as a red flag here, since it implies that people who live in other times and places with other economic arrangements are automatically laboring under inauthentic community. What made the communication/community (these are functionally the same for Dewey) in these locales so remarkable, so genuine? Dewey believes community arises organically out of mutual relationships of interdependence which might be typical of a small town of rough equality (much like Dewey's Burlington, Vermont in the 1860s and '70s). The mismatch that Lippmann sees isn't the fault of citizens failing at omnicompetence but institutional and political structures having gone awry. After all, these structures should have emerged out of the needs discovered in communicating without them. The government and its agencies should exist to solve problems that arise out of what he will later call the "felt need" of a group. Once created, however, the institutions grow to the scale of county, state, and country, and eventually become unmoored from the community relations that grounded them. As stranger sociality becomes a structural necessity, the modes of communication that made the government structures function dissipate. The public of the small town could recognize itself as such—maybe even by all standing in the town square together. But the modern public is so dispersed that they cannot recognize themselves as a public: "If a public exists, it is surely as uncertain about its own whereabouts as philosophers since Hume have been about the residence and make-up of the self."[24]

The self-consciously deliberating public that Lippmann sets as an ideal may prove elusive. Partly this is because we have, in Dewey's view, flipped cause and effect. We didn't create institutions so that a public would emerge, but rather the institutions emerged in response to the situational elements that also give rise to publics: these institutions "served a purpose; but the purpose was rather that of meeting existing needs which had become too intense to be ignored, than that of forwarding the democratic idea." The problem of the public, then, is one contained in what we are calling rhetorical sociology, which explores the systemic and structural background necessary for rhetoric to serve specific purposes. For example, the rhetoric described by Aristotle required the background of not only the institutions of classical Athens (the court and the assembly) but a specific set of social conditions flowing from both Athenian culture and Cleisthenes's reforms in BCE 508. Dewey's functionalism is in general an organic and holistic one, and he doesn't postulate a simple correspondence between institutions or systems and specific functions. What does Dewey have to say about a rhetorical sociology, in this context? "To learn to be human is to develop through the give-and-take of communication an effective sense of being an individually distinctive member of a community; one who understands and appreciates its beliefs, desires and methods, and who contributes to a further conversion of organic powers into human resources and values. But this translation is never finished." But even with these relationships in place, people cannot make good decisions about their affairs (writ large and small) if they labor under various kinds of ignorance, specific and general. The circulation and appraisal of knowledge both happens through a public and enables it: "The prime condition of a democratically organized public is a kind of knowledge and insight which does not yet exist. In its absence, it would be the height of absurdity to try to tell what it would be like if it existed."[25] Why did we ever think that publics could achieve the ideal that Lippmann mocks, a kind of cross between a jury and a meeting of scientists? Probably because a few examples existed, but they were achieved only under an unusual or unsustainable rhetorical sociology, generalized from the behavior of rational economic actors or an idealized version of scientists.

In short, Lippmann and Dewey come to much the same conclusion—the "public" isn't doing the democratic work that we need it to. And to an extent they agree about why: a deformed and defective rhetorical sociology. Lippmann thinks that individuals aren't up to the feats of intellectual and rational work required by the deliberating public because they are limited and fallible as thinkers, and the system of democratic institutions provides them neither the space nor the motivation to bear the burden of decision-making. Dewey actually expands this critique, taking the focus off democratic institutions and redirecting his diagnosis to larger social structures. The tendency has been to see Lippmann as the arch-realist, whose despair at the failure of the public is warranted and implies that we just have to lower expectations; the opposing tendency is to see Dewey as the nebulous idealist who believes in the public that Lippmann has just dismantled. But this is selling Dewey short, since if his diagnosis is correct then reform is possible through education (and not just in the schools).

Another way to see the harmony in their respective accounts is to pose the question this way: how does relationality improve the circulation of accurate information, and how does accurate information improve relationality? Effective democratic publics need a system that can answer this question. From Lippmann's perspective, we might invent institutional mechanisms to improve the circulation of reliable information. From Dewey's perspective, we might create the social conditions for making a system of weak ties possible in which friendships between strangers became a norm when trying to solve public problems. We would argue that friendships between strangers would be much easier inside a system that freely circulated careful and accurate information. We'd also argue that we'd be less prone to the kinds of divisive forms of hatred, racism, and xenophobia that seem so prevalent in our own moment if we had a better system of weak ties underpinning public life. To the extent Robert Putnam's claims in *Bowling Alone* are true, they are part of the reason that Russian propaganda was able to influence the 2016 American election. We ought to think about concerns with relationality and concerns with objectivity of information as deeply related components of building a contemporary democratic ecology fit for our moment.

The Virtues of Rhetorical Sociology and the Legacy of Dewey/Lippmann

If we stop thinking about Lippmann as the champion of expertise and Dewey as the champion of "ordinary" citizens, and start thinking about Lippmann as caring about communication as the accurate transmission of information and foregrounding the importance of reliable and trustworthy evidence and Dewey as caring about communication as relationality and foregrounding the importance of relationships, then we can think about them both as articulating complementary components of effectively managing public discourse and complementary ways of suggesting we look for a rhetorical sociology that can do all that we need it to do. The conclusion forced on us is that while things are no better than a century ago, by the terms of this analysis they aren't really any worse. Since the 2016 US elections, any number of scholars and commentators have tried to make the point that we are in a crisis, one created by the intersection of damaged institutions (including legislative and journalistic) and the possibilities of information sharing made possible by the internet. This argument has become so familiar that it seems obviously valid. Take, for example, Kathleen Hall Jamison's meticulously argued

Cyberwar: How Russian Hackers and Trolls Helped Elect a President, in which she makes the case that not only did Russian operatives attempt to interfere in the 2016 election by changing the signal-to-noise ratio in the overall public discourse but that they could have tipped the election to Trump with well-constructed interventions with the right voting populations at the right time. Even if one is skeptical about Jamison's argument, we can note that the diagnosis is pretty much the same as Dewey and Lippmann claimed: if people don't have at least shallow civic relationships of the kind Dewey described, then every bad outcome that Lippmann foresaw will come to pass. Social media has only revealed the poverty of civic relationships; Robert Putnam is right that these bonds weakened over the last half of the twentieth century, but that is consistent with Dewey's analysis that the further we are from the interdependencies of small-town life (even with all the prejudice and exclusions they supported) the less likely we are to see the kind of communication that sustains a functioning democracy. If the internet were going to fix community, it has failed, since it generates at least as many toxic communities as functional ones; from the horrors of sites like 4chan or 8kun to the local noxiousness of Nextdoor, a site for local residents to share ideas and information that manages to both bring neighborhoods together, divide them, spread rumors, and make people paranoid.[26]

The gist of the problem is that the internet and media systems are no better than we are; fixing them will not fix us. Dewey is often lambasted for his suggestion that we need to replace the Great Society with the Great Community, but practicalities aside, he seems to be correct. As we have struggled toward a more socially just society, we've made progress, albeit imperfect progress, in creating inclusion for groups who used to be invisible or excluded, and certainly were from the Vermont small towns of Dewey's childhood. This is a hopeful sign. The larger notion of community may have to function like Habermas's ideal speech situation, which still leaves the problem of how we get there from here. For Dewey that answer is almost always education. For Lippmann it seems that the answer might be better institutions populating our democratic ecology. Social movements are both "social" in that they rely on relationality and institutional in that they need and use the structures of our ecology. American pragmatism, Chicago sociology, and the Lippmann/Dewey exchanges all remind us that we ought not separate these two concerns.

In the end, Dewey and Lippmann do not give us communication practices; they describe and prescribe a communication system, and if we read them as prescribing and describing systems level problems and solutions then we can learn from both of them. The same systems-level problems and solutions that plagued them plague us now. In some sense, those systems-level problems are likely enduring problems for any democracy. What changes from one time to another are the kinds of institutions and forms of relationality that are possible and desirable in any given moment. The institutions and relationships that may have worked in democratic Athens wouldn't work for us, and the kinds that governed the nineteenth century in the United States were not fit for the twentieth century. The work of building a democratic ecology is never finished or perfect and requires attention to both issues of relationality and institutional structures. We are best able to manage public discourse in democratic societies when we can foster the kinds of relationships that Dewey's optimistic spirit articulated *and* when institutions of the kind that sober-minded and cynical Lippmann saw as necessary are freely circulating reliable evidence and information. One test of our current moment is to ask just how good our democratic system is at achieving these two ends. Our answer will tell us a lot about whether we are able to make good decisions as a public.

Notes

1. Keith and Danisch, "Dewey on Science, Deliberation, and the Sociology of Rhetoric."
2. Pielke, *Honest Broker*.
3. Blumer, *Symbolic Interactionism*, 2.
4. See Mead, *Mind, Self, and Society*.
5. For an example of how one might ground a rhetorical theory in Mead's view of symbolic interactionism, see Nienkamp, *Internal Rhetorics*.
6. Park and Burgess, *The City*.
7. Park, "Human Ecology," 13–14.
8. For more on this idea of deliberation, see Gastil, *Political Communication and Deliberation*.
9. Dewey, *Public and Its Problems*, 206.
10. Dewey, *Liberalism and Social Action*, 56.
11. Dewey, *Public and Its Problems*, 16.
12. Dewey, 126, 155.
13. Westbrook, *Dewey and American Democracy*, 309.
14. Dewey, *Public and Its Problems*, 211, 141.
15. Dewey, 208.
16. Dewey, *Later Works of John Dewey*, 227.
17. Lippmann, *Phantom Public*, 28.
18. Gastil, "Beyond Endorsements and Partisan Cues."
19. Knobloch et al., "Did They Deliberate?"; Gastil, Richards, and Knobloch, "Vicarious Deliberation."

20. Jansen, "Phantom Conflict"; Schudson, "'Lippmann-Dewey Debate'"; Rakow, "Family Feud."
21. Dewey, *Public and Its Problems*, 123–24.
22. Sproule, *Propaganda and Democracy*.
23. Dewey, *Public and Its Problems*, 111.
24. Dewey, 117.
25. Dewey, 118, 154, 166.
26. See https://www.cc.gatech.edu/people/home/keith/pubs/nextdoor-chi2014.pdf; https://hbr.org/2018/05/how-nextdoor-addressed-racial-profiling-on-its-platform; https://www.chicagotribune.com/opinion/commentary/ct-perspec-nextdoor-neighborhood-news-paranoia-0504-20180502-story.html.

Bibliography

Blumer, Hans. *Symbolic Interactionism: Perspective and Method*. Berkeley: University of California Press, 1986.
Dewey, John. *The Later Works of John Dewey*. Vol. 14. Carbondale: Southern Illinois University Press, 1988.
———. *Liberalism and Social Action*. Amherst, NY: Prometheus Books, 1999.
———. *The Public and Its Problems*. New York: Holt, 1927.
———. "The Reflex Arc Concept in Psychology." *Psychological Review* 3 (1896): 357–70.
Gastil, John. "Beyond Endorsements and Partisan Cues: Given Voters Viable Alternatives to Unreliable Cognitive Shortcuts." *Good Society* 23 (2014): 145–59.
———. *Political Communication and Deliberation*. Thousand Oaks, CA: Sage, 2008.
Gastil, John, Richard C. Richards, and Katherine Knobloch. "Vicarious Deliberation: A Case Study of the Oregon Citizens' Initiative Review and Electoral Deliberation." *International Journal of Communication* 8 (2014): 62–89.
Jamison, Kathleen Hall. *How Russian Hackers and Trolls Helped Elect a President: What We Don't, Can't, and Do Know*. New York: Oxford University Press, 2018.
Jansen, Sue Curry. "The Phantom Conflict: Lippmann, Dewey and the Fate of the Public in Modern Society." *Communication and Critical/Cultural Studies* 6 (2009): 221–45.
Keith, William, and Robert Danisch. "Dewey on Science, Deliberation, and the Sociology of Rhetoric." In *Trained Capacities: John Dewey, Rhetoric, and Democratic Culture*, edited by Brian Jackson and Greg Clark, 27–46. Columbia: University of South Carolina Press, 2014.
Knobloch, Katherine R., John Gastil, Justin Reedy, and Katherine Cramer Walsh. "Did They Deliberate? Applying an Evaluative Model of Democratic Deliberation to the Oregon Citizens' Initiative Review." *Journal of Applied Communication Research* 41 (2013): 105–25.
Lippmann, Walter. *The Good Society*. New York: Little, Brown, 1936.
———. *The Phantom Public* (1925). New Brunswick, NJ: Transaction, 1993.
———. *Public Opinion* (1922). New York: Free Press, 1997.
Mead, George Herbert. *Mind, Self, and Society*. Chicago: University of Chicago Press, 1966.
Nienkamp, Jean. *Internal Rhetorics: Toward a History and Theory of Self-Persuasion*. Carbondale: Southern Illinois University Press, 2001.
Park, Robert E. "Human Ecology." *American Journal of Sociology* 42 (1936): 1–15.

Park, Robert E., and Earnest Burgess. *The City: Suggestions for Investigation of Human Behavior in the Urban Environment.* Chicago: University of Chicago Press, 1984.

Pielke, Roger A. *The Honest Broker: Making Sense of Science in Policy and Politics.* Cambridge: Cambridge University Press, 2007.

Putnam, Robert. *Bowling Alone: The Collapse and Revival of American Community.* New York: Simon and Schuster, 2001.

Rakow, Lana F. "Family Feud: Who's Still Fighting About Dewey and Lippmann?" *Javnost—the Public* 25 (2018): 75–82.

Schudson, Michael. "The 'Lippmann-Dewey Debate' and the Invention of Walter Lippmann as an Anti-Democrat, 1986–1996." *International Journal of Communication* 2 (2008): 1031–42.

Sproule, J. Michael. *Propaganda and Democracy: The American Experience of Media and Mass Persuasion.* Cambridge: Cambridge University Press, 1997.

Westbrook, Robert. *Dewey and American Democracy.* Ithaca, NY: Cornell University Press, 1991.

CONTRIBUTORS

Kristian Bjørkdahl is Associate Professor of Rhetoric at the University of Oslo. He is the author of *Live, Die, Buy, Eat: A Cultural History of Meat* (with Karen V. Lykke), as well as the editor of several volumes, including *Rhetorical Animals* (with Alex C. Parrish) and *Do-Gooders at the End of Aid: Scandinavian Humanitarianism in the Twenty-First Century* (with Antoine de Bengy Puyvallée).

Nathan Crick is Professor in the Department of Communication and Journalism at Texas A&M University and former reporter at the *Adirondack Journal*. He is the author of *Democracy and Rhetoric: John Dewey on the Arts of Becoming*, *Dewey for a New Age of Fascism: Teaching Democratic Habits*, and *The Rhetoric of Fascism*.

Robert Danisch has a PhD in communication from the University of Pittsburgh (2004) and a BA from the University of Virginia in history and philosophy. He is a full professor in the Department of Communication Arts at the University of Waterloo. He writes about rhetoric, pragmatism, and democracy.

Steve Fuller is Auguste Comte Professor of Social Epistemology at the University of Warwick. He is the author of twenty-five books, including *Post-Truth: Knowledge as a Power Game*, *Nietzschean Meditations: Untimely Thoughts at the Dawn of the Transhuman Era*, and *A Player's Guide to the Post-Truth Condition: The Name of the Game*.

William Keith is Professor of Rhetoric and Argumentation at the University of Wisconsin-Milwaukee. He has written widely about the history of public participation in the United States and its relationship to communication pedagogy. His publications include *Democracy as Discussion* and, most recently, *Beyond Civility: The Competing Obligations of Citizenship* (with Robert Danisch).

Bruno Latour (deceased) was Professor Emeritus at the Sciences Po Médialab. A philosopher, anthropologist, and sociologist, and one of the most important thinkers of his time, Latour was the author of numerous books, including *Laboratory Life* (with Steve Woolgar), *We Have Never Been Modern*, *Politics of Nature: How to Bring the Sciences into Democracy*, and, most recently, *After Lockdown: A Metamorphosis*.

John Durham Peters is María Rosa Menocal Professor of English and of Film and Media Studies at Yale University. He is the author of, among other books, *Speaking into the Air: A History of the Idea of Communication*, *The Marvelous Clouds*, and

Promiscuous Knowledge: Information, Image, and Other Truth Games in History (with the late Kenneth Cmiel).

Patricia Roberts-Miller is former Director of the University Writing Center and Professor Emeritus in the Department of Rhetoric and Writing at the University of Texas at Austin. She is the author of numerous books, including *Speaking of Race: Constructive Conversations About an Explosive Topic, Demagoguery and Democracy,* and *Fanatical Schemes: Proslavery Rhetoric and the Tragedy of Consensus,* as well as various book chapters and articles.

Michael Schudson is Professor of Journalism at Columbia Journalism School. He is the author of eleven books and coeditor of four others concerning the history and sociology of the American news media, advertising, popular culture, Watergate, and cultural memory—most recently *Journalism: Why It Matters, Why Journalism Still Matters,* and *The Rise of the Right to Know.*

Anna Shechtman is Klarman Fellow at Cornell University, where she will begin as an assistant professor in the Department of Literatures in English in 2024. Her book *The Riddles of the Sphinx* is forthcoming from HarperOne, and she is currently working on a genealogy of the American media concept.

Slavko Splichal is Professor of Communication and Public Opinion at the Faculty of Social Sciences, University of Ljubljana, and an associate member of the Slovenian Academy of Sciences and Arts. He is the founder and director of the European Institute for Communication and Culture and of its journal *Javnost—the Public.* He is the author of *Transnationalization of the Public Sphere and the Fate of the Public, Principles of Publicity and Press Freedom,* and *Public Opinion: Developments and Controversies in the Twentieth Century.*

Lisa S. Villadsen is Professor of Rhetoric and Head of the Section of Rhetoric at the Department of Communication at the University of Copenhagen. Her research interests revolve around contemporary political rhetoric—particularly issues of rhetorical citizenship, populism, and official apologies as civic discourse.

Scott Welsh is Associate Professor and Chair in the Department of Communication at Appalachian State University in Boone, North Carolina. He is author of the book *The Rhetorical Surface of Democracy.*

INDEX

Achieving Our Country (Rorty), 4
activism and participation of public
    changing participatory forms of democracy, 104
    Dewey's call for, 83, 147
    education of public needed for, 92–98, 101, 104–6
    "folk theory of democracy," 201
    Lippmann on social movements as "instruments of progress," 9, 29–31
    participation and technology, 64, 66n26
    in response to government failure, 49–50, 52–54, 58
    symbols by individuals to attract votes, 185, 193–96
    tripartism and, 171–72
Addams, Jane, 41–42, 221
"administrative" tradition, communication studies, 68–69, 72–74, 85n41
Adorno, Theodor, 77–78
Allport, Floyd, 10, 70, 72–74, 77
American Revolution, 113
Areopagitica (Milton), 97
Aristotle, 119, 218, 233
Asen, Robert, 141, 210

Barnes, Harry Elmer, 71
Becker, Gary, 129, 130
Benoit-Barné, Chantal, 141, 148
Bernays, Edward, 122–23
Berry, Jeffrey, 205–6
Best and the Brightest, The (Halberstam), 18–19
Bitzer, Lloyd F., 140
Blair, Tony, 129, 131
Blumer, Herbert, 220
Bolshevik Revolution, 116
Bolsonaro, Jair, 2, 3
Borgerlyst. See Civic Desire
Boston Common, Lippmann's writing for, 33
Bourne, Randolph, 10, 70–71, 74–78, 126
Bowling Alone (Putnam), 234
Brandal, Nik, 167

Brexit (film), 4–5
Brooks, David, 24–25
Bryce, James, 89, 100
Buck, Carrie, 208
Burke, Kenneth, 205
Bybee, Carl, 22

Camic, Charles, 80
Campbell, Donald, 130
Carey, James, 6, 10, 20, 31–32, 68–70, 79–83, 163
Center (Center for the Study of Democratic Institutions), 20
Champlin, Dell, 200
Chicago school of sociology, 220–24
citizenship, rhetorical. *See* propaedeutic rhetorical citizenship
Citizens Initiative Review (Oregon), 231
Civic Desire *(Borgerlyst)*
    aesthetics emphasized in, 149–50
    Conversation Salon exercise, 143–46, 149, 153, 156, 157n21
    peer-to-peer interaction fostered with, 148–49
    People's Election/Choice exercise, 143, 145–46
    as propaedeutic rhetorical citizenship case study, 140, 154–55
    as societal laboratory, 142–46
Clark, Gregory, 150
class
    elites' misreading of, in contemporary era, 1–5
    Halberstam on Vietnam War decision-making and, 19
    Norwegian tripartism and, 168
    The Revolt of the Elites and the Betrayal of Democracy (Lasch), 79–80
    See also education; Marxism
Clinton, Hillary, 3
Cold War terminology, coined by Lippmann, 114
collective bargaining, 178n4
    See also tripartism

communication studies
 "administrative" tradition of, 68–69, 72–74, 85n41
 "critical" tradition of, 69, 74–78
 on industrial capitalism, 226
 See also interpersonal communication; rhetoric
community-building. *See* propaedeutic rhetorical citizenship
Comte, Charles, 113
confirmation bias, 97–98, 125, 204, 210
 See also rhetorical sociology
conflict partnership, 166, 168, 176–78
 See also Norwegian social democracy
conservatism, appropriation of (1980s), 129
contemporary politics and controversies.
 data mining of public opinion, 102–6
 Dewey's relevance to, 82–83
 expert and nonexpert deliberation, recent research, 204–9
 Lippmann's distrust of technology, 64
 Lippmann's relevance to, 6
 on-line expertise, 106–7
 political pragmatism and, 192–96
 populism increase worldwide, 1–5, 138–39
 public opinion and data mining, 102–6
 public participation and technology, 64, 66n26
 2016 US elections and need for rhetorical sociology, 234–36
 See also journalism and media
conversation
 conversation democracy, Koch on, 142
 Conversation Salons (Civic Desire project), 143–46, 149, 153, 156, 157n21
 decision-making via, 210, 213
 public opinion as, 98–99
 See also interpersonal communication
cosmopolitanism, 126
Creel, George, 40
crisis of representation, 45–67
 partisan detection by public, 54–61
 public's capacity to understand political issues, 46–51
 Public vs. publics, 49–54
 realist vs. reformist approach to democracy and, 45–46, 61–65
 as twentieth-century *Prince* (Machiavelli), 45–46
"critical" tradition, communication studies, 69, 74–78

Critique of Public Opinion (Tarde), 95–96
Cummings, Dominic, 4
Cyberwar (Jamison), 234–35

Dahl, Robert, 24, 105
Danisch, Robert, 13, 141
data exploitation, 4–5
"datafication" of public opinion, 10, 88, 90–91, 99–102, 105–6
deliberation, 200–216
 confirmation bias and decision-making, 97–98, 125, 204, 210
 decision-making via mediation vs. direct knowledge, 12–13
 defined, 225
 "deliberative polling experiment," 104
 "epistemological populism," 206
 expert and nonexpert deliberation, contemporary research, 204–9
 experts' role and "intelligence work," 164–65, 190–92
 knowledge of journalists, 26–27, 47–48, 128
 "Lippmann/Dewey debate," and public opinion theory, 91
 "Lippmann/Dewey debate," as misread on, 200–204
 Lippmann on insiders' vs. outsiders' knowledge, 9, 20, 22–24, 47–48, 54, 64–65, 186–87
 Lippmann on "omnicompetent" citizens, 19–21, 43, 63, 226, 229–32
 as process vs. identity, 209–13
 public's capacity to understand political issues, 46–51
 rhetorical sociology for decision-making, 229–34
 rhetoric and public knowledge, 140–41
 See also activism and participation of public; experts and expertise; journalism and media; public opinion; rhetorical sociology
democracy, 1–16
 conversation democracy, 142
 democratic deliberation, dominant ways of thinking about, 206–7
 democratic socialism, Dewey on, 30, 76–77, 83
 disagreement about premise of, 203–4
 human ecology theory of, 222–26, 228–29, 234–36
 as "idea" vs. "ideal," 190–92, 197, 226
 liberal democracy as impermanent, 7
 liberalism and, 1, 2, 62, 113

optimism vs. risk in contemporary era, 1–5
pragmatism and early twentieth-century perspective, 185–90
See also activism and participation of public; crisis of representation; deliberation; neoliberalism; Norwegian social democracy; pragmatism; Progressivism; publics
Democracy, Deliberation and Education (Asen), 210
Democracy Index *(Economist)*, 2
Denmark, Civic Desire project in. *See* Civic Desire
Descartes, R., 220–21
Dewey, John
 at Columbia University, 74
 contradictory ideas of, 70–72
 on democratic socialism, 30, 76–77, 83
 on eclipse of the public, 63, 68, 71, 74, 93, 138
 as emergentist, 132–34
 Experience and Nature, 160
 on experts as partisans, 65n9
 Forum Movement and, 121
 German Philosophy and Politics, 78
 on Great Community, 63, 69, 73–74, 103–4, 225, 227–28, 235
 John Dewey and the Artful Life (Stroud), 149–50
 public as defined by, 227
 on "reconstruction," 82–83
 "The Reflex Arc Concept in Psychology," 220–21
 See also education; interpersonal communication; "Lippmann/Dewey debate"; *The Public and Its Problems*
Dial, The, Dewey on World War I in, 75
Dialectic of Enlightenment (Adorno and Horkheimer), 77–78
Dryzek, John, 139–40

Eberly, Rosa, 153–54, 156
eclipse of the public, Dewey on, 63, 68, 71, 74, 93, 138
economics
 Dewey on democratic socialism, 30, 76–77, 83
 The Good Society (Lippmann) on, 225
 Great Society and welfare debate, 130–32
 human capital theory, 128–30
 "Lippmann/Dewey debate" as Progressive politics vs. Marxist, 79–81, 82, 112–14, 121–22, 131

Lippmann on capitalism, 62–63
 social democracy and twentieth-century Progressivism, 111–14, 122–23, 129–30, 132
 See also tripartism
Economist, Democracy Index of, 2
education
 Dewey's legacy to, 122
 for expanded public participation, 92–98, 101, 104–6
 Fishkin on "deliberative polling experiment" and, 104
 political pragmatism of Lippmann and Dewey, 183–84
 public opinion theory and need for public education, 92–98, 101, 104–6
 thinking encouraged by, 212–13
Einstein, Albert, 132
elites. *See* experts and expertise; journalism and media; politicians and political leadership
Emerson, Ralph Waldo, 115
Erdoğan, Recep Tayyip, 3
eugenics, 208–9
Everybody's Magazine, Lippmann's writing for, 33
Experience and Nature (Dewey), 160
experimenting society (Campbell), 130
Expert Political Opinion (Tetlock), 211
experts and expertise
 deliberation, expert and nonexpert, 204–9
 "intelligence work" and, 164–65, 190–92
 "Lippmann/Dewey debate" and public opinion theory, 91–92
 Lippmann's theories misread by others, 65n9
 Lippmann's use of "we," 22–23, 25
 objectivity and, 17–19, 24–27, 51–54, 207–9
 online access to, 106–7
 propaedeutic rhetorical citizenship and, 147
 See also journalism and media; pragmatism

Fabian Society, 33, 38, 122, 127, 130–31
Finansforbundet (Norwegian union), 175
Fisher, Irving, 128, 129
"folk theory of democracy," 201
For a Left Populism (Mouffe), 3
Forum Movement, 121
"foxes," 211
Frankfurt School, 77–79

Freedom House, 2
Freedom in the World index, 2
French Revolution, 113
Freud, Sigmund, 34, 121
Fuller, Steve, 3

Gallup, George, 100
Gardner, Dan, 211–12
Gastil, John, 231
Gemeinschaft und Gesellschaft (Tönnies), 95
German Philosophy and Politics (Dewey), 78
Golden Day, The (Mumford), 76
Good Society, The (Lippmann), 225
Goodwin, Jean, 147, 200, 201
Great Community
　for democracy improvement, 225
　Great Society transformation and, 63, 69, 227–28, 235
　for "inclusive" communication, 73–74, 103, 225
　internet as, 103–4
Great Society
　origin of term, 65n2, 122
　The Phantom Public (Lippmann) on, 46, 53, 59, 63–65
　Progressivism and, 127–32
Great Society, The (Wallas), 127
Gunster, Shane, 206

Halberstam, David, 18–19
Harding, Warren G., 71
Harvard University, 32–33
Hauglie, Anniken, 173–74
Hauser, Gerard, 141, 148, 151–52, 156
Hearing the Other Side (Mutz), 155
"hedgehogs," 211
Hegbloom, Maria T., 141
Hegel, Georg, 58, 59, 60, 82, 89, 118, 119
Hersh, Seymour, 116
Hibbing, John, 203–4
Hirsch, Fred, 132
Hitler, Adolf, 78, 205
Hobbes, Thomas, 133–34
Holmes, Oliver Wendell, 65n14
Hook, Sidney, 160
Horkheimer, Max, 10, 70, 74, 77–78
Hull House, 221
human capital theory, 128–30

identity politics
　deliberation as process vs., 209–13
　as elitism, Lasch on, 79–80
　phantom of identity, Lippmann on, 59–60

Immigration Act (1924), 208
Inquiry (Wilson administration task force), 40
insiders vs. outsiders. *See* experts and expertise
Institute of Communications Research, University of Illinois, 80
institutional mechanisms/solutions
　Aristotle on institutionalism, 218
　Dewey on building social relationships between strangers, 13, 223–29, 234–36
　Lippmann on information accuracy, 13, 223–29, 234–36
International, Lippmann's writing for, 33
interpersonal communication
　communication as means and end, 148–50, 165
　Great Community for, 73–74, 103, 225
　political pragmatism and, 192
　public discourse management problem, 218, 219–26
　tripartism and, 169–72
　See also Civic Desire; conversation; rhetorical sociology
interwar period, 69, 70, 101

Jackson, Brian, 150
James, William, 32, 115, 119, 125
Jamison, Kathleen Hall, 234–35
Jansen, Sue Curry, 27, 69, 163, 231
Jefferson, Thomas, 118
John Dewey and the Artful Life (Stroud), 149–50
Johnson, Boris, 129
Johnson, Lyndon, 114, 128–31
journalism and media
　decision-making via mediation vs. direct knowledge, 12–13
　Dewey on purpose of news, 31
　Horkheimer on mass-mediated democracy, 70
　knowledge limitation of journalists, 26–27, 47–48, 128
　knowledge limitation of journalists, "citizen journalists," 26
　mass media vs. interpersonal communication, 121
　mediation of information and decision-making, 203, 210–11
　muckrakers, 115–16
　"outrage industry," 205–6
　public opinion as conversation, 98–99

Public Opinion (Lippmann) on
    journalists' role in democracy, 22,
    23, 26
JPMorgan bank, 33

Kant, Immanuel, 89, 97, 104
Katz, Elihu, 80
Keith, William, 13
Kennan, George, 114
Kennedy, John F., 18–19
Keynes, John Maynard, 83, 130
Kingdon, John, 21–22
Knight, Frank, 132–33
Knoedler, Janet, 200
Knowledge for What? (Lynd), 85n41
Koch, Hal, 142
Kock, Christian, 141–42, 152
Koht, Halvdan, 168
Kritik der öffentlichen Meinung (Tarde), 95
Kuttner, Alfred Booth, 34

Laclau, Ernesto, 3
Lasch, Christopher, 79–80
Lasswell, Harold, 71
Laughlin, Harry, 208, 211
Lazarsfeld, Paul Felix, 85n41
League of Nations, 115, 117
Leave campaign, 4–5
Lee, Harper, 125
Lenin, Vladimir, 116
Levitsky, Steve, 207
liberalism
    ambiguity of, 62
    French Revolution and American
        Revolution, 113
    "illiberal" democracy, 1, 2
    See also democracy; neoliberalism
Liberty and the News (Lippmann)
    on journalists' knowledge and reliance
        on outside expertise, 26–27
    on "manufacture of consent," 92,
        123
Lincoln, Abraham, 116
Lippmann, Walter
    Cold War terminology by, 114
    as dualist, 132–34
    education of, 32–33
    elitist reputation of, 19, 29–30
    The Good Society, 225
    as iconclast and socialist, 31–34
    presidential administration roles of,
        115–16
    on social movements as "instruments of
        progress," 9, 29–31

"The 'Lippmann-Dewey Debate' and
    the Invention of Walter Lippmann
    as an Anti-Democrat, 1985–1996"
    (Schudson), 79–80
    twentieth-century crisis events covered
        by, 81
    *Walter Lippmann and the American
        Century* (Steel), 132
    Walter Lippmann Colloquium (Paris,
        1938), 112, 113
    on Zionism, 126
    See also experts and expertise; *Liberty
        and the News*; "Lippmann/Dewey
        debate"; *Phantom Public*; *Preface to
        Politics*; *Public Opinion*; stereotypes
"Lippmann/Dewey debate," 68–87
    "administrative" tradition critiques of
        Dewey, 68–69, 72–74, 85n41
    Carey's schema of, 6, 10, 31–32, 68–70,
        79–83, 163
    crisis as common theme of, 81–83
    "critical" tradition critiques of Dewey,
        69, 74–78
    Dewey's contradictory ideas and, 70–72
    as false dilemma, 11–12, 160–66,
        176–78
    future envisioned in, 182–85, 190–93,
        198
    intellectual environment of, 9–11
    as misread, 200–204
    public opinion as conceptualized by,
        88–89, 91–95
    realist vs. reformist approach to
        democracy and, 9, 45–46, 61–65
    as straw men fallacy, 20, 69–70, 163
    as "struggle for soul of Progressivism,"
        10–11, 111–14
    as typology of democracies, 5–8
    World War I timeframe and influence
        on, 40–43, 69, 81–83
    See also activism and participation
        of public; deliberation; experts
        and expertise; Norwegian
        social democracy; pragmatism;
        Progressivism; propaedeutic
        rhetorical citizenship; public
        opinion theory; rhetorical sociology
"'Lippmann-Dewey Debate' and the
    Invention of Walter Lippmann as
    an Anti-Democrat, 1985–1996, The"
    (Schudson), 79–80
Lloyd, Andreas, 142, 147
Lodge, Milton, 209–10, 213
Lynd, Robert Staughton, 85n41

Machiavelli, Niccolò
The Phantom Public (Lippmann), Latour on, 9, 45–46, 48–49, 50, 54, 57, 61
The Phantom Public (Lippmann) and praise for, 65n7
public opinion theory in context of, 89, 90, 93
Main Agreement (Norway, 1935), 167–68
Mann, Michael, 206
Mansbridge, Jane, 23
"manufacture of consent," Lippmann on, 123
Marx, Karl, 121–22
Marxism
  democratic socialism vs., 76–77
  on French Revolution vs. American Revolution, 113
  Lippmann as socialist, 31–34
  "Lippmann/Dewey debate" and Progressive politics vs., 79–81, 82, 112–14, 121–22, 131
Masses, Lippmann's writing for, 33
McIntyre, Alasdair, 150
McNamara, Robert, 18
Mead, George Herbert, 124, 220–21
media. *See* journalism and media
"melting pot," 123–26
Mill, John Stuart, 91, 119–20, 130
Milton, John, 97
Monroe Doctrine, 117
Mont Pèlerin Society, 112
Mouffe, Chantal, 2–3
Mounk, Yascha, 1, 3
muckrakers, 115–16
Müller, Jan-Werner, 205–7, 213
Mumford, Lewis, 10, 70, 74–78
Murray, Charles, 129
Mutz, Diana, 155

neoliberalism
  as individual interests vs. society, 59–61
  Norway's social democracy and, 178n7
  Rüstow on, 112
  sociology vs., 60
  twentieth-century Progressivism and influence of "Lippmann-Dewey debate," 111–14, 122–23, 129–30, 132
New Freedom policy (Wilson), 127–28
New Republic
  Bourne's writing for, 126
  Dewey's analysis of *The Phantom Public* (Lippmann) in, 63, 68
  Lippmann as editor of, 40
  Lippmann on insiders vs. outsiders in, 20

Lippmann on League of Nations, 119
New York Times
  Brooks on Trump's support by Republican Party, 24–25
  Halberstam on Vietnam War and, 19
Niebuhr, Reinhold, 10, 70, 74–78
Nixon, Richard, 114, 127
Noelle-Neumann, Elisabeth, 100
Norwegian social democracy, 160–81
  as "conflict partnership," 166, 168, 176–78
  culturalized tripartism, 172–75, 176–77
  "Lippmann/Dewey debate" as false dilemma, 11–12, 160–66, 176–78
  as "together-talking," 168–72

objectivity. *See* deliberation; experts and expertise
Olstad, Finn, 167, 168
"omnicompetent citizens," Lippmann on, 19–21, 43, 63, 226, 229–32
  See also deliberation
On Liberty (Mill), 91
L'opinion et la foule (Tarde), 95, 96
Orbán, Victor, 2, 3
Oregon, vote-by-mail in, 230–31
Orwell, George, 193
"outcomes-based ethics," 207
"outrage industry," 205–6

Park, Robert, 221, 223
partisans
  detecting, 54–61
  Dewey on experts as partisans, 65n9
  Lippmann on stereotypes and, 190
"Part of the Same Future" (Hauglie), 173–74
Pass, Nadja, 142, 147
Peace and Bread in Time of War (Addams), 41–42
People's Election/Choice (Civic Desire project), 143, 145–46
People vs. Democracy, The (Mounk), 1, 3
Peters, John Durham, 6, 27
Phantom Public, The (Lippmann)
  contemporary relevance of, 6
  definition of phantom public, 59–60, 68
  Dewey on phantom public concept, 187
  on Great Society, 46, 53, 59, 63–65
  on humans as passive spectators, 39–43
  on insiders vs. outsiders, 20, 23
  A Preface to Politics and Lippmann's changed views in, 9, 29, 30, 39–43
  realist vs. reformist approach to democracy and, 9

stereotypes, phantom public's use of, 100
  as twentieth-century *Prince*
    (Machiavelli), 9
  See also crisis of representation;
    "Lippmann/Dewey debate"; publics
Pielke, Roger, 218–19
Plato, 119, 127, 128
politicians and political leadership
  failure by, and public activism, 49–50,
    52–54, 58
  Lippmann on political indifference,
    34–39
  Lippmann on statesmanship, 29
  "routineers," 36–37
  self-contained community, 23
  symbols by individuals to attract votes,
    185, 193–97
  understanding of political issues by,
    21–23
polling. *See* public opinion
pragmatism, 182–99
  adjustment needed for representation,
    52–53, 61–65
  Allport on causation and, 72–74
  democracy, early twentieth-century
    perspective, 185–90
  democracy as "idea" vs. "ideal," 190–92,
    197, 226
  democracy as rhetorical politics, 197–98
  "folk pragmatism," 207
  future envisioned by Lippmann and
    Dewey, 182–85, 190–93, 198
  "left critiques" of Dewey's theories on,
    74–78
  rhetorical pragmatism, 141
  rhetorical sociology and, 220–24
  symbols produced to attract votes, 185,
    193–97
  See also crisis of representation; realism
A Preface to Politics (Lippmann), 29–44
  on humans as willful vs. rational, 34–39
  The Phantom Public and changed views
    from, 9, 29, 30, 39–43
  on social movements as "instruments of
    progress," 9, 29–31
Prince (Macchiavelli). *See* Machiavelli,
    Niccolò
Progressivism, 111–37
  Dewey as emergentist vs. Lippmann as
    dualist, 132–34
  Great Society and, 127–32
  "Lippmann/Dewey debate" as
    Progressive politics vs. Marxist,
    79–81, 82, 112–14, 121–22, 131

  "melting pot" as test for, 123–26
  public's role and, 10–11, 111–14
  social democracy and "Lippmann/Dewey
    debate" influence on, 111–14
  state role and, 119–23
  Wilson vs. Roosevelt, Lippmann's
    changed allegiance, 114–19
Prohibition, 84n11
propaedeutic rhetorical citizenship, 138–59
  Civic Desire project as, 140, 142–50,
    154–55
  collective level, propaedeutics at, 153–54,
    156
  Danish pedagogy, Dewey's influence
    on, 142
  definition of propaedeutics, 153
  Dewey on interpersonal communication
    importance and, 11, 138–40
  rhetorical citizenship, defined, 152–53
  rhetoric study, Dewey's influence on,
    140–42
  vernacular rhetoric, reticulate public
    spheres, trust, and, 151–53
Public and Its Problems, The (Dewey)
  on "blindness" of public, 47
  Carey's "Lippmann/Dewey debate"
    schema on, 68
  contemporary relevance of, 6
  democratic faith of, 165–66
  on democratic realism, 71
  on Great Community, 228
  on interpersonal communication
    importance, 11
  on optimism about democracy, 1
  on philosophy of interaction, 221–22
  political pragmatism of, 183, 186, 190–91
  politics, definitive statement on, 119
  public opinion theory in context of,
    88–89, 95
  race discussion as conspicuously absent
    from, 123
  on scientific method in social sciences,
    72, 228–29
  on Wallas, 127–28
  See also "Lippmann/Dewey debate";
    pragmatism; publics
publicity agents, 184, 194–96
Public Opinion and the Crowd (Tarde), 95,
    96
Public Opinion (Lippmann), 17–28
  Carey's "Lippmann/Dewey debate"
    schema on, 68
  contemporary relevance of, 6
  on cultural beliefs, 223

Public Opinion (Lippmann) (*continued*)
  on experts' role and objectivity, 17–19, 24–27
  on insiders vs. outsiders, 9, 20, 22–24, 47–48, 54, 64–65, 186–87
  on journalists' role in democracy, 22, 23, 26
  on "omnicompetent citizens," 19–21, 43, 63, 226, 229–32
  political pragmatism of, 182, 183, 186, 190
  on politicians' understanding of political issues, 21–23
  on problem of inquiry and communication, 228
  on public interest as changing, 121–22
  public opinion theory in context of, 95
  public's capacity for understanding political issues, 8–9
  on race as stereotype, 123
  on self-contained community, 23
  See also "Lippmann/Dewey debate"; pragmatism; publics
public opinion theory, 88–110
  "datafication" of, 10, 88, 90–91, 99–102, 105–6
  data mining of, in contemporary era, 102–6
  Lippmann's and Dewey's conceptualization of, 88–89, 91–95
  symbols by individuals to attract votes, 185, 193–96
  Tarde's and Tönnies's early sociological theories about, 10, 89–91, 94–99, 101
  vernacular rhetoric, reticulate public spheres, and trust, 151–53
public relations, inception of, 123
publics
  Dewey on eclipse of the public, 63, 68, 71, 74, 93, 138
  Dewey on private vs. public activity, 72
  Dewey's definition of, 227
  Dewey's "publics" and political pragmatism, 193
  elites' misreading of, in contemporary era, 1–5
  identity politics and, 59–60, 79–80, 209–13
  Lippmann/Dewey "debate" on democratic deliberation, 5–8
  Lippmann on public's capacity to understand political issues, 46–51
  Lippmann's post-World War I change of view on, 38–40
  listening to the masses, 4, 14n16
  partisan detection by, 54–61
  problem of, as rhetorical sociology, 231–34
  Progressivism and role of, 10–11, 111–14
  Prohibition and role of, 84n11
  proto-publics, 153–54, 156
  public, defined (Lippmann), 54
  Public vs. publics, 49–54
  reticulate public spheres, 148, 151–53
  See also activism and participation of public; propaedeutic rhetorical citizenship; public opinion theory
Putnam, Robert, 234, 235

race and racism, 118, 123–26, 204–5, 208
Rakow, Lana, 6, 163
Reagan, Ronald, 79–80, 129
realism
  Niebuhr's critiques of Dewey on, 76–77
  The Public and Its Problems (Dewey) on democratic realism, 71–72
  realist vs. reformist approach to democracy, 9, 45–46, 61–65
"The Reflex Arc Concept in Psychology" (Dewey), 220–21
representation, crisis of. *See* crisis of representation
Republic (Plato), 128
reticulate public spheres, 148, 151–53
  See also propaedeutic rhetorical citizenship
Revolt of the Elites and the Betrayal of Democracy, The (Lasch), 79–80
rhetoric
  Aristotle on, 233
  citizen engagement and, 139–40
  Committee on Public Information (Wilson administration), 40
  democracy as rhetorical politics, 197–98
  Lippmann on political indifference and, 35–36
  listening to publics, 4, 14n16
  in macro context, 217–18
  of Nazis, 77, 78, 205, 208
  of "outrage industry," 205–6
  See also propaedeutic rhetorical citizenship; public opinion theory; rhetorical sociology; vernacular rhetoric

rhetorical sociology, 217–38
  decision-making improved with, 229–34
  defined, 232–33
  Lippmann's and Dewey's legacies combined as, 13, 226–29, 234–36
  as problem of the public, 231–34
  public discourse management problem and, 218, 219–26
  rhetorical structures in, 222, 223
  as rhetoric in macro context, 217–18
Riccio, Barry, 34
Riesman, David, 24
Robbins, Lionel, 112, 130–31
Rokkan, Stein, 166
Roosevelt, Franklin Delano, 114
Roosevelt, Theodore, 30, 114–19
Rorty, Richard, 4
"routineers," 36–37
  See also politicians and political leadership
Rusk, Dean, 18
Rüstow, Alexander, 112

Santayana, George, 32, 115
Saurette, Paul, 206
Schmitt, Carl, 50–51
Schudson, Michael, 69, 163, 201–3, 207, 208
Sejersted, Francis, 168, 172–73
Shame of the Cities, The (Steffens), 116
Shechtman, Anna, 6
Siim, Birte, 166–67
Skjeie, Hege, 166–67
Smith, Adam, 112–13
Sobieraj, Sarah, 205–6
social democracy. *See* Norwegian social democracy; Progressivism
Social Laws (Tarde), 106
social movements. *See* activism and participation of public
sociology
  neoliberal thought vs., 60
  Public Opinion (Lippmann) as predating study of, 26
  public opinion theories of Tarde and Tönnies, 10, 89–91, 94–99, 101, 103, 105
  symbolic interactionist school of, 124, 220–24, 228–29
  Weber on, 134
  See also public opinion theory; rhetorical sociology
Spencer, Herbert, 112

state, role of. *See* Progressivism
statesmanship, Lippmann on, 29
statistical analysis
  "datafication" of public opinion, 10, 88, 90–91, 99–102, 105–6
  Lippmann on public opinion data, 112
  Tarde's "crowd-public" dichotomy, 96
Steffens, Lincoln, 33, 115–16
Stengers, Isabelle, 63
stereotypes
  decision-making and bias, 202, 203, 207–8, 210
  Lippmann on "backwardness" of groups, 214n32
  Lippmann's definition of, 84n5, 164
  phantom public's use of, 100
  political pragmatism and, 188–90, 191
  Progressivism and "melting pot," 123–26
  See also symbols
Stroud, Scott, 149–50
Superforecasting (Tetlock and Gardner), 211–12
"surveillance capitalism," 4–5
symbols
  interactionism, symbolic, 124, 220–24, 228–29
  used by individuals to attract votes, 185, 193–96

Taber, Charles, 209–10, 213
Tarde, Gabriel
  Critique of Public Opinion, 95–96
  on "crowd-public" dichotomy, 96
  early sociological theories of Tönnies and, 10, 89–91, 94–99, 101
  Kritik der öffentlichen Meinung, 95–96
  L'opinion et la foule (Public Opinion and the Crowd), 95, 96
  public opinion theory of, 89–91, 94–99, 101
  Social Laws, 106
Tell, Dave, 31
10% Less Democracy (Jones and Garret, eds.), 1
Tetlock, Philip, 211–12
Thatcher, Margaret, 129
Theiss-Morse, Elizabeth, 203–4
Thoreau, Henry David, 204–5
Thorsen, Dag Einar, 167
Tilden, Samuel J., 139
"together-talking." *See* Norwegian social democracy
To Kill a Mockingbird (Lee), 125

Tönnies, Ferdinand
    Gemeinschaft und Gesellschaft, 95
    Hobbes translated by, 134
    public opinion theory of, 89–91, 94–99, 101
tripartism
    corporatist mechanism of, 166–67, 172, 176
    cultural significance of, 172–75, 176–77
    as "together-talking," 168–72
    tripartite negotiations, defined, 161–62, 178n4
    See also Norwegian social democracy
Trotsky, Leon, 116
Trump, Donald
    Brooks on Republican Party's support of, 24–25
    conservatism appropriation (1980s) and, 129
    democracy at risk in contemporary era, 1–5
    press conferences of, 115
trust between strangers. *See* propaedeutic rhetorical citizenship
truth
    activity vs., 31
    Lippmann on truth in politics, 57
    "post-truth" era, 2–3
"Twilight of the Idols" (Bourne), 74

University of Chicago. *See* Dewey, John
University of Illinois, 80
US Constitution, 118, 120

vernacular rhetoric
    defined, 141, 151
    reticulate public spheres, trust, and, 148, 151–53
    thick moral vernaculars, 156
    See also propaedeutic rhetorical citizenship
Vietnam War, 18–19, 114
Villadsen, Lisa, 141–42

Wallas, Graham, 65n2, 122, 127–28
Walter Lippmann and the American Century (Steel), 132
Walter Lippmann Colloquium (Paris, 1938), 112, 113
Weber, Max, 134
welfare debate, 130–32
Wellborn, Charles, 40
Welsh, Scott, 12
Westbrook, Robert, 202, 210, 228
White, Morton, 71
Wilson, Woodrow, 75, 114–19, 127–28
Women's International League for Peace and Freedom, 41–42
World War I
    Dewey on American intervention in, 74–76
    League of Nations, 117–19
    "Lippmann/Dewey debate" timeframe and influence on, 40–43, 69, 81–83
    Lippmann on British Foreign Office during, 17
    Lippmann on public's understanding of, 9, 30–31, 40–41, 193
    pragmatism of Lippmann and Dewey about, 184
    Treaty of Versailles, 40, 75, 76, 118
World War II
    Cold War terminology coined by Lippmann, 114
    Nazi rhetoric, 77, 78, 205, 208
    public opinion theory in context of, 88–89
Wright, Benjamin F., 30

Young, Michael, 131

Zask, Joëlle, 63
Ziblatt, Daniel, 207
Zionism, Lippmann on, 126
Zuckerman, Michael, 23

RHETORIC AND DEMOCRATIC DELIBERATION

Other books in the series:

Karen Tracy, *Challenges of Ordinary Democracy: A Case Study in Deliberation and Dissent* / Volume 1

Samuel McCormick, *Letters to Power: Public Advocacy Without Public Intellectuals* / Volume 2

Christian Kock and Lisa S. Villadsen, eds., *Rhetorical Citizenship and Public Deliberation* / Volume 3

Jay P. Childers, *The Evolving Citizen: American Youth and the Changing Norms of Democratic Engagement* /Volume 4

Dave Tell, *Confessional Crises and Cultural Politics in Twentieth-Century America* / Volume 5

David Boromisza-Habashi, *Speaking Hatefully: Culture, Communication, and Political Action in Hungary* / Volume 6

Arabella Lyon, *Deliberative Acts: Democracy, Rhetoric, and Rights* / Volume 7

Lyn Carson, John Gastil, Janette Hartz-Karp, and Ron Lubensky, eds., *The Australian Citizens' Parliament and the Future of Deliberative Democracy* / Volume 8

Christa J. Olson, *Constitutive Visions: Indigeneity and Commonplaces of National Identity in Republican Ecuador* / Volume 9

Damien Smith Pfister, *Networked Media, Networked Rhetorics: Attention and Deliberation in the Early Blogosphere* / Volume 10

Katherine Elizabeth Mack, *From Apartheid to Democracy: Deliberating Truth and Reconciliation in South Africa* / Volume 11

Mary E. Stuckey, *Voting Deliberatively: FDR and the 1936 Presidential Campaign* / Volume 12

Robert Asen, *Democracy, Deliberation, and Education* / Volume 13

Shawn J. Parry-Giles and David S. Kaufer, *Memories of Lincoln and the Splintering of American Political Thought* / Volume 14

J. Michael Hogan, Jessica A. Kurr, Michael J. Bergmaier, and Jeremy D. Johnson, eds., *Speech and Debate as Civic Education* / Volume 15

Angela G. Ray and Paul Stob, eds., *Thinking Together: Lecturing, Learning, and Difference in the Long Nineteenth Century* / Volume 16

Sharon E. Jarvis and Soo-Hye Han, *Votes That Count and Voters Who Don't: How Journalists Sideline Electoral Participation (Without Even Knowing It)* / Volume 17

Belinda Stillion Southard, *How to Belong: Women's Agency in a Transnational World* / Volume 18

Melanie Loehwing, *Homeless Advocacy and the Rhetorical Construction of the Civic Home* / Volume 19

Kristy Maddux, *Practicing Citizenship: Women's Rhetoric at the 1893 Chicago World's Fair* / Volume 20

Craig Rood, *After Gun Violence: Deliberation and Memory in an Age of Political Gridlock* / Volume 21

Nathan Crick, *Dewey for a New Age of Fascism: Teaching Democratic Habits* / Volume 22

William Keith and Robert Danisch, *Beyond Civility: The Competing Obligations of Citizenship* / Volume 23

Lisa A. Flores, *Deportable and Disposable: Public Rhetoric and the Making of the "Illegal" Immigrant* / Volume 24

Adriana Angel, Michael L. Butterworth, and Nancy R. Gómez, eds., *Rhetorics of Democracy in the Americas* / Volume 25

Robert Asen, *School Choice and the Betrayal of Democracy: How Market-Based Education Reform Fails Our Communities* / Volume 26

Stephanie R. Larson, *What It Feels Like: Visceral Rhetoric and the Politics of Rape Culture* / Volume 27

Billie Murray, *Combating Hate: A Framework for Direct Action* / Volume 28

David A. Frank and Francis J. Mootz III, *The Rhetoric of Judging Well: The Conflicted Legacy of Justice Anthony M. Kennedy* / Volume 29

Milton Keynes UK
Ingram Content Group UK Ltd.
UKHW012255060324
438913UK00003B/83